fresh pantry

fresh pantry

Eat Seasonally,
Cook Smart & Learn to
Love Your Vegetables

AMY PENNINGTON

AWARD-WINNING AUTHOR OF URBAN PANTRY

SKIPSTONE

Published by Skipstone, an imprint of Mountaineers Books
Printed in the United States of America
17 16 15 14   1 2 3 4 5

Copy editor: Lisa Cooper Anderson
Design: Jane Jeszeck/Jigsaw, www.jigsawseattle.com, and Emily Ford
Layout: Emily Ford
Cover photograph: Della Chen
Back cover photographs: Tomato–Melon Soup with Poached Shrimp & Summer Herbs (Photo by Amy Pennington); Oregano and Winter Squash Pasta (Photo by Kenneth Dundas); Carrot Marmalade (Photo by Della Chen)

Photography by the author except where otherwise noted and for the following: pages 2, 8, 10, 14, 20, 64, 80, 83, 84, 102, 130, 156, and 198 by Della Chen; pages 5-7, 24, 42, 63, 133, and 194 by Kenneth Dundas.

Library of Congress Cataloging-in-Publication Data
Pennington, Amy, 1974-
  Fresh pantry : eat seasonally, cook smart & learn to love your vegetables / by Amy Pennington.
    pages cm
  Includes index.
  ISBN 978-1-59485-817-8 (paperback) — ISBN 978-1-59485-818-5 (ebook) 1. Cooking (Vegetables) 2. Seasonal cooking. I. Title.
  TX801.P46 2014
  641.6'5—dc23
                        2013047382

ISBN (paperback): 978-1-59485-817-8
ISBN (ebook): 978-1-59485-818-5

Skipstone books may be purchased for corporate, educational, or other promotional sales. For special discounts and information, contact our sales department at 800-553-4453 or mbooks@mountaineersbooks.org.

Skipstone
1001 SW Klickitat Way
Suite 201
Seattle, Washington 98134
206.223.6303
www.skipstonebooks.org
www.mountaineersbooks.org

LIVE LIFE. MAKE RIPPLES.

CONTENTS

LIST OF RECIPES

ACKNOWLEDGMENTS

I OWE A DEBT OF gratitude to one of my favorite collaborators, Kate Rogers, who is not only editor in chief of an amazing, environmentally conscious publisher, Mountaineers Books, but a longtime colleague whom I now consider a friend. Kate's patience, support, and candid advice was much appreciated throughout the duration of this long project. Thank you, Kate!

This book project may never have come together if not for the spontaneous suggestion from managing editor extraordinaire, Margaret Sullivan. Margaret's voice and ability to organize my thoughts helped these pages flow. Thank you, Margaret!

Thank you, as well, to the team at Skipstone—Emily White for her marketing magic, Emily Ford for her design and ebook prowess, and Doug Canfield and others for their continued assistance in my book endeavors.

Thank you to Della Chen for her picture-perfect images, many of which are included in the print book and throughout the original ebook series. And a big thanks to *all* of my friends who helped my own photography efforts and recipe testing by lending their homes, kitchens, dishes, linens, and opinions: Rusty Blackwood, Ruth True, the Bartholomew clan, Seth and Sarah Pennington, and my entire Facebook posse.

All of my writing is first passed to my dear friend, Ritzy Ryciak, who is an ever-present resource for editorial suggestions, positive reinforcement, and her convivial nature. She helped me immensely throughout this project, and I'm forever appreciative and grateful to call her a friend. Namaste, guuurl.

And finally, I also owe a huge thank you to Kenneth Dundas, who let me overtake his kitchen for testing and writing, taught me how to wield a camera properly, and spent many weekends helping me to shoot recipes for the book. I am quite happily beholden to him in more ways than I can count, and thankful for his love, patience, and support.

PREFACE

I THINK ABOUT THE ORDER of ingredients in two ways: every kitchen has a dry pantry and a fresh pantry. The dry pantry holds those ingredients that are shelf-stable and keeps them accessible all year—things like grains, beans, nuts, and dried fruits. My first book, *Urban Pantry: Tips & Recipes for a Thrifty, Sustainable & Seasonal Kitchen,* introduced new homemakers to pantry cooking concepts and ingredients, provided experienced cooks with organizational inspiration, and helped cooks of all skill levels create sustainable and thrifty kitchens. But that book's approach and ingredients mostly reflect those dry, shelf-stable, or preserved goods. A *fresh* pantry, however, needs stocking more frequently as it holds food that will spoil easily; when I talk about the "fresh" pantry, I'm referring to meat, milk, and, especially, produce that changes with the season and, in turn, requires flexibility in the kitchen.

For anyone trying to eat a sustainable diet, vegetables and fruits are pantry musts, so I wanted to create a new tool for home cooks by taking and applying the ideas from *Urban Pantry* to fresh, seasonal fruits and vegetables. This new book, *Fresh Pantry: Eat Seasonally, Cook Smart & Learn to Love Your Vegetables,* picks up where *Urban Pantry* leaves off—by continuing the conversation about living sustainably. Eating fresh, local, and seasonal foods is a healthy act that everyone can get behind! To support home cooks in their efforts to eat this way (as much as possible), I focus on one seasonal vegetable or fruit for each month of the year. Of course, seasons vary across the country, but *Fresh Pantry* features some of our most common produce, as well as a few regional specialty extras like warm-weather-loving pomegranates and citrus. You'll realize that, over the course of the year, it's easy to use in-season ingredients to efficiently and deliciously add color and flavor to the canned and dried foods already in your pantry.

More and more, people are turning to farmers markets for local, fresh food, and that's rad to see and be a part of; people have an ongoing interest in seasonal eating for themselves and their families. (My always-full canning classes prove it!) As with my first book, I've tried here to provide a selection of awesome tasting and easy-to-make recipes, but this time to encourage you to cook more with *fresh* foods, rather than preserving them. There is true pleasure to be had in eating "real" food at its freshest. I also make it easier to identify just what a seasonal food is. With the plethora of options available at grocery stores, it's hard to tell anymore. Each chapter here is peppered with facts about how vegetables and fruits grow, so you can start making educated choices, whether at your local supermarket or farmers market.

When you commit to eating seasonally, you're faced with cooking produce that comes in and out of the markets and rotates often. This means you can't cook the same dishes all year long (which is refreshing), but it also means you have to shake up your repertoire (which can be intimidating). Adhering to this more natural schedule for seasonally available produce demands adaptability and creativity in the kitchen, so as not to fatigue the palate, bore the cook, or rely on processed or non-seasonal foods. Everyone knows a fresh sliced tomato goes well with mozzarella and basil. Here, we flip that concept on its head and pair juicy tomatoes with a spiced, firm yogurt instead. Carrots are offered as main ingredients for dinner, blueberries are served alongside halibut, and beet juice becomes part of a cocktail. I aim to provide a mix of flavors and techniques to keep your time in the kitchen interesting and fun—life is too short to make the same twelve dishes over and over again!

ONE MONTH AT A TIME

I'VE ORGANIZED THIS BOOK INTO monthly chapters that each focus on a single vegetable or fruit, loosely following a typical agricultural growing season. Of course, growing and harvesting seasons overlap and meld across the year. For example, you might see fresh tomatoes in your own garden as early as July and as late as October. Here in the Northwest, summer finally gets going in July and lasts through September. So, use this book as a rough calendar for when things will be at their best, but seize the moment when something appears at your farmers market a bit earlier.

The recipes are healthy, original, and wholesome, exploiting the virtues of a single vegetable or fruit across the day—from breakfast to dessert. Cooking in this fashion allows you to master one ingredient at a time. Each recipe uses affordable food and incorporates pantry ingredients you already have around—nothing esoteric, though there are a few special ingredients. And while each month teaches various techniques that can be applied broadly to many dishes, you won't find any recipes with too many complicated steps. Instead, you'll find simple, slightly elevated home cooking that really delivers on flavor. Just choose your recipe and run with it!

I hope that *Fresh Pantry* will help expand the way you think about seasonal food so that you're able to maximize the season and enjoy individual fruits and vegetables while they are fresh, afford-able, and at their peak.

Orange-Flower & Raspberry Jelly

LEARN TO LOVE WHAT'S IN SEASON

SEASONAL EATING IS NOT SOMETHING that came particularly naturally to me. I had been growing food for a few years when I decided I wanted to try to eat locally all winter long. I had come to discover that in-season food tasted better, and it made sense to buy only the best. Additionally, I'm an environmentalist and believe that one person *can* make a difference, so I liked the idea of making my eco-footprint smaller.

Eating this way is a learning process, however, and it takes some getting used to. Summers are easy, but the first winter I ventured into local-only territory, I ate the same dishes over and over again, and quickly tired of potatoes. One of the more valuable lessons I learned over that year was to relax a little. It's okay to supplement local fare with produce from other states or regions—the key word being *supplement*. But most importantly, I learned that I needed more options. I taught myself how to vary recipes by using what was in season. If I found a watermelon salad I loved, I tried it with roasted squash during winter. With renewed vigor and a little ingenuity, I eventually figured out how to vary my meals well enough that cooking with the seasons is now an effortless endeavor.

Fresh pantry veggies are an asset in the kitchen, providing substance, bulk, and nutritional fiber that we need for fuel. Where once meat prevailed, vegetables are now a stronger staple in our diets and continue to move further into the spotlight. No longer relegated to side dishes and salads, many vegetables can make up the main components of a meal. Your food should range in taste and texture, and you can use a selection of alternating aromatics and spices to enliven dishes and complement the sugars and starches that naturally occur in fruits and vegetables. Aim for biodiversity—a plate full of a varied selection of veg that rotates often.

STOCKING THE FRESH PANTRY

I AM AN URBAN FARMER and have been growing my own food for many years, so I'm something of a seasonal food missionary. I can tell you that food eaten in season really does taste better! Sunlight allows sugars to develop in fruits and vegetables—the reason many taste best at their peak, picked fresh from the vine, stem, or tree. No worries, though, if you don't grow your own food. Farmers markets, small grocery stores, and some supermarkets typically offer a revolving selection of seasonal, local produce. Even better, purchasing produce that comes from a regional farm ensures it has been harvested when ripe—a benefit of it traveling only a short distance from the field to your plate.

Much of the produce available in most supermarkets and "big box" stores, however, is harvested well before it's fully ripened, to extend its shelf life and help it survive the often long transport process from commercial farms to the store. It's true that for some cooks, these stores may be the only shopping option, so don't sweat it. The process of eating seasonally and sustainably is a work in progress—one that requires constant rethinking. *Fresh Pantry* is a seasonal guide, so anytime you select a vegetable or fruit during its season, you're eating something healthy. When you can, however, be sure to purchase what is both *local* and seasonal. I'm sure I sound like a broken record by now, but farmers markets are a great resource. Yes, they can be a pain to get to—but get there. It's worth the extra effort.

In addition to tasting better, seasonal fruits and veggies are often cheaper: buying watermelon from Peru in December will cost far more than if you buy local melons when they are in season (between June and September, depending on where you live). Purchasing food in season takes advantage of the inevitable economic scale of supply and demand. When tomatoes are ripe and ready, and every farmer at the market has boxes to sell, it forces the price down. At these moments, it's smart to be opportunistic and stock up. Buying seasonal food by the box will always equal savings.

At home, I aim to be as self-sufficient as possible—this means I do as much as I can on my own. I grow most of my own herbs and some lettuces in addition to herbaceous flowers, like scented geraniums. I have also accepted that I'll have to set aside some time to work in the kitchen on a near-daily basis. Yes, it takes longer to make homemade crackers or to cut and freeze summer fruit for later, but at the end of the day I'm using whole ingredients, I know what's in every bite, it's less expensive, *and* it tastes far better.

Eating seasonally benefits from a sharp eye, which allows you to discern quality and, therefore, value in the marketplace. It's not about being a food elitist and preferring expensive organic produce or appreciating the perfume of a ripe tomato (which, of course, a ripe tomato does have!). Instead, it's about making the best choice for your health and the health of your community. To make sure you're choosing the freshest ingredients, use all your senses. You want produce that has a real vibrancy to it—a vitality. It should look, smell, and feel like it's just been harvested.

Ignore wilted greens and anything with sliminess between the leaves, which indicates decay. Pay attention to any green spots that are turning yellow and avoid them. Touch all of the produce you purchase and leave behind anything with notable soft spots or anything that has gone limp. And of course, use your nose! Take a whiff and note any moldy smells or the slight fermentation of fruits. Everything you choose should smell good and look fresh. Be choosy when selecting fresh produce, but don't be squeamish. For instance, it's quite normal for winter squash skins to scar, leaving behind a dense web of unsightly tissue. This will not affect the taste of the fruit's flesh and actually helps preserve the squash a little bit longer. Ditto for things like dirty and rough-looking winter carrots or knobby celery root: they may not be pretty, but they still taste great. Conveniently, buying produce while it's in season alleviates the selection process a bit, because seasonal food is always pretty darn fresh—particularly when it comes straight from the farm.

When you're shopping for seasonal produce, it is wildly helpful to let go of any hard-and-fast rules about what you need, or think you need, to take home. It's best to allow availability and price to motivate your purchases instead of the short, demanding lines of a recipe. Use all of your senses and choose the best looking fruits and vegetables that day. And if something is going out of season, that's cause enough for throwing some money down! Try to be aware; if you're at the farmers market, talk to the farmers and grab the last offerings before they're gone for another year. I missed nectarine season by a week last year because I neglected to ask when the end of their season was. I walked away totally deflated—I'd have to wait another year.

It is also helpful, when shopping seasonally, to understand the naming mechanisms for fruits and vegetables. At large supermarkets, produce is often labeled only by the obvious—"peppers," "radish," "Bibb lettuce"—making it easy to grab what you need. Farmers markets, on the other hand, favor calling a spade a spade and will often label produce with the name of the particular variety they harvested—Chioggia beet, Nantes carrot, Little Gem lettuce. This can be slightly confusing, as the naming structure of fruits and vegetables is not always solid. One farmer's "pickling cucumber" could be another farmer's "gherkin," though they're the same cucumber—a small, prickly cuke that is bred to be pickled. It's not a matter of concern, but it's helpful to understand that they are in fact the same veg.

Produce comes and goes from the markets, and the time frame relies almost completely on Mother Nature. When you eat seasonally, you have a direct relationship with the weather, which is ever shifting and sometimes unreliable. A late summer allows for an extended tomato harvest, so instead of eating peppers and kale, you may be opting for another bowl of Perfect Tomato Salsa. In spring, a late frost can knock out entire fields of lettuce starts, or spring showers can flood fields and destroy loosely rooted snap peas. You'll find it's best to adapt to the varying weather conditions and make do with anything the farmers have available.

STORING THE FRESH PANTRY

WITH THE DRY PANTRY, THE goal is to stock your cupboards well enough to put together a meal with ease. Items in a dry pantry are re-stocked every few weeks, perhaps, but those dried beans and grains only get you so far. A fresh pantry is key to cooking healthy meals at home, although ingredients will ebb and flow with each month. Some vegetables can be treated more as part of your permanent, or "dry," pantry, due to their shelf life and longevity. This mostly applies to fall and winter vegetables—many of which can be stored in a cool cellar or garage for extended periods of time—and to daily recipe staples that should be stocked regularly. For instance, I always have onions, ginger, garlic, and lemons on hand, and they all store well.

Buying in bulk and then storing or preserving food provide excellent ways to add some thrift in the kitchen. When you store produce properly, you extend your dollars and keep your kitchen organized. Almost all produce, with few exceptions, should be washed, dried, and stored between single layers of linen or paper towels, then rolled and held in the crisper. Water and oxygen lead to decay, so when moist leaves touch, they won't last long. I have several thin, white tea towels (or flour-sack towels) for wrapping produce, and they work fantastically well and spare the cost and waste of using paper towels. This wrapping extends the life of vegetables for many days, in particular for leafy greens like lettuce and herbs.

All fruits taste best at room temperature, so I try to store them on the counter when possible. Fruits must be covered, either with a loosely wrapped linen cloth or a small, netted tent that sits over plates of food. This keeps gnats and other insects off the fruit. Additionally, any time a fruit or vegetable needs ripening, leaving it out on the counter at room temperature can help it mature. The longer fruit sits on the counter, the more it will sweeten and soften. Storage onions, ginger, garlic, apples, citrus, potatoes, winter squash, and more can all be kept at room temperature without much fear of decay. They will last for a week or two before showing signs of deterioration. In the same way, to retard maturation (if you have the perfect cherries, for example), store them in the fridge. Cold storage slows maturation and keeps fruits perfectly ripe for longer.

Many fruits and vegetables can be stored long-term by taking advantage of cold storage, freezing, or preserving. Generally, soft fruits freeze well on their own and require no effort other than to wrap them in a resealable plastic bag. To freeze fruit (tomatoes and tomatillos included), lay clean individual pieces of fruit out on a sheet pan, making sure not to overlap much. Place the entire sheet pan in the freezer and leave there until frozen through. This process, known as IQF, or Individually Quick Frozen, helps maintain the shape and quality of the fruit and allows for easy grabbing later on. You'll never have to cut through a frozen mass of stuck berries again. Each chapter in this book includes additional notes about storing specific produce and recipes.

WHAT I MEAN BY HEALTHY

I OFTEN TOSS AROUND THE description "healthy" as it relates to food, but I haven't explained what I mean. Please allow me to climb up on my soapbox for a moment and clarify why the term keeps showing up in my recipes: It is very (very!) important to me that recipes be good for you in some way. This is not to say I shy away from using butter or good fats like coconut oil. It means that I like to challenge the conventional way we tend to think about cooking. For instance, if I read a recipe that calls for loads of oil or cheese, I want to know *why* it's there. If there's not a good reason (maybe a specific taste or texture?), then I prefer to find a more healthful substitute.

Conversely, if I'm reading a healthy recipe that is technically good for me but seems to lack flavor, I ask myself, "Why would anyone want to eat that?" Then I work to improve the dish. This is how I channel my creative energy. Combined with my desire to remain fit and active, this drive has led me to the way I cook and eat today. I enjoy a well-balanced diet with lots of fruits and vegetables, no processed foods, minimal carbohydrates, and a limited reliance on protein as my main source of calories. Do I eat ice cream? *Hell, yes!* Do I fight off anyone within one foot of the crispy skin from a roast chicken? *Yes, I do!* But you have to have balance, and I strive for that in any recipe I write. I hope you find the recipes in *Fresh Pantry* equally healthy *and* delicious.

WINTER

DEPENDING ON WHERE YOU LIVE, eating locally and seasonally in the winter is, quite simply, a challenge. Winter officially begins just before the holidays on December 21st and lasts until March 21st. The first winter I experimented with eating only local food, I failed utterly. I probably caved by purchasing a big, plastic clamshell of hydroponic butter lettuce, leaving the store feeling both guilty and hypocritical. Now older and (hopefully) wiser, I have accepted that ingenuity is the way to make it through winter, along with a healthy dose of perseverance and the good grace to give yourself a break.

For much of the country, winter offers little from the fields, so what is available are mostly cellared fruits or vegetables, or those that were grown in late summer and held in the ground. Cellaring is the art of storing produce effectively over winter in order to make it last. Starch-heavy fruits and vegetables can be cellared efficiently: winter squash, potatoes, carrots, beets, turnips, parsnips, apples, pears. And even some summer melons can last through early winter if their shells are hard enough. Cellaring encompasses strategies like burying food in sand, wrapping fruit in newspaper, or hanging produce in nets, and then storing them in a cool, dry place like a cellar, garage, or refrigerated room. Tender greens, of course, would not survive such conditions. Their high water content renders them too delicate for long storage.

It's worth pointing out that much of the produce you find at big-box grocery stores in winter has been stored but not technically "cellared," and it's helpful to understand the difference. Modern agricultural practices like cold storage allow for immature fruits and vegetables to be held at cool temperatures with sterile air (i.e., no oxygen, which promotes decay) in order to last for many months in refrigerated warehouses and shipping trucks. These long-stored fruits and vegetables should be avoided when you shop for food in winter, as they are often pulled from the fields not because they are ripe and ready, but rather because they will store and travel well. (Slightly immature fruits maintain their shapes and are more difficult to bruise when handled.) Knowing what is in season and understanding your local options are the first line of defense for eating healthy and making good and delicious choices for you and your family. Local farmers may use refrigeration to store vegetables short term, but they're just as likely to use their fields as a type of ground storage when the weather turns cold in winter and vegetables are insulated in the earth.

It is easy to tire of what little winter has to offer that is truly seasonal. Roasted squash with butter and sage is delicious, of course, but you can't survive on that all winter. Your palate grows tired of the same flavor profile and texture. In order to combat the dinner doldrums, I use a two-pronged strategy: 1) pull from many cultures and 2) mix up the cooking techniques.

Flavors and textures vary widely from culture to culture, and varying spices alone will introduce new flavors to a standard winter vegetable. It's easier to eat sustainably when your meals are culturally rich. For example, the unexpected flavor of puréed winter squash stuffed in a wonton wrapper is one of my favorites.

Texturally, you want a range of mouthfeels across your meals, and varying the cooking technique helps to accomplish this goal. Baking produces soft flesh for most fruits and vegetables, whereas roasting at a high temperature allows natural sugars to caramelize and crisp. These are two very different results, achieved simply by adjusting the heat of your oven. Sautéing, which is done on the stovetop, preferably in a heavy-bottomed pan (I splurged on a cast-iron pan this year, and it's now practically the only pan I use), is similar to oven cooking, except you can control the heat more. This immediate control allows you to cook vegetables to any desired consistency—overcook for a soft core, or undercook for an al dente bite.

Winter is a great time to mix up cooking techniques and try something new. We tend to slow down a bit in winter—so take advantage of shorter days by cooking at home on the weekend or coming home immediately after work a night or two during the week. This extra personal time leaves space to enjoy the process—no need to rush through meals. Roasting broccoli, braising greens, baking breads, puréeing squash flesh, blanching carrots, frying onions—these are all techniques to employ and revisit over winter when the pickings are slim and you're spending more time indoors.

One more note about winter strategies in the kitchen: around the winter solstice, as we crest past holidays and settle into the slower routine of darker days, is an excellent time for food preservation. You wouldn't necessarily think so, as winter is generally an infertile time of year without bounty to put aside. Citrus, however, comes into season starting in December and offers a myriad of fruit selections through March. Even though citruses are not local fruits to people living in the north, winter is still an excellent time to take advantage of supple citrus skins and lively citrus flesh for both fresh eating and stocking the pantry. Marmalades, candied zests, and juice-based drinks are excellent indulgences that should not be missed, because as you know . . . every fruit has its season! And winter is where citrus really shines.

DECEMBER

CABBAGE

I GREW UP IN NEW YORK, which still has a vibrant Irish culture and community. For us, St. Patrick's Day was (and is) a legitimate holiday to celebrate, not just an excuse to drink green beer. Every St. Patrick's, my mom made (and still makes!) corned beef and cabbage, and it was one of my favorite meals growing up. I loved the velvety texture of salted cabbage against the stringy meat. And so my love affair with cabbage began. When I moved out of my mom's and started cooking for myself, I would often make steamed cabbage, just like she did, and eat it simply with salt and butter. It wasn't until later that I branched out and experimented with making slaws or using cabbage leaves as a stuffing vehicle—fully embracing all the potential of this ingredient.

Cabbage grows in a tight cluster of leaves that form into a heavy globe as they mature. Most cabbages are planted in summer for fall or winter harvest, though spring cabbages also can be sown and grown. These come into the markets from May to midsummer and are smaller and lighter than their autumn counterparts. Cabbage is one of the ultimate winter vegetables due to its long-lasting nature—it will keep in storage for months. Cabbages are members of the *Brassica* genus, alongside Brussels sprouts, collards, cauliflower, broccoli, and kale. Cabbage is a very nutritious vegetable—it sustained many families during the Great Depression—and it's especially high in vitamin C and fiber. Many people opt for cabbage when eating for health.

Most cabbages are sold with the tougher outer leaves removed and are typically pale in color. Cabbage varieties grown for sale in supermarkets are thick-ribbed, heavy, and uniform, and guarantee high yields from the field—but this doesn't necessarily mean they're the best tasting. Just remember that color means health, so select the greenest cabbage head you can find. Red cabbage, too, can be found year-round, and the same benefits apply—they are long-lasting vegetables packed with nutrients. Other varieties have crept into the marketplace recently and show up in fall—savoy cabbage being the most well known. Savoy leaves are densely crinkled and bright green in color, with smaller inner heads. These cabbages are sweet and pretty, adding texture and visual appeal to meals. Choose this cabbage when opting for a stuffed-leaf dish, like Pork & Apple Stuffed

Cabbage, as the leaves are malleable and wide. Round heads aside, Chinese cabbage is also available in both summer and fall. This elongated cabbage has a frilly edge and soft leaves and makes a great choice for recipes like the Turkey Meatball & Cabbage Soup.

Cabbage can be eaten raw, fermented, or cooked. If it's to be served raw, it's best to slice it very thin, particularly when using market-bred cabbages. The softer the leaves, the wider you can slice them. To soften the leaves, slice them into strips or chunks, massage in a small amount of salt, and let the cabbage sit for a few hours. This process draws water out and takes some of the work out of chewing. Big, thick heads of cabbage are also the best choice for homemade kraut or kimchee—both of which are fermented and relatively easy to make at home. For cooked cabbage, you can use any variety interchangeably, though red cabbage may color broths, liquids, or other vegetables. Cooking a cabbage will turn the strong leaves into a soft mass of velvet-like texture, so mind your cooking time and control the outcome. (Personally, I love when they are supple and melt in your mouth.)

Ideally, store cabbages in a cold garage or cellar, where they will keep for several months. Keep them stacked in a crate or box, in between torn newspaper strips. If the exterior leaves mold or decay, just strip them off and eat the inner cabbage leaves—don't let a bit of mold intimidate you. You may also keep cabbages in the house, in the vegetable drawer or crisper of the fridge, where they will keep for months. Wrap any unused cabbage in a dry linen or paper towel, so it doesn't come in contact with other fruits and vegetables, which may accelerate decay. If you're out of space in the fridge and don't have a cool, dry garage, cabbage may also be blanched, drained, and frozen in resealable plastic bags, where it will hold in good condition for several weeks.

Cabbage is one of the more affordable and functional vegetables available, so it's wise to take advantage of its virtues all winter long. Add cabbage to soups, where it will add bulk to feed many mouths, roast a head in the oven to bring out its sweetness, or put some up as kraut to enjoy as a garnish for meals. This versatile vegetable should not go neglected.

DECEMBER RECIPES

Cabbage

Cabbage & Potato Burek
Cabbage–Apple–Carrot Slaw
Cabbage Focaccia with Olives
Creamy Cabbage with Bacon & Cranberries
Steamed Savoy Cabbage with Dill Butter
Turkey Meatball & Cabbage Soup
Red Cabbage Pasta
Pork & Apple Stuffed Cabbage
Red Cabbage Sauerkraut

Seasonal Extras

Aunt Janet's Broccoli & Potato Pasta
Deep-Roasted Broccoli with Charred Garlic

Cabbage & Potato Burek

MAKES 4 TO 6 SERVINGS

I tasted burek on my first trip to Croatia to meet my extended family, and I often think of it with longing. This traditional pastry is eaten in the morning or afternoon and stuffed with meat, cheese, potatoes, cabbage, or even apples. Here, phyllo dough is used to wrap a savory filling of cabbage and potatoes, and then rolled and pressed into a baking tin. Each burek bakes up golden brown and crispy and can be eaten warm or at room temperature.

6 to 8 tablespoons butter, divided
1 tablespoon olive oil
1 cup diced onion
$\frac{1}{4}$ teaspoon salt
$\frac{1}{8}$ teaspoon pepper
$\frac{1}{2}$ pound cabbage, sliced into thin strips (about 2 cups)
$\frac{1}{2}$ pound potatoes, cooked and smashed (about 1$\frac{1}{2}$ cups)
3 tablespoons white vermouth or wine
$\frac{1}{2}$ cup water
12 sheets phyllo

In a large pot, warm 1 tablespoon of the butter and the olive oil over medium-high heat. When the butter has melted, add the onion, salt, and pepper, and cook until the onion softens and starts to brown, about 10 minutes. Add the cabbage, and stir until it starts to wilt. Once the cabbage has wilted, add the potatoes and cook, stirring often, until the vegetables start to stick to the pan. Add the vermouth and deglaze the pan, scraping up any brown bits, about 2 minutes. Once all of the vermouth has evaporated, add the water to the pan, cover, and reduce the heat to low. Cook, stirring occasionally, until the cabbage and potatoes are very soft and can be easily mashed together with the back of a fork, about 20 minutes.

Remove from the heat and set aside to cool.

To form the burek, lay the phyllo sheets out and cover them with a damp dish towel. Melt the remaining butter over low heat. Remove 2 pieces of phyllo from under the towel and set them out on the counter, stacked, with the longest edge nearest you. Using a pastry brush, brush the entire top sheet with butter. Get 2 more sheets of phyllo and stack them over the first 2 sheets. Brush butter over this entire layer as well. Cut the stacked phyllo in half widthwise, so you have 2 new layered sets about 8 inches wide and 13 inches long.

Preheat the oven to 425 degrees F.

Spread a row of the cooled filling along the short end of the phyllo dough, about 1 inch from the bottom edge. The filling should be no more than 1 inch wide and should leave a 1-inch allowance along the side edges. Fold the bottom flap of the phyllo up over the filling and brush some melted butter over the fold. Roll the pastry into a long cylinder. Brush more butter over the phyllo as you roll, ending with the seam facing down against the counter. Starting from one side, snake the rolled phyllo into a small, loose

CABBAGE TO KRAUT—WHAT IS FERMENTATION?

My friend Margaret's grandmother used to say that the only way to guarantee a good and healthy year was to eat a serving of sauerkraut on New Year's Eve. I couldn't agree more. Cabbage is a deeply sustaining food and has been a staple of many cultures over the years. Sauerkraut, which is the sour and tangy result of fermenting cabbage, has also been made for centuries. The process of fermentation preserves it for many months at a time, which was very helpful before refrigeration, and the resulting sauerkraut had the added benefit of being a very healthy food. It's no wonder many cultures across Asia and Europe have relied on sauerkraut for sustenance.

Fermenting at home is easy, but the process is bound to leave beginners with unanswered questions. Some fermented foods take advantage of the natural process of converting sugar to alcohol (as with wine) or creating lactic acid and using bacteria to ferment foods (as in yogurt). This conversion happens with the addition of lactic bacteria (good bacteria) to help the process along. The process results in a bubbling batch of ingredients that eventually settle down, tasting tangy and sour in a good way.

Cabbage can be fermented in small batches on the countertop. It is a simple process, though one that requires common sense and faith in your powers of observation. We eat many fermented foods today, with little thought to how they are made—artisan breads, beer, coffee, kimchi, miso, yogurt—all of these foods are fermented. In our daily environment, microbes, bacteria, and yeast naturally surround us. They live in our air and provide the basis for fermentations. Sauerkraut harnesses these naturally occurring organisms to transform cabbage into a tangy side dish.

Cabbage undergoes several phases before the final outcome of "kraut" is reached. Grated cabbage is covered and submerged in a saltwater brine. This salted brine attracts "good" bacteria to the cabbage and eventually helps to produce sauerkraut. The more salt used, the more acidic the final kraut will be. The brine also protects the cabbage from "bad" bacteria and microorganisms—the salted environment is inhospitable for these types of spoilers. For this reason, the cabbage must always remain submerged in its own salted vegetable juice brine. If the top layer of kraut does come in contact with air and mold or decay forms, you can simply scoop off the first discolored inches of cabbage and continue with the fermentation; the cabbage under the layer in contact with air remains healthy and fine. Fermentations can occur in as quickly as

→

a few days or may take up to several months. It's the choice of the cook to determine when the preferred flavor is reached. For details on how best to start your own batch of sauerkraut, check out the detailed recipe for Red Cabbage Sauerkraut.

Fermented foods are tremendously healthy for us. They offer good microorganisms to our digestive systems. Gut health is thought to be one of the most vital components for a healthy life—90 percent of the serotonin our body produces originates in the gut. Serotonin contributes to our mood, appetite, sleep, learning, and memory. A healthy gut equals a healthy equilibrium throughout our bodies.

The introduction of these microbes also helps to support a strong immune system, has been linked to cancer prevention, and may keep asthma and other respiratory ailments at bay. By adding fermented foods to your diet, you naturally support a microbial diversity that is vital for optimal health. Personally, I try to eat a fermented food at every meal. I have kefir stirred into a juice drink in the morning, a small spoonful of fermented carrots on toast for lunch, and maybe some kraut or kimchi over my stews, soups, or roasts for dinner. Try some at your next meal!

---

coil, taking care to bend the fold creases gently. Place the phyllo coil, or burek, along the edge of a 9-inch round baking pan. There will be room for more. Continue making stuffed phyllo coils in this fashion until you run out of filling, placing them in the pan in a circular pattern. Brush the tops with any remaining melted butter.

Put the pan in the oven and bake until the phyllo is deeply golden brown, about 30 to 40 minutes. Remove from the oven and let it cool slightly before serving.

PANTRY NOTE: This pastry is a great way to use up leftover potatoes or cabbage. Burek holds up okay in the fridge for one day before going soggy. Crisp up leftovers in the oven before serving.

Cabbage-Apple-Carrot Slaw

MAKES 6 SERVINGS

Winter slaws offer a perfect way to freshen up the typically heavy dishes that predominate when the weather turns cold. In this slaw, thinly shaved cabbage is paired with sweet apple and grated carrots, and then tossed with a simple vinaigrette. Slaws are best left to macerate for some time before serving, so plan ahead and let this one rest at least a few hours before the meal. You can play with the flavor profile by adding chopped cilantro, a pinch of cayenne pepper, or a handful of raisins.

½ pound cabbage

3 medium carrots, peeled and grated
(about 2 cups)

1 large apple, cut into thin matchsticks
(about 1½ cups)

¼ cup olive oil

1 tablespoon fresh lime juice

1 tablespoon rice wine vinegar

2 teaspoons sugar

2 tablespoons poppy seeds (optional)

Using a sharp knife and working slowly, cut off very thin slices of cabbage—almost shaving them off. The thinner you slice the cabbage the more appetizing it is. Put the shaved cabbage in a large bowl. Add the carrots and apple to the cabbage and toss the ingredients to combine. Add the oil, lime juice, vinegar, sugar, and poppy seeds, if desired, and stir well to combine. Cover with a plate or plastic wrap and set aside on the counter or in the fridge for at least 3 hours before serving.

PANTRY NOTE: Slaw will last for several days in the fridge, covered.

Cabbage Focaccia with Olives

MAKES ONE 12 X 16-INCH "LOAF"

Focaccia is flat and spongy Italian bread. Bread flour lends a chewy texture to the finished "loaf," much like that of a golden pizza crust. The addition of charred cabbage and olives gives the bread a flavorful punch, accelerated by an indulgent sprinkle of fresh rosemary and a drizzle of olive oil. You can use any cabbage or combination of cabbages for this recipe—savoy, traditional green heads, or red cabbage varieties all work equally well and provide a mix of color.

Olive oil for sheet pan

DOUGH

2 cups warm water

3 teaspoons active dry yeast

1 tablespoon honey

3½ to 4 cups bread flour

1 teaspoon salt

TOPPINGS

1 pound mixed cabbage, shredded
(about 4 cups)

10 cloves garlic, peeled and smashed

4 tablespoons olive oil, divided

¼ teaspoon salt

1 teaspoon red chile flakes

2 tablespoons chopped fresh rosemary

½ cup pitted Kalamata or cured black
olives

Coarse salt, for dusting

Olive oil, for drizzling

Lightly oil the bottom of a sheet pan and set it aside.

To make the focaccia dough, combine the warm water, yeast, and honey, and stir until the yeast is nearly dissolved. Set aside until the yeast dissolves completely and the mixture is foamy, about 10 to 15 minutes.

Fit an electric mixer with a dough hook. In the mixer bowl, combine 3 cups of the bread flour with the teaspoon of salt. Turn the machine to low and pour in half of the yeast mixture. Mix until well combined and then add the remaining yeast mixture. Mix on low to medium-low speed for 5 minutes. If necessary, add more bread flour in quarter-cup increments until the dough is no longer tacky. (Do not add more than 1 cup in total.) Turn the dough out onto a lightly floured work space and hand-knead for 3 minutes. The dough should not need more flour and should easily pull away from your work surface. Set the dough on the prepared sheet pan and cover loosely with plastic wrap, topped with a clean dish towel. Set the dough in a warm place to rise, about 45 minutes to an hour, until it has doubled in size.

Preheat the oven to 450 degrees F. While the dough is rising, make the toppings. Put the cabbage and cloves of garlic on a second large sheet pan and toss them with 2 tablespoons of the olive oil and the ¼ teaspoon of salt. Spread this mixture evenly across the pan (you may need yet another sheet pan in order to spread the cabbage evenly, avoiding overlaps) and put the pan in the oven. Roast until the cabbage edges are charred and browned, about 15 to 20 minutes, stirring occasionally. Remove from the oven and set aside.

Meanwhile, in a small bowl, combine the remaining olive oil, the chile flakes, and the rosemary, and set aside.

Once the cabbage is cooked and the dough has risen, remove the dough from its pan and punch it down, turning it over once or twice and kneading lightly. When most of the air has been removed, move the dough back to a freshly oiled sheet pan. Using your fingertips, stretch the dough into a rectangular shape nearly the size of the pan, leaving the dough about ½ inch thick. Using your fingertips, make several depressions in the surface of the dough. Sprinkle the charred cabbage and garlic evenly over the top. Add the olives, pressing them lightly down into the dough. Pour the reserved olive oil mixture over the entire surface of the dough. (It's okay if olive oil pools in the depressions you've made with your fingertips!) Cover the dough with plastic wrap, topped off with a dish towel. Set it in a warm space to rise for a second time, about 45 minutes to an hour; allow it to rise until it's doubled in size and stands about 1 inch thick.

Preheat the oven to 475 degrees F. Remove the plastic wrap and sprinkle the dough with a liberal pinch of coarse salt. Put the focaccia in the oven and bake until golden brown, about 15 minutes. Remove from the oven and allow it to cool slightly before serving. Serve alongside a small bowl of olive oil for dipping.

PANTRY NOTE: Focaccia leftovers can be wrapped in parchment and held at room temperature for one day. Leftover focaccia can be sliced horizontally and used as panini bread or charred on the grill for panzanella salad. You can also freeze focaccia in resealable plastic bags, where it will keep for about one month.

Creamy Cabbage with Bacon & Cranberries

MAKES 4 SERVINGS

This side dish is deceptively healthy and easy to make. Steamed cabbage is tossed with melted butter and plain yogurt, which results in a velvety and tangy sauce. The butter and bacon appear in small proportion to the greens, giving the sensation of richness without a heavy cream component. The browned bacon and sweet plumped cranberries create a perfect flavor profile—salty, sugary, and tart, all in one bite.

- ½ cup chopped bacon
- ½ pound cabbage, cut into thin strips (about 2 cups)
- ½ cup dried cranberries
- 6 tablespoons butter
- 4 tablespoons plain nonfat yogurt
- ⅛ teaspoon salt
- ⅛ teaspoon pepper

In a small saucepan over medium-high heat, cook the bacon until golden brown. Drain off the fat and set the crisped bacon aside.

Bring a large pot of salted water to a boil, and drop in the cabbage and cranberries. Cook until the cabbage is wilted and just tender, about 5 minutes. Drain and put the cabbage and cranberries in a serving bowl. Sprinkle the bacon on top, and cover, keeping it warm.

In a small frying pan or saucepan, melt the butter, then remove it from the heat and pour it into a small bowl. Once it has cooled slightly, stir in the yogurt, salt, and pepper. Pour this mixture over the cabbage and toss to coat evenly. Serve immediately.

PANTRY NOTE: This side dish will hold in the fridge, covered, for about three days. Heat up gently before serving.

Steamed Savoy Cabbage with Dill Butter

MAKES 4 SERVINGS

I grew up eating corned beef and cabbage. My mom would cut the cabbage into big wedges and submerge it in beef broth until it was practically falling apart. Here, wedged savoy cabbage is steamed, resulting in a bright green leaf that is appetizing yet has a soft texture, just like Mom's.

- 1 small head savoy cabbage, quartered
- 1 stick butter, melted
- 3 tablespoons fresh dill, finely chopped
- ¼ teaspoon salt
- ⅛ teaspoon pepper

In a large pot over high heat, bring an inch of water to a boil, then put all the cabbage in the pot and cover, reducing heat to low.

Meanwhile, in a small saucepan, melt the butter over medium heat. Once the butter has melted, remove it from the heat and sprinkle in the dill, salt, and pepper, stirring to combine.

HOW TO GROW CABBAGE

Cabbage is a crop best grown in gardens with extra space, in my opinion—they take a fair amount of time to develop heads and need extra room for their large bottom leaves. If you have the space, however, cabbages are great crops to grow as they require little attention and produce big, nutritious heads for harvest.

Cabbages can be grown in spring, summer, or autumn; different varieties will thrive across the seasons. Be sure to select the proper variety and time your planting accordingly. Spring cabbages produce smaller, more tender heads, and can be planted as starts, under protection, as early as March in mild climates—later for areas with hard frost. If you're direct-seeding, sow later to allow the soil to warm and help with germination.

Late cabbages are planted in summer for a pre-winter harvest. These varieties have big, strong cores that can withstand light frosts but are meant to be harvested before a hard frost and either cellared or used in krauts. Some varieties are also bred for over-wintering. These will be planted sometime in early to mid-autumn and should survive the winter, assuming they put on enough growth before winter sets in. Come spring, overwintering varieties start to put on size and can be harvested in March and April when there is otherwise not much in the garden for eating.

Cabbages take up a lot of space—rows should be about four feet apart, and cabbages spaced anywhere from eighteen inches to three feet, depending on the seed type and time of year. They do well in conditioned soils but don't need much extra attention or amendments. Overwintering cabbages (as with most overwintering crops) do well with a compost side-dress in spring, which helps support their last bit of growth before harvest.

Chinese cabbages should be treated differently in the garden. They are not as hardy and will not overwinter well. Sow Chinese cabbages in spring, and they will be ready for summer harvests. These cabbages bolt quickly if the temperature turns warm without warning, so their success in the garden depends on how cool or warm spring is.

Cabbages are reasonably shallow rooted and therefore do well in containers. One cabbage head fits in a medium container—it must be about eighteen inches deep and have a diameter wide enough to support the head. Use potting soil and mix in several handfuls of composted manure or a few spoonfuls of nitrogen and be sure to water regularly. Inconsistent watering stresses all plants and leads to disease. For winter, mulch the soil and wrap the pots in burlap to help prevent the roots from freezing.

Steam the cabbage until a knife inserted in it goes easily through, about 15 minutes. Remove the cabbage from the heat and, using a slotted spoon, drain off the excess water and place the cabbage on a serving platter. Pour the dill butter over the cabbage and serve immediately.

PANTRY NOTE: Leftover cabbage can be used as filling for burek or chopped into pieces and added to the filling for stuffed cabbage leaves.

Turkey Meatball & Cabbage Soup

MAKES 4 TO 6 SERVINGS

This is one of my all-time favorite meals—I make it whenever I need a little extra TLC. Light and wholesome turkey meatballs are flavored with Asian-inspired ingredients like green onions, cilantro, and sesame oil. Dropped into home-made chicken broth spiked with cooking wine and heaped with cabbage, this soup is the ulti-mate miracle elixir, promising good health and good eating all winter long.

GARNISH
1/2 pound shiitake mushrooms
1 tablespoon olive oil

BROTH
1 tablespoon olive oil
4 cloves garlic, peeled and smashed
1 pound cabbage, chopped (about 2 cups)
1/4 cup Chinese cooking wine, such as
   Shaoxing

5 cups homemade chicken broth
3 green onions, trimmed and cut in half
   lengthwise

MEATBALLS
1 pound ground turkey
2 tablespoons finely chopped green
   onion
2 tablespoons chopped cilantro
1 tablespoon grated fresh ginger
2 teaspoons sesame oil
1/4 teaspoon salt
1/4 teaspoon pepper
2 tablespoons olive oil
Chopped cilantro, for garnish (optional)

Preheat the oven to 425 degrees F.

Place the mushrooms on a sheet pan and drizzle them with 1 tablespoon of olive oil. Using your hands, toss the mushrooms to coat well with the oil, then put them in the oven. Bake, stirring occasionally, until the mushrooms are dehy-drated and crisped, about 20 minutes. Remove from the oven and set aside. These will garnish the individual servings.

Put the remaining tablespoon of olive oil in a large pot over medium-high heat. When the oil is rippling and the pan is hot, add the garlic and cabbage, turning them over continuously to pre-vent burning. Cook until all the cabbage is wilted and the garlic is beginning to stick to the bottom of the pan. Add the wine to the pan to deglaze it, scraping up any brown bits, stirring continu-ally until the wine is nearly evaporated. Add the chicken broth and bring to a boil. Reduce heat to the lowest setting and cover.

To make the meatballs, put all the meatball ingredients except the oil into a large bowl and use your hands to combine well. Shape the ground turkey into small meatballs and set them aside. Heat the olive oil in a large sauté pan over medium-high heat. When the oil is hot, drop in the meatballs and brown them on all sides (about 2 minutes per side), then drop them immediately into the soup broth.

Add the halved green onions to the soup and cover, cooking until the meatballs are cooked through and the cabbage is very tender, about 30 minutes.

To serve, spoon a portion of the soup into a soup bowl and garnish with a few roasted mushrooms and a sprinkle of the chopped cilantro, if desired.

PANTRY NOTE: This soup is even better the second day and can remain in the fridge, covered, for up to five days. Leftovers freeze well and will keep for a month in the freezer.

Red Cabbage Pasta

MAKES 4 TO 6 SERVINGS

This recipe is a new way to think about serving pasta. Long noodles are cooked and twirled with roasted red cabbage, then doused with a crispy layer of garlic-infused toasted bread crumbs.

The texture of al dente pasta with something crisp is universally appealing, and this combo is packed with flavor.

> ½ pound red cabbage, shredded (about 2 cups)
> 4 tablespoons olive oil, divided
> ¼ teaspoon salt
> 1 tablespoon butter
> 2 anchovy fillets
> 4 cloves garlic, chopped
> ½ cup bread crumbs
> 1 pound spaghetti
> Parmesan, for grating (optional)

Preheat the oven to 450 degrees F.

Place the cabbage on a large sheet pan and toss it with 2 tablespoons of the olive oil and the salt. Spread the cabbage evenly across the pan in a single layer, then set it in the oven. Roast until the cabbage edges are charred and browned, about 15 to 20 minutes, stirring occasionally. Remove from the oven and put the cabbage in a large bowl until ready to use.

In a medium sauté pan, heat the remaining olive oil and the butter over medium-high heat. When the butter is melted, add the anchovies and garlic, cooking them and stirring constantly until the garlic begins to brown, about 5 minutes. Stir in the bread crumbs. They will seem dry at first, but keep stirring and eventually they will turn glossy from absorbing the oils. Stir continually until the bread crumbs are golden brown and fragrant, about 4 to 5 minutes more. Remove from the heat and set aside.

Bring a large pot of salted water to a boil and drop in the spaghetti. Cook until al dente, about 10 to 12 minutes (or according to the package instructions). Drain the pasta and immediately add it to the bowl with the cabbage, tossing with tongs to combine.

Portion the pasta into shallow bowls and sprinkle on a liberal helping of the prepared bread crumbs. Grate Parmesan over the tops, if desired. Serve immediately.

PANTRY NOTE: Leftover pasta keeps well for one day in the fridge, covered. Reheat quickly or eat cold.

Pork & Apple Stuffed Cabbage

MAKES 4 SERVINGS

Stuffed cabbage rolls, a traditional peasant food, vary in their contents across many different cultures. I started making them years ago and filled them with anything I had in the house—some leftover steamed barley, mashed potatoes, or maybe even some sautéed greens. In this recipe, cabbage leaves are stuffed with a classic fall pairing—pork and apples—and then baked in a wine broth until sweet and tender. Here, the cabbage leaves are peeled from the head and blanched, but you may also freeze the entire head two days before making the dish and then defrost it, which also wilts the leaves and spares the extra work. You can vary the flavor by swapping out stuffing

ingredients or even altering the braising liquid—try adding sautéed onions and tomato sauce to the braise.

1 cup brown rice

2¼ cups water

1 large head green cabbage, about 2 to 3 pounds

1 tablespoon olive oil

1 pound pork sausage (about 2 cups)

1 apple, finely diced (about 1½ cups)

2 teaspoons smoked paprika

1 teaspoon salt

¼ teaspoon pepper

1½ cups dry white wine

1½ cups beef stock or water

2 carrots, roughly chopped

4 tablespoons dried thyme (or a handful of fresh leaves)

2 cloves garlic, smashed

½ onion, thinly sliced (about 1 cup)

2 tablespoons butter, chopped into small pieces

In a medium saucepan over high heat, bring the rice and water to a boil. Reduce the heat to low, cover the pot, and steam until the rice is very tender and broken, about 30 to 60 minutes. Remove from the heat and, without removing the cover, set aside.

While the rice is steaming, prepare the cabbage leaves. Set the top of the cabbage on the counter and, using a sharp knife, cut the leaves away from the stem, slicing alongside the stem to release the leaves, one by one. Gently peel each leaf away from the cabbage head and set them aside. Continue working in this fashion until you have about 16 leaves.

Bring a large pot of salted water to a boil and add the leaves to the pot, blanching until the ribs are very soft, about 15 minutes. Remove the leaves from the water and set them in a colander or strainer to drain further and cool slightly.

While the cabbage is cooling, in a large sauté pan, heat the olive oil over medium heat. When it's warm, crumble in the sausage and cook it until golden brown, about 15 minutes. Remove from heat and put the sausage in a large bowl.

Add the apple, paprika, salt, pepper, and steamed rice to the bowl. Stir well, folding to combine. Taste for seasoning and adjust, if desired.

Preheat the oven to 300 degrees F.

To make the cabbage rolls, lay 1 leaf flat on the counter and place a spoonful of filling (about ¼ cup) in the center of the leaf. Working from the bottom up, fold the leaf up and over the filling. Fold in the sides, creating a compact envelope, then continue rolling until the cabbage leaf is closed. Set the roll aside, seam side down, and continue making rolls until all of the filling is gone. Don't worry about small tears in the leaves or oddly shaped rolls—they will cook well and taste great, regardless.

In the bottom of a large Dutch oven, put the wine, beef stock or water, carrots, thyme, and garlic. Place the cabbage rolls directly on top of these ingredients, stacking them in layers, as need be. Once all of the rolls are in the pot, layer the sliced onions on top. Place the butter evenly over the onions and cover the pot with aluminum foil. Add a lid to the pot and put it in the oven to cook.

After 2 hours, remove the pot from the oven and set it aside to cool before serving. To serve, plate up the cabbage rolls, spooning over a little bit of the pan broth to moisten.

PANTRY NOTE: Leftover cabbage rolls can be kept in the fridge, covered, for up to three days. They taste even better on the second day.

Red Cabbage Sauerkraut

MAKES 2 TO 4 CUPS

Homemade sauerkraut makes for a strong and pungent side dish with an incomparable flavor— and the homemade version tastes very different from commercially produced sauerkraut. Sauer- kraut is a fermented product and is considered a "live" food: it is packed with healthy micro- flora that will help maintain a healthy gut and strengthen your immune system, deliciously. As fermentation is not an exact science, use this recipe as a guide and be prepared to use your common sense. Any fermentation smell- ing "off" or offensive should be composted and restarted, but don't be intimidated—you can do it! (And check out the sidebar Cabbage to Kraut—What Is Fermentation? for more tips on home fermentation.)

1 medium head red cabbage
1 tablespoon sea salt
2 cloves garlic, minced
2 teaspoons grated fresh ginger
1 teaspoon caraway seeds

Cut the cabbage head into quarters, leaving the core intact. Using a food processor with the grater attachment (or a box grater on the largest holes), grate the cabbage into fine pieces, working in batches if necessary.

Put the grated cabbage in a large bowl (or a large stockpot if you don't have a large enough bowl) and add the salt, garlic, ginger, and caraway seeds. Stir to combine.

Using your hands, toss and gently squeeze the cabbage pieces, working to extract some moisture. When the cabbage starts creating moisture and is slightly softer, pack it into a tall, narrow container like a wide-mouth quart or half-gallon jar. Fill the jar to the top and, using your fist, press down firmly to pack down the cabbage and extract some more water for the salt brine. Pack it as tightly as you can before covering.

To cover the cabbage, use a clean weight small enough to fit inside the top of the jar—a small plate, a clean stone, or a smaller glass jar filled with water all work well. You may also use a resealable plastic bag filled with brine (dissolving 1 teaspoon of salt in 1 cup of hot water), which is malleable and heavy enough to keep the vegetables submerged. (If it leaks, brine won't affect fermentation.)

The weighted cabbage will continue releasing water and creating a saltwater brine. The brine should rise up to cover the cabbage—this takes anywhere from 6 to 12 hours. The cabbage must be fully submerged under a saltwater brine for the duration of the ferment, lest it develop mold.

If the brine does not rise high enough to cover the cabbage after 8 hours, add some saltwater to the jar by dissolving 1 teaspoon of salt in 1 cup of hot water. Stir to dissolve the salt and let it cool completely before adding it to the jar.

Set the jar aside on a counter, or in a cool dark cupboard, to ferment for a few days or longer. The kraut should be ready in about five days and will have a pleasant smell and crisp texture. Taste it and decide if you'd like to ferment it further. I prefer to ferment for somewhere between 1 and 2 weeks, but you can ferment kraut for many weeks or even months, if so desired.

Sometimes the kraut on top will discolor, or the fermentation will create bubbles or "blooms" of mold. In the event of any discoloration, just scoop it from the top of the kraut before serving. With surface blooms or bubbles, use a spoon to remove as much as you can, but don't worry too much about it. It's typical of the brine coming into contact with air.

When done, the cabbage will be translucent. Remove the weight from the kraut, cover it with a lid, and store it in the fridge.

PANTRY NOTE: Kraut will hold in the fridge, covered, for many weeks or even months. Use it as a relish, a garnish for winter stews, or a condiment on a cheese platter.

Aunt Janet's Broccoli & Potato Pasta

MAKES 4 SERVINGS

My Aunt Janet has been making this Italian pasta dish for as long as I can remember. I clearly recall thinking as a kid, "Potatoes with pasta?!" as I peered over the edge of her stove. But the end result is a deeply satisfying bowl of vegetables and noodles that everyone will love.

2 large stalks broccoli

2 small boiling potatoes, diced (about 1½ cups)

6 tablespoons olive oil

6 cloves garlic, cut in quarters

½ teaspoon salt

¼ teaspoon pepper

4 cups penne pasta

½ cup grated Parmesan or Pecorino

To prep the broccoli, cut off the stems along the main broccoli stalks, and break or cut off small pieces of the florets. Use a vegetable peeler to shave the outer, tough layer of broccoli stalks, and finely chop the smaller stems and the peeled stalks. Fill a large saucepan with 2 cups of water and bring to a boil over high heat. Add the broccoli florets, chopped stems and stalks, and the potatoes; cover, reducing heat to medium-low. Simmer until the broccoli and potatoes are very soft and can be easily smashed with a fork, about 25 to 30 minutes. Drain the broccoli and potatoes and set aside.

In a large, deep-sided sauté pan, warm the olive oil over medium heat, then drop in the garlic cloves and salt, and cook until the garlic is translucent and crisped on the outside, about 15 minutes. You do not want the cloves to brown, so reduce the heat if they are cooking too quickly.

Meanwhile, bring a large pot of salted water to a boil and drop in the penne. Cook until al dente, about 12 minutes (or according to the package directions). Drain, reserving ¾ cup of the pasta water, and set aside.

Add the steamed broccoli to the garlic and oil, leaving the mixture to poach instead of turning it often. Just stir it 2 or 3 times—about every 5 minutes or so. Cook until very soft and starting to brown just slightly, about 15 minutes in total. Using the back of a fork, smash the broccoli, potatoes, and garlic into small pieces. Add another spoonful of oil if the pan goes dry.

Turn the heat to high. When the broccoli starts sticking to the pan, stir in the reserved pasta water and the cooked penne. Remove from the heat and serve immediately, portioning into shallow bowls and dividing the grated Parmesan evenly over the top of each serving.

PANTRY NOTE: Leftover pasta holds in the fridge, covered, up to three days and is delicious eaten cold.

Deep-Roasted Broccoli with Charred Garlic

MAKES 4 SERVINGS

This roasted broccoli dish is deceptively easy, but packs such a delicious punch it's worth including in your regular lineup of dishes. High heat is the crucial component here—it cooks the broccoli quickly but also guarantees burned and crispy florets that are addictive. Smashed garlic also turns deep brown and can be eaten by the clove, so add more if you're a garlic lover.

- 3 stalks broccoli
- 8 cloves garlic, peeled and smashed
- 3 tablespoons olive oil
- ½ teaspoon salt
- ¼ teaspoon pepper

Preheat the oven to 450 degrees F.

To prep the broccoli, cut off the stems along the main broccoli stalks, and break or cut off whole florets. Use a vegetable peeler to shave the outer, tough layer of the main broccoli stalks; quarter the stalks lengthwise, then chop them into 3-inch-long pieces.

Place the broccoli stalk and floret pieces and the garlic on a large sheet pan and drizzle with the olive oil. Sprinkle on the salt and pepper. Using your hands, toss the pieces to combine, making sure all of the broccoli is glossy and coated. Spread evenly across the pan, making sure not to overlap any broccoli pieces.

Put the baking sheet in the oven and cook until the broccoli edges are charred and crispy, turning and redistributing once or twice, for about 15 to 17 minutes total. Remove the pan from the oven and serve immediately.

PANTRY NOTE: Leftover charred broccoli can be held in the fridge, covered, for up to three days. Serve leftovers as a garnish over bean stews or use as a filling for burek.

JANUARY

WINTER SQUASH

IN WINTER, THERE ARE NOT a lot of options for fresh vegetables, which is a challenge for me. As someone who likes to cook and eat at home, and prefers to work with fresh ingredients, I scan produce labels at my local grocery store to figure out where each vegetable or fruit was grown. Anything from South America is out—it never tastes great, it's often expensive, and freshness is always in question. Hello? How long ago was that picked? I also avoid any produce that is way out of season—summer fruits like tomatoes or strawberries. Strawberries in winter are rarely sweet and delicious; instead, they are slightly green and acidic. For most of us, this means there are not a lot of seasonal and fresh vegetables to choose from during winter.

Enter the often overlooked winter squashes. These vegetables (technically fruits) can be eaten whole, mashed into a smooth buttery purée, grated into batters, and sautéed to a crisp. They pair beautifully with roasted winter meats or simple seared and baked fish. Nutritionally speaking, winter squashes, with their varying shades of orange flesh, are packed with benefits: vitamins A and C, along with an excellent dose of fiber. Squashes are low in calories, which makes them superb options for anyone focused on weight loss or eating healthy. Economically speaking, because they are not high-demand vegetables, winter squashes are quite affordable, often costing somewhere in the ballpark of a dollar a pound.

Beyond creamy butternut squash soup or split squashes that are sweet-roasted with cinnamon, however, many home cooks simply do not know what to do with winter squashes. Countless recipes call for butter, sugar, cinnamon, and a roasting pan, which is tasty but gets really boring after two or three meals. Other common and, in my opinion, unfortunate, squash recipes add loads of dried fruit and other sweet ingredients. But winter squashes are already delightfully sweet, so there is little need to candy them up with additional sugars. Happily, there are many more interesting ways to cook with winter squash, and I'm sharing ten of them here, from breakfast to dessert.

Harvested in late fall, winter squashes last through early spring if stored properly. Thanks to this longevity, squashes are plentiful throughout the season at most grocery stores. Because they are slow to spoil, you can buy them in bulk, which further reduces their price. Store a box of squash in your cool garage (or in an insulated shed) so you always have a fresh vegetable on hand.

Of course, winter squashes require a bit of muscle to make them work; the thick skins can be intimidating—another reason that some home cooks avoid them. But it's nothing a sharp knife and some strategic cutting techniques can't overcome. Once the squash is open, you can remove the seeds and pulp by scraping them out with a metal spoon. Save the seeds and roast them for a recipe garnish or an easy snack later. For DIY kitchen enthusiasts, you can also dry and hull squash seeds to remove the internal seed, known as a pepita (see the sidebar Seed Saver: How to Make Home-made Pepitas in this chapter). The process is time-consuming but fun, and a great way to keep kids busy while you're in the kitchen.

Winter squashes come in a sweeping variety of shapes and sizes, but don't be daunted when picking them out. Although variety names may change between regions (or countries), at the end of the day there are a handful of squashes that you can purchase anywhere. I've listed my favorites below. Make sure to avoid gourds, however, which are strictly ornamental.

Pumpkins. Most pumpkins are bred for size, not flavor. If opting for pumpkin, choose a Sugar Pie or other cooking variety like New England Pie or cheese pumpkins.

Butternut Squash. Among the most popular types, butternut is one of the creamier squashes, lending itself nicely to mashes and purées. Peeling a butternut is reasonably easy, immediately rewarding you with a good portion of thick flesh.

Acorn Squash. Easily identifiable and most often used for roasting, this squash has tender pulp that tears easily from ribbed skin into succulent and buttery strings. Shaped like an acorn, it holds together nicely when baked.

Delicata Squash. As gorgeous as they are delicious, delicatas have come into favor in recent years, perhaps because of their cylindrical and scalloped shape. They are thin-skinned, so you need not peel them before cooking. Delicatas make an excellent sautéed squash and, when hollowed, their long boat shape turns them into a perfect vehicle for stuffing.

Hubbard, Turban, and Kabocha Squashes. Some of the larger, lesser known squashes include Hubbard (a gray-blue, often pear-shaped squash), turban (which features bubbled and ribbed skin of orange, green, and white that looks like two very different squashes have accidentally grown together), and kabocha (a dark green, squat squash with a bright and starchy flesh).

Winter squashes vary in texture and flavor, but when you're choosing a squash, don't get caught up in what variety is best for a specific dish. Rather, choose one that looks interesting and try it. In these recipes, particular varieties of squashes are called out only occasionally; most varieties can easily be substituted for one another.

JANUARY RECIPES

Winter Squash

Winter Squash Bread with Streusel
Crispy Winter Squash Croquettes
Winter Greens & Squash Salad with Prosciutto
Vanilla Bean Delicata
Crisped Squash with Mint & Pine Nuts
Harissa-Roasted Acorn Squash
Oregano & Winter Squash Pasta
Baked Squash Shepherd's Pie
Butternut Squash & Shrimp Wontons in Green Onion Broth
Chocolate–Squash Tart

Seasonal Extras

Pomegranate–Celery–Citrus Salad with Chile
Brussels Sprouts with Smoked Fish Aioli & Parmesan

Winter Squash Bread with Streusel

MAKES 1 LOAF

In my family we have tea and sweets in the late afternoon—my grandma would approve of this breakfast bread and its crispy-sweet topping for a tea-time treat. I wanted to make something sweet using winter squash in an unusual way. Zucchini bread is a typical way to use a bumper crop of summer squash, and pumpkin bread recipes using mashed pulp tend to show up every fall. Why not combine the two ideas?

Here, I grate winter squash into an easy morning loaf to be served as a breakfast bite. I replaced the oil traditionally called for in quick breads with yogurt, which is healthier and richer. (You can also substitute applesauce for the yogurt, if you prefer.) Use any variety of winter squash on hand for this bread.

BREAD
2 eggs
¾ cup yogurt
1 tablespoon vanilla extract
¾ cup sugar
1½ cups grated winter squash
1½ cups whole wheat pastry flour
    (all-purpose flour is okay too)
1 teaspoon ground cinnamon
¼ teaspoon freshly ground nutmeg
¼ teaspoon ground cloves
½ teaspoon baking powder
½ teaspoon baking soda

STREUSEL
½ cup sugar
½ cup brown sugar
½ cup whole wheat pastry flour
Pinch of salt
4 tablespoons butter, very cold
¼ cup chopped pecans

Preheat the oven to 350 degrees F. Liberally grease the inside of a loaf pan and set aside.

In a medium-sized bowl, beat the eggs lightly. Add the yogurt (or applesauce, if using), vanilla extract, sugar, and grated squash. Mix to combine and set aside. In another medium-sized bowl, add the pastry flour, all the spices, baking powder, and baking soda. Stir to combine evenly.

Add the dry ingredients to the wet ingredients, folding with a rubber spatula until well combined. Don't mix aggressively, as overmixing will activate the gluten in the flour and make the bread tough. Instead, fold the batter in gentle circles until it's just mixed. Pour the batter into the loaf pan and set aside.

To make the streusel topping, put the sugars, flour, and pinch of salt into a medium-sized bowl and stir to combine. Cut the butter into small cubes. Using your fingertips, massage the sugar-butter mixture together until it forms coarse crumbs and larger clumps. Mix in the pecans, then sprinkle the crumbs directly on the batter in the loaf pan, spreading a thick layer evenly over the top.

Bake for 45 minutes to an hour, until just cooked through. Check for doneness by inserting a butter knife into the center of the loaf. If it comes out clean, remove from the oven and cool slightly before serving. If the batter is still gooey, let it bake another 15 minutes at most. Remove from the oven and cool slightly before serving.

PANTRY NOTE: For longer storage, wrap the entire loaf (after cooling) with plastic wrap, which extends the life of the bread for several days. Store at room temperature, tightly wrapped, or freeze for up to two months.

Crispy Winter Squash Croquettes

MAKES 8 TO 10 CROQUETTES

Croquettes are little fried patties, typically made with boiled potatoes or fish. My grandmother's Italian neighbor in Queens used to season leftover mashed potatoes and shape them into flat-bottomed domes, then shake them in a brown bag filled with bread crumbs. "Rita used to make hundreds," my mom recalled, "and everybody loved them."

Inspired by this same idea, the squash here is steamed and mashed as a binder, then liberally seasoned before being shaped and briefly shallow-fried, just to brown the crust before they are finished off in the oven. These crispy croquettes are delicious. Using a starchy squash (such as Hubbard or kabocha) will help them hold their shape better. For frying, I use vegetable oil or olive oil interchangeably.

1 pound winter squash (Hubbard or kabocha), seeded and cut into large pieces
1 tablespoon olive oil
1 tablespoon butter
½ cup finely diced onion
10 sprigs fresh thyme, leaves picked and roughly chopped
Salt
Pepper
1 cup seasoned bread crumbs
1 egg
Splash of milk
½ to 1 cup vegetable or olive oil

In a large stockpot, put the squash in about 1 inch of water. (You don't want to submerge the squash; you only want to provide enough water to steam.) Cover and bring to a boil, then reduce to a simmer and let the squash steam until very soft, about 20 to 30 minutes. Turn off the heat and drain the water from the stockpot. Replace the lid so the squash continues steaming, and set aside.

In a medium sauté pan, heat the tablespoon of olive oil and the butter over medium-high heat. When the butter starts to bubble, add the onion, thyme, and a pinch of salt. Stir the onion mixture often, until very soft and brown, for about 10 minutes. Remove from the heat and set aside.

Scoop the soft flesh from the squash pieces and add it to the sauté pan. Mash the squash and the onion mixture together to combine well. Season with salt and pepper to taste. Move the squash-onion mixture to a bowl and refrigerate until very cool, preferably overnight but at least an hour. (Chilling the squash will help the croquettes maintain their shape later, so don't scrimp on time here!)

Once the mixture has thoroughly cooled, set up your frying station. Put the bread crumbs on a small plate. Beat the egg with a splash of milk in a shallow bowl to create an egg wash and set aside. Put about ½ cup of the oil in a deep-sided sauté pan and set over medium heat.

Remove the squash-onion mixture from the fridge. Using a large spoon, scoop and shape it into football-like dumplings, working quickly so it doesn't warm too much. Using a fork, gently coat each dumpling in the egg wash and then immediately move it to the bread crumbs. Roll softly with the fork, until the entire croquette is covered. Push it to the edge of the bread crumb plate, then shape two or three more croquettes. Handle the croquettes as little as possible so they maintain their shape, and only form as many as you can fry at one time.

Preheat the oven to 350 degrees F.

Test the oil for heat by dropping in a small pinch of bread crumbs. You want the oil hot, but not smoking hot. When the oil is heated well, the bread crumbs will start frying immediately, though not vigorously. If they are only slightly fizzy, wait until the oil is a bit hotter.

When the oil is ready, gently roll the croquettes into the oil, being careful not to overcrowd the pan. They will start to brown immediately. When one side is brown, quarter-turn the croquettes to brown another side. Work in this fashion until all sides are golden brown. The process for one croquette should take about 6 to 8 minutes total. When it's brown on all sides, remove the croquette with a spatula and slide it onto a shallow roasting pan. Continue until all croquettes are browned.

Put the roasting pan in the oven and bake for 20 minutes. Remove and serve immediately.

PANTRY NOTE: These croquettes store well in the fridge, loosely covered, for one day; reheat in oven or sauté pan, or eat cold. Any leftover mashed squash can be used in Baked Squash Shepherd's Pie or as filling for Butternut Squash & Shrimp Wontons in Green Onion Broth.

Winter Greens & Squash Salad with Prosciutto

**MAKES 2 SERVINGS AS A LUNCH
OR 4 AS A SIDE SALAD**

In winter, it's nice to have a refreshing salad, but tender lettuce is hard to come by. Instead, opt for robust winter leaves like chicories and spicy greens. The bitterness from radicchio and arugula is contrasted and complemented by sweet squash in this recipe. Use any combination of winter greens you can find—frisée,

Creamy Cabbage with
Bacon & Cranberries, p. 33

OPPOSITE
TOP LEFT Cabbage & Potato Burek, p. 28
TOP RIGHT Red Cabbage Sauerkraut, p. 38
BOTTOM Cabbage Focaccia with Olives, p. 31

TOP Red Cabbage Pasta, p. 36
BOTTOM Turkey Meatball & Cabbage
Soup, p. 35 (Photo by Kenneth Dundas)

OPPOSITE
TOP Winter Squash Bread with Streusel,
p. 46 (Photo by Kenneth Dundas)
BOTTOM Crispy Winter Squash
Croquettes, p. 47 (Photo by Kenneth Dundas)

TOP Miami Rolls, p. 69 (Photo by Kenneth Dundas)
BOTTOM LEFT Spiced Leek Fritters,
p. 68 (Photo by Kenneth Dundas)
BOTTOM RIGHT Homemade Onion Dip,
p. 71 (Photo by Kenneth Dundas)

OPPOSITE
Vanilla Bean Delicata,
p. 49 (Photo by Kenneth Dundas)

TOP Roasted Onion Soup,
p. 73 (Photo by Kenneth Dundas)

OPPOSITE
Smoky Stuffed Onions,
p. 76 (Photo by Kenneth Dundas)

Chard & Carrot Tart,
p. 95 (Photo by Della Chen)

OPPOSITE
TOP Cardamom–Carrot
Latkes, p. 88 (Photo by Della Chen)
BOTTOM Roasted Carrots &
Sesame Yogurt, p. 90
(Photo by Della Chen)

TOP Steamed Clams in Lime–Carrot Juice, p. 92 (Photo by Della Chen)
BOTTOM Carrot Marmalade, p. 97 (Photo by Della Chen)

OPPOSITE
TOP Healthy Carrot Cake, p. 96 (Photo by Della Chen)
BOTTOM Carrots & Eggs with Anchovy Crumbs, p. 91 (Photo by Della Chen)

escarole, Treviso, dandelion, and fennel all work equally well.

To soften up the bite, the radicchio is tossed with the vinaigrette early, which helps slightly break down the leaves. The squash is cooked until golden in a sauté pan and added to the salad bowl while still warm, making this a homey dish. Salty prosciutto is crisped up and added for texture, and I've been known to place a fried egg over the top for the ultimate lunchtime fare.

VINAIGRETTE
3 tablespoons olive oil
1 tablespoon apple cider vinegar
½ teaspoon Dijon mustard
1 teaspoon honey

1 small head radicchio (about 5 ounces),
   cut into 1-inch by 3-inch thin ribbons
2 tablespoons olive oil, for frying
½ pound winter squash, peeled and cut
   into 1-inch cubes
4 slices prosciutto
2 cups arugula
Salt and pepper

In a large bowl, whisk together all the vinaigrette ingredients. Add the radicchio, tossing with tongs to coat completely. Set aside.

In a medium-sized sauté pan, heat the 2 tablespoons of olive oil over medium-high heat. Distribute the squash into a single layer in the pan. Do not move the squash pieces; rather, cook until one side is golden brown, about 4 minutes.

Flip and cook another side of the squash pieces until brown, about 2 to 3 minutes. Continue until all sides of the squash pieces are golden and crispy. Remove the squash from the sauté pan and set aside to cool on a small plate.

Lay the prosciutto in the sauté pan, taking care not to overlap the slices. Cook until brown and crispy on one side, about 1 to 2 minutes, then flip. Brown the other side, another minute or so, and remove from the heat. Let the prosciutto cool slightly and cut it into ribbons. Add the prosciutto to the radicchio, then add the warm squash. Gently fold in the arugula until just coated. Season with salt and pepper to taste and serve immediately on a large platter or on individual salad plates.

PANTRY NOTE: This salad will not store well, as the vinegar continues to break down the greens and will turn the salad slimy.

Vanilla Bean Delicata

MAKES 4 TO 6 SERVINGS

Delicata squash is a small, long, and narrow winter squash with light yellow, green-flecked skin. Its fluted shape gives the appearance of a flower when cut crosswise. Delicatas can be eaten whole and do not require peeling as the skin is quite thin. This recipe highlights the sweetness of the squash by cooking it in butter along with real vanilla bean. The subtle, warming flavor of fresh vanilla complements the creamy flesh of the squash. Try this recipe for a weeknight side dish, as it comes together quickly.

> 1 delicata squash, washed and patted dry, cut in half lengthwise, seeds removed
> 1 tablespoon olive oil
> 3 tablespoons butter
> ½ teaspoon salt
> ¼ teaspoon pepper
> 1 fresh vanilla bean

Cut the delicata squash halves into ½-inch-thick half moons. Heat the olive oil and butter in a large sauté pan over medium-high heat. When the butter is frothy, add the squash, salt, and pepper, stirring once to coat. Let the mixture sit in a single layer over the heat until brown, for about 4 minutes.

Meanwhile, split the vanilla bean lengthwise, leaving the very top intact. Holding one end of the pod, open up the split pods and scrape down the center with the back of a knife to remove the seeds. Scrape them directly into the sauté pan, over the squash. Stir to combine the vanilla beans with the squash, then again let the mixture sit in a single layer over the heat.

Continue cooking, only stirring occasionally, until both sides of the squash pieces are brown and crisp and the squash is tender and cooked through, about 15 minutes total. Transfer the squash to a platter and serve immediately.

PANTRY NOTE: Delicata squash becomes starchy and grainy over time, so this dish does not keep well. Any leftovers can be finely diced and added to a savory bread pudding; otherwise, plan to eat everything you cook on the same day. Vanilla beans are expensive, but split pods can be rinsed and dried, then ground with sugar for a delicious vanilla sugar. Placed in a glass jar, this homemade scented sugar will keep indefinitely.

Crisped Squash with Mint & Pine Nuts

MAKES 4 SERVINGS

This is one of my favorite ways to eat winter squash because it offers up a new texture. Squash is a soft vegetable, which is why it's so lovely to mash, but mash gets old after a while. Sautéing squash in a small pool of olive oil allows it to brown nicely. It cooks and crisps quickly, making a side dish that is ready to go in no time. Any squash that is easy to peel works well for this recipe—butternut, kabocha, Hubbard, and so on. The addition of cool, fresh mint, fatty pine nuts, and spicy red chile flakes complements the sweetness of the lean squash perfectly, making this recipe a bowl of perfection. Invest in the fresh mint here; it really does make a difference.

> 1 pound winter squash, trimmed and cut in half, seeds removed
> 4 to 6 sprigs fresh mint, leaves picked
> ½ cup pine nuts

2 tablespoons olive oil

2 tablespoons butter

½ teaspoon red chile flakes

Salt and pepper

Cut or peel off the tough outer skin of the squash and cut the flesh into 1-inch cubes. Set aside. Stack and roll the mint leaves into a tight, cigar-shaped bundle. Cut crosswise into super-thin ribbons and set aside.

Set a medium-sized saucepan over medium-high heat. Toast the pine nuts in the heated pan, stirring frequently until brown. Pine nuts color quickly (and are expensive!), so pay attention and stay close, moving them around the pan continuously. Once they are brown, remove them from the pan and set aside.

Add the olive oil and butter to the saucepan. When the butter is frothy, add the squash and the red chile flakes, stirring once to coat evenly. Add a pinch of salt and pepper. Let the mixture sit in a single layer over the heat until brown, about 4 minutes. Once it's golden brown on one side, flip the squash and let it sit over the heat until brown, another 2 to 3 minutes. Continue until all sides of the squash pieces are golden and crispy.

Remove the squash from the heat and add the pine nuts and fresh mint, stirring to combine, before placing everything on a platter. Season to taste with salt and pepper if desired and serve immediately.

PANTRY NOTE: This dish can be made ahead and served at room temperature, but wait to cut and add the fresh mint until just before serving. Any leftovers keep well in the fridge for up to two days.

Harissa-Roasted Acorn Squash

MAKES 4 SERVINGS

Harissa is a Middle Eastern oil-based relish made from crushed chiles, garlic, and spices such as coriander. Although it may sound exotic, you can find harissa in most international sections of the grocery store or in smaller ethnic markets. It can be used on its own as a condiment for many meals.

Several years ago, I cooked a harvest dinner for a handful of friends. I wanted to use all local, seasonal ingredients, and winter squash was plentiful. In a quest to shake up everyone's palates, I combined slices of acorn squash with a spoonful of spicy Moroccan harissa, tossed it together, and baked it. The dish was a perfect pairing and took only about ten minutes to prepare. Don't worry about peeling the squash. Diners can scoop the flesh out on their own, and the skin helps hold the slices together. Add a garnish of plain yogurt for a nice cooling element.

1 acorn squash, washed well, cut in half, seeds removed

3 tablespoons harissa

2 tablespoons olive oil

½ teaspoon salt

Preheat the oven to 350 degrees F.

Cut the squash into 2-inch-wide slices and put them in a large bowl. Add the harissa, olive oil, and salt, tossing with your hands to coat evenly. Put the squash in a shallow roasting pan, making sure the slices do not overlap. Scrape up any harissa remaining in the bowl and add it to the squash pieces, then put the pan in the oven.

After 20 minutes of baking, toss the squash lightly to recoat with the harissa, and return the pan to the oven. Bake for another 10 to 25 minutes (30 to 45 minutes total), until the squash is tender and the harissa starts getting crispy and thick. Serve immediately, with spoons, so guests can scoop the soft flesh out of each slice.

PANTRY NOTE: Any leftover Harissa-Roasted Acorn Squash can be mashed and used as a filling or added in chunks to a chickpea stew during the final stages of cooking. You can also purée Harissa-Roasted Acorn Squash with chicken stock for a spicy squash soup.

Oregano & Winter Squash Pasta

MAKES 4 SERVINGS

Simple veggie-centric pasta dishes are my new favorites: they are inexpensive, healthy, fast to come together, and great for a crowd or a solo dinner. This concept depends on mixing and matching the season's freshest ingredients. Be sure to finish this dish with an indulgent portion of freshly shaved Parmesan. The flavor in this recipe comes from the liberal amount of fresh herbs, in addition to the broth created by adding a bit of pasta water for a "sauce." It's important that you work quickly so the broth doesn't evaporate out of the pan. Many herbs work with this pasta dish, so use what you like or what you have in the pantry.

    4 tablespoons olive oil
    4 tablespoons butter
    1½-pound winter squash, peeled and
        cut into 1-inch cubes
    ½ teaspoon red chile flakes
    2 tablespoons vermouth
    ½ cup fresh oregano leaves, packed
    1 pound pasta
    Parmesan, for shaving
    ½ lemon (optional)

Set a large stockpot of heavily salted water (for the pasta) over high heat and bring to a boil.

While the water is heating, set a large, straight-sided sauté pan over medium-high heat and begin to heat the olive oil and butter. When the butter is frothy, add the squash and chile flakes, stirring once to coat and then letting the cubes sit in a single layer over the heat until brown on the bottom, about 4 minutes.

Once the squash is golden brown on one side, flip and let sit to brown another side, about 2 to 3 minutes. Continue until all sides are brown and crispy. Deglaze the pan with the vermouth, stirring to scrape up any brown bits, then immediately remove from the heat. Sprinkle the oregano leaves over the squash and set aside.

Drop the pasta into the boiling water and cook until just al dente, anywhere from 8 to 12 minutes, depending on the chosen pasta. Follow the packet instructions! When the pasta is just about done (meaning it has about 1 minute left), return the sauté pan to high heat. Just as the pasta is finishing, your squash pieces will start sizzling. Using tongs or a slotted spoon, grab the cooked pasta from the stockpot and put into the sauté pan—the water from the pasta creates a nice broth. Do this until all the pasta is in the sauté pan, stirring once or twice to coat the pasta in the broth and mix all the ingredients together, about 2 minutes total.

Remove the sauté pan from the heat and plate up the pasta immediately into 4 large shallow bowls. Shave a generous amount of Parmesan over the top, squeeze on a bit of lemon juice if desired, and serve.

PANTRY NOTE: This dish holds well and can be kept in the fridge and eaten the next day, tasty as a cold noodle lunch.

Baked Squash Shepherd's Pie

MAKES 4 SERVINGS

This super-healthy version of shepherd's pie, made with stew meat and winter vegetables, is as hearty as it gets. For this baked dish, however, lose the cream and potatoes found in traditional recipes. Instead, rely on nonfat yogurt and mashed squash as a topping. Leave the vegetables chunky—they allow for a deliciously satisfying robust texture. I tested out this recipe on my friend Ritzy, adding dried prunes because I absolutely love the combination of hearty roasted meat and fruit. We ate the entire pie.

This technique of using steamed and mashed squash for a topping can be used for any savory pie fillings. For variety, try ground meat with cumin and potatoes or traditional chicken pot pie. Any squash type will work well, as the yogurt introduces a creaminess to the squash's flesh.

TOPPING
2-pound winter squash, well scrubbed
½ cup nonfat plain yogurt
Salt and pepper

PIE
¼ cup all-purpose flour
1 teaspoon salt
1 tablespoon ground paprika
Pinch of pepper
1 pound stew meat, cut into 1-inch cubes
2 tablespoons olive oil
1 tablespoon butter
1 large onion, cut in half and sliced into
   ¼-inch half moons
3 cloves garlic, peeled and smashed
6 stalks celery, cut into 2- to 3-inch
   pieces
4 carrots, peeled and cut into 1-inch
   pieces
8 prunes, pitted and cut in half
1 tablespoon coriander seeds, crushed
3 tablespoons lager beer (or white
   wine, vermouth, brandy—something
   flavorful and boozy)

HOW TO CUT A SQUASH

Most winter squashes have hard exterior shells, making them a real challenge to break into, but I've learned a few tips and tricks to guarantee success and ease of mind for anyone wielding a sharp implement around an unyielding shell. First and foremost, a sharp knife in the kitchen is crucial. If you don't have a home sharpening block (I do not), be sure to take your knives out regularly for this service. Most specialty kitchen stores offer knife sharpening or can refer you to a service.

Follow the number-one rule of cutting and chopping: always work with a flat surface. Most squashes are round or odd-shaped. Solve this imbalance by shaving off a small piece and making your own flat surface. From there you have better leverage. Acorn squashes benefit greatly from creating this flat surface, which makes them easier to cut into wedges (for Harissa-Roasted Acorn Squash) or halves.

To cut round squashes, such as kabocha or blue Hubbard, set the squash in the center of your cutting board. As you would with a cake, cut the squash into wide wedges, removing the seeds from each wedge individually. For butternut squash, first cut off the neck of the squash, which provides a whole piece of flesh. Remove the skin one of two ways: use a vegetable peeler or place cut side down on a cutting board and slice off thin layers of skin, turning the squash as you go. From there, place the bottom of the squash, flat side down, on your cutting board and remove the skin in the same fashion. Then the squash can be cut in half, seeds removed, and cut further into desired shapes. Peel the lower portion of the butternut similarly.

The thin-skinned delicata squash does not need to be peeled. Cut in half lengthwise and scoop out the seeds. If you'd like to cook with rings, cut the ends off the delicata and scoop out the seeds with a small spoon. This process is a bit labor intensive but will allow you to cut even rings of scalloped squash for such recipes as Vanilla Bean Delicata.

Preheat the oven to 350 degrees F.

In a large stockpot, put the squash in about 1 inch of water. (You don't want to submerge the squash; you just want to provide enough water to steam.) Cover the pot and bring to a boil over high heat. Reduce to a simmer and let the squash steam until very soft, about 20 to 30 minutes. Turn off the heat and drain. Replace the lid so the squash continues steaming and set aside for it to cool.

Stir together the flour, salt, paprika, and pepper on a large dinner plate. Put the stew meat in the flour mixture, coating well, and set it aside. In another large stockpot, heat the olive oil over medium-high heat. Once it's hot, add the stew meat in a single layer, leaving it to sit over the heat and brown. Stir occasionally, to sear all sides of the meat, about 6 to 8 minutes total. Transfer the meat to a platter.

Add the butter, onions, and garlic to the same stockpot, working to scrape up any brown bits in the oil. Once the onions are softening, about 2 minutes, add the celery, carrots, prunes, and coriander seeds. Cook and stir until the vegetables start to stick to the bottom of the stockpot. Deglaze the pot with the beer, scraping the bottom, then remove from the heat. Add the meat to this mixture and stir to combine. Place the mixture in a shallow pie pan or round baking dish, spreading it evenly over the bottom of the pan; set aside.

Now that the squash is cool enough to handle, take it out of the pot and remove the flesh by scraping the skin with a spoon. Measure out 3 cups of cooked squash and put it in a large mixing bowl. Add the yogurt and season with salt and pepper to taste, mashing all with a fork to combine well. Place the squash mash over the top of the savory pie filling and put in the oven to bake.

Bake 1 hour or until the top of the squash mash is golden brown and crispy. Let it cool 5 minutes before serving in shallow bowls.

PANTRY NOTE: Any leftovers can be kept in the fridge, covered, for two days.

Butternut Squash & Shrimp Wontons in Green Onion Broth

MAKES ABOUT 30 DUMPLINGS, OR 6 SERVINGS

Easy to make, wontons offer an entertaining challenge for passionate home cooks. Inside store-bought wrappers, the combination of squash and shrimp makes for a surprising filling. Satiny smooth squash is mixed with chopped shrimp and traditional Asian flavors like sesame and green onion, then wrapped in a delicate pouch. Drop the dumplings into the green onion- and ginger-scented broth for a quick poach that produces an eye-catching bowl of soup.

You may also use spring roll wrappers and fill them as you would an eggroll before frying. A note about the broth: you can use either homemade chicken stock or miso broth with great results. Aromatics scent the soup, and Chinese cooking wine (Shaoxing) adds depth of flavor. It is worth it to source Chinese cooking wine at an Asian marketplace—they will all carry this Asian pantry staple.

WONTONS

1½ pounds butternut squash, scrubbed, cut in half and seeds removed

½ pound shrimp (about 15 medium), cleaned and shells removed

1 tablespoon cornstarch (optional)

1-inch-long piece fresh ginger, peeled and grated

3 green onions, finely chopped

½ cup finely chopped fresh cilantro

½ teaspoon sesame oil

1 teaspoon soy sauce

1 package store-bought wonton wrappers

More fresh cilantro leaves, for garnish (optional)

BROTH

6 cups homemade chicken stock or miso broth

2 tablespoons Chinese cooking wine (optional)

1-inch-long piece fresh ginger, peeled and julienned

5 green onions, trimmed and cut in half lengthwise

To make the filling, cut the squash into several big pieces—don't worry about removing the skin. Place the squash slices, skin side down, in another large saucepan with about 1 inch of water. Set over high heat and bring to a boil. Once it's boiling, reduce the heat to a low simmer and cook, steaming the squash until very soft, about 20 to 25 minutes. Make sure you don't burn the bottom of the saucepan—add small amounts of water as necessary. It is important that you don't boil the squash, but steam it, so be sure no squash flesh is submerged in the water at any time. When the squash is completely cooked through, remove from the heat, drain the water, and set aside to cool.

While the squash is cooling, chop the shrimp into a semi-coarse mash with a chef's knife. Aim to have some larger chunks of shrimp along with very finely chopped pieces. Put the chopped shrimp in a large mixing bowl and add the cornstarch (if you have it), grated ginger, chopped green onions, cilantro, sesame oil, and soy sauce. Stir to combine.

Once the squash is completely cool, scoop out the flesh using a spoon and measure 1½ cups of squash mash. Add this to the mixing bowl of shrimp and fold to combine. (Save any leftover squash for another use.)

To make the wontons, first prepare your workspace, making sure the countertop is perfectly clean and dry. Fill a small cup with water and keep it close. Lay four wonton wrappers on your workspace and place a small spoonful (about 1 tablespoon) of squash filling in the center of each wrapper. Then dip the tip of your finger into the water and trace along the outside edges of the wonton wrapper.

If using square wonton wrappers, fold the wrapper in half diagonally (into the shape of a triangle), and press the dough together around the filling, removing all air bubbles. Work your way out to the edges of the wrapper, pressing out the air as you go. Turn the wonton so the longest edge is facing you and the tip of the triangle points away. Fold in the sides of the wonton to create a little envelope, sealing the edges with water if they need some coaxing to stick together. Note: This is the easiest and fastest way to make filled wontons, but there are many other shapes and techniques to try!

If using round wrappers, fold the wrapper in half to create a half moon, pressing the dough together around the filling, removing all air bubbles. Work from the center out to the edges, pressing out any air as you go. Pleat the top of the half moon to create a small fold on top.

No matter which style of wrapper you are using, continue shaping the wontons, placing them on a sheet pan as you go, until they are ready to use.

In a large saucepan, warm the stock or miso over medium heat and add the Chinese cooking wine (if desired), ginger, and half of the green onions intended for the broth. Bring to a low simmer and cover.

To put the soup together, bring the broth up to a low boil and add the reserved green onion halves. Set up a steaming pot using either a bamboo steamer or a stainless steel steaming basket. If using stainless steel, lightly oil the bottom of the basket.

Add the wontons to the steamer, making sure they don't overlap or touch, and cook until the wrappers become just translucent, about 5 minutes. Once they are cooked, place 5 dumplings apiece in large shallow soup bowls and ladle on 1 cup of the broth, being sure to portion out the green onions and ginger evenly. Serve immediately with fresh cilantro as garnish if desired.

PANTRY NOTE: This soup does not keep well, so plan to eat all of the dumplings you steam. Dumplings, made and shaped, can be frozen for up to two months. Make sure to freeze them individually on a sheet pan so they maintain their shape.

Chocolate–Squash Tart

MAKES ONE 9-INCH TART

This tart is made from crumbled-up cookies and a simple winter squash custard. Chocolate cookies go well with the smooth squash flavor, but you can use any cookie on hand for this sweet, crisp crust. Simply add a few shakes of cocoa powder to turn the cookie crumble chocolaty. Steamed squash is the perfectly creamy filling, very much like canned pumpkin flesh in pies. Since tart pans are shallow, you don't end up with heavy mouthfuls of filling.

6 ounces crisp chocolate cookies or
    biscotti
3 tablespoons sugar
1/4 teaspoon salt
4 tablespoons butter, melted
1 pound winter squash, cut in half and
    seeds removed
3 eggs
3/4 cup brown sugar
1/2 teaspoon ground cinnamon
1 teaspoon freshly grated ginger
1/4 teaspoon freshly ground nutmeg
Pinch of salt
2 ounces bittersweet chocolate, bar or
    block

Preheat the oven to 350 degrees F.

In a blender or food processor, grind the cookies, sugar, and salt into fine crumbs and put this in a mixing bowl. Pour in the melted butter, stirring to combine well, until the crumbs are well coated and moist and take on an oily look. Press the crumbs into a 9-inch tart pan, spreading evenly across the bottom and pressing into the fluted sides. The crust will be thin. Put it in the oven and bake for 12 to 15 minutes, until the crumb crust is crisp and dry.

For the filling, cut the squash into several big pieces—don't worry about the skin. Put the chunks of squash, skin side down, into a large saucepan with 1 inch of water. Bring to a boil over high heat. Once it's boiling, reduce to a low simmer and cook, steaming the squash until very soft, about 20 to 25 minutes. Don't burn the bottom of the pan—add small amounts of water as

necessary. It is important that you don't boil the squash but steam it, so be sure no squash flesh is submerged in the water at any time. When the squash is completely cooked through, remove it from the heat, drain, and set aside to cool.

Scoop out the squash flesh with a spoon after it has cooled. Using an electric mixer on medium speed, mix the squash until smooth, removing any stringy lumps. Add the eggs, brown sugar, spices, and salt, mixing well. The squash filling will be thick and smooth, like a heavy cream. Pour the squash mixture into the tart shell, to just under the tart pan edges. Bake about 40 minutes, until the filling is firm and does not jiggle in the middle when shaken lightly.

While the tart is baking, shave pieces of the bittersweet chocolate into curls using a vegetable peeler or the blade of a chef's knife. When the filling is set, remove the tart from the oven and sprinkle the chocolate curls over the top. Serve when it's cool.

PANTRY NOTE: Extra squash filling will keep for three days in the fridge and may be used in any other tart or pie shell or baked in a ramekin as you would a crème brûlée. This tart can be kept at room temperature, lightly covered with parchment, for three days.

HOW TO GROW WINTER SQUASH

Winter squash is a beguiling plant to grow—it's a creeping vine thick with hairy, pointed leaves and wiry tendrils searching for something to grab on to. Squash plants are true creepers and can cover large lengths of the garden if left to their own devices.

Winter squashes include many members—pumpkins, gourds, butternut squash, and acorn squash among them. They are ready for harvest in early to mid-fall, right around Halloween. Seeds are sown in midsummer in order to make this harvest in time; the juicy vines would never last through winter. Squashes require warm days for ripening their fruit, so they do best in warm gardens and open fields.

They are also sensitive to temperature during germination and only sprout readily in warm, but not too wet, soil. Unlike most seeds, these don't need constant moisture to germinate well. Winter squash starts are also relatively easy to find—just be sure to time the planting accordingly. Squashes are planted in hills, which are essentially mounds of dirt within the garden beds. I mound up soil in the corners of the beds, allowing the squash plants to grow out and away from the other plants. They'll easily overrun anything in their path.

Toward the end of their life, the squash leaves will eventually be taken over by powdery mildew in cooler, damp climates. This is not a problem for the fruit, but you may need to harvest it immature if the mildew is particularly bad. For summer-forming mildew, it is best to pull the plant before it spreads to other garden members.

As with tomatoes, to encourage ripening you may need to thin the fruit from the squash vines as the weather gets cooler. Remove any very small or young squashes from the vine, which allows bigger fruits to mature in the dwindling warmer days of autumn.

Choose a variety that works in your climate. Anyone with a shorter summer should opt for small squashes like delicata—these mature faster than larger varieties. For hot summers, indulge in large squashes like butternut and kabocha. Ditto for pumpkins— Sugar Pie pumpkins do well in milder climates, whereas big Jack-O-Lanterns do well when they have time to grow and mature.

Pomegranate–Celery–Citrus Salad with Chile

MAKES 4 SERVINGS

Take advantage of the season's last pomegranate seeds and try this crunchy, refreshing winter salad. Celery is a summer/fall crop in the north and a winter crop in the south, so any northern states are getting their celery from southern neighbors. Use the entire stalk of celery—leaves and all—and don't trim off the fat white base, which is delicious. This salad is a harmonious blend of crunchy, sweet, acid, and spice. I eat it near daily in the winter, and add an avocado whenever I can get my hands on one. You can also embellish this salad with nuts or a hard-boiled egg to make a lunchtime meal of it.

4 celery stalks
1 orange
¼ cup pomegranate seeds
2 tablespoons olive oil
1 tablespoon apple cider vinegar
½ teaspoon Dijon mustard
½ teaspoon honey
¼ teaspoon red chile flakes

Using a mandoline, cut the celery stalks at an angle into very thin slices, including the tops. Chop the leaves fine with a knife. (If using a knife to cut the stalks, work slowly and cut them as close to paper-thin as possible.) Put the sliced celery into a large bowl.

To prep the orange, cut off the top and bottom and set the orange on its end. Using a sharp knife, carefully cut the skin from top to bottom, working with the curve of the fruit. To cut out the sections, insert the blade just next to the membranes on both sides and remove the fruit wedges. Add the orange wedges to the bowl.

Add the pomegranate seeds, olive oil, vinegar, Dijon, honey, and chile flakes to the bowl and fold to combine well, making sure no lumps of mustard or honey are left. Serve immediately.

PANTRY NOTE: This salad holds well in the fridge, covered, for a day. If held longer, revive with additional fresh celery and another orange.

Brussels Sprouts with Smoked Fish Aioli & Parmesan

MAKES 4 SERVINGS

This dish sounds like an odd pairing, but I think it's a real candidate for some winter dinner shake-ups this year. Homemade aioli infused with smoked fish is tossed with still-warm roasted Brussels sprouts. The aioli melts into an irresistibly thick and creamy sauce around the crispy sprouts. You can also use store-bought mayo, but in this Brussels sprouts recipe, it will change the texture slightly. A few shaves of Parmesan add sharpness.

1 pound Brussels sprouts, trimmed and halved (about 4 cups)
2 tablespoons olive oil
¼ teaspoon salt
¼ teaspoon pepper

SEED SAVER: HOW TO MAKE HOMEMADE PEPITAS

Pepitas are the small green "nuts" found in the center of squash seeds. Soft and delicious, they can be used as other seeds and nuts are—in quick breads, in granola, or ground to a pulp for sauces. Pepitas are turning up in the nut section of many grocery stores, so look there if you need a large amount.

For cooks interested in maximizing their dollar and getting crafty with kitchen DIY projects, making your own pepitas is a rewarding overnight project. If you have plans to cook with a lot of squash or you attend a pumpkin-carving party in autumn, this is a great technique. It's not for the faint of heart, however. Hulling seeds is a lot of work, but I think it's worth the investment—if only for the bragging rights.

The white seeds in the center of the squash are actually the seed's hull, the exterior coating that protects the interior kernel. This kernel is what makes up pepitas: the bright green seed of a pumpkin. To get at that kernel, remove the hull. To do this, seeds must be completely dry, dry enough so the hull becomes brittle. To dry out the seeds, first wash them free of any residual squash pulp. Lay a thin linen cloth on a sheet pan, and fan out the seeds in a single layer to dry overnight. The next morning, preheat the oven to 250 degrees F. Remove the cloth and bake the seeds for thirty minutes, until they are totally dry but not toasted. You are aiming to dry out the hull.

Once they're completely dry and brittle, cool the seeds completely (about an hour), then pour them into a large resealable plastic bag. Using a rolling pin, smash and roll the seeds, breaking apart and cracking the hulls. This takes about three to five minutes—you want to beat them enough to break the hulls but not enough that you smash the pepitas. Fill a large bowl with water and pour in the smashed seeds. Stir vigorously. If the hulls have been dried and smashed, they will float to the top, while the pepitas will sink to the bottom. Break apart the few hulls that have not released their pepitas.

Skim off the white hulls and discard. Using a strainer or slotted spoon, strain the pepitas out of the water and lay them flat on a clean linen cloth to dry completely overnight. Toss them occasionally to distribute air. Once the pepitas are completely dry, store them in a glass jar in the cupboard, where they'll keep for several weeks.

2 egg yolks
1 teaspoon Dijon mustard
1 cup vegetable oil
1 tablespoon fresh lemon juice (or
    vinegar)
¼ cup finely diced smoked trout
Additional salt and pepper
2 ounces shaved Parmesan

Preheat the oven to 425 degrees F.

Place the Brussels sprouts on a sheet pan and toss with the olive oil, salt, and pepper until well coated. Set the pan in the oven and roast until the Brussels sprouts are charred and the outer leaves are crisp, about 20 minutes.

While the Brussels sprouts are cooking, make the aioli. In a medium-sized bowl, whisk together the egg yolks and Dijon mustard. While whisking continuously, begin to drizzle in the vegetable oil at a near trickle. When you notice the mixture getting fluffy, pour in the rest of the oil in a slow, steady stream, whisking all the while. Your arm will get veeeery tired, but don't give up! When the aioli is emulsified and thick, whisk in the lemon juice.

Divide the aioli, reserving half for another use, and fold the trout into the portion you will use for this recipe, mashing any large pieces of trout with the back of a fork. The mixture will look like a thick paste. Put the trout-aioli mixture in a large bowl and set aside.

When the Brussels sprouts are cooked through and tender, remove them from the oven, and immediately put them in the bowl with the aioli. Using a rubber spatula, fold all of the ingredients until they are well combined—the aioli will soften. Season with salt and pepper to taste. To serve, place on a platter and sprinkle the shaved Parmesan on top.

PANTRY NOTE: Leftover aioli is excellent as a more substantial dip for crudité or toasts. Aioli will keep in the fridge for about five days. Fold in fresh herbs for a new flavor—tarragon is one of my favorites.

Harissa-Roasted Acorn Squash

FEBRUARY

ONIONS

ONIONS DON'T USUALLY COME TO mind when you want to make a delicious meal. Alliums of all kinds (including chives, garlic, onions, and leeks) are typically relegated to recipe bases and play the role of flavor builders. However, onions perfume dishes as no other vegetable can, and often meals will fall flat if you omit them. Called for in many recipes, alliums tend to be staples in the kitchen. I grew up in a house that would sooner run out of water than garlic. My sister buys medium-sized yellow onions in a twenty-five-pound bag, and I tend to overbuy at the grocery, picking up an onion, shallot, or globe of garlic with every trip.

Onions come into season starting in the spring, but these (known as, not surprisingly, "spring onions") are best eaten fresh. They tend to be more delicate than the yellow onions commonly available at the grocery store, and they often have their greens still attached. Walla Wallas, ramps, and torpedo onions are all considered spring onions and come into season throughout spring and summer. Storage onions, the ones more commonly thought of as kitchen staples, are available year-round but are harvested in late summer through winter. These large storage onions (so named because they can be stored for many months without decay) are traditionally dried, or cured, and held in cold storage until ready to use. The dry paper skins around onions and garlic protect the soft interior flesh. Onion availability may vary from state to state, but nationally (even globally!) you can purchase yellow, white, or red onions throughout the year.

Onions are one of the least expensive vegetables you can buy, often selling for less than a dollar a pound, which adds up to quite a bargain for anyone on a budget or trying to feed a crowd. While we tend to think of onions as secondary players, these recipes aim to move them into the spotlight by highlighting some uncommon dishes using onions as the star ingredient. In the kitchen, onions can easily span across meals, and should. Used in savory dishes, onions pair well with just about anything—roasted meats, other vegetables, delicate broths, and bread. They can be eaten raw or roasted, shaved, pickled, and sautéed with excellent results. Onions are one of the rare ingredients used in every culture—cooks from Asia to South America and everywhere in between use them nearly daily.

In my own kitchen I use mostly yellow onions, because they are always available, but varying the onion will also vary the flavor and texture of your dish. Yellow onions, perfect for cooking, offer an all-around mellow onion flavor. White onions are sweeter than yellows and are often called for in Mexican dishes. Red onions are a bit sweeter, turn whatever you're making rose-colored, and provide a pungent oniony bite when eaten raw. Green onions are best eaten fresh—their greens can be chopped as you would chives (see Grow Your Own Green Onions). Small, tender whole onions (like ramps and torpedoes) are excellent charred in the oven or on a grill and eaten whole—greens and all.

Garlic is, of course, a crucial ingredient in so many dishes and can be grated and used raw or roasted into a sweet paste. Leeks, best for sautéing or braising, present the softest, most delicate onion flavor and cook quickly. My favorite allium may just be the shallot—I use minced shallots occasionally for perfect homemade vinaigrettes.

Here, we go from starters to sides, offering new and creative ways to use onions—the whole onion—in your meals. These recipes come together easily, providing novel and exciting flavor profiles. One of my favorites is Smoky Stuffed Onions—you'll love them. Be sure to try the healthier spin on Homemade Onion Dip for your next party. While there are some new ideas here, traditional recipes like Roasted Onion Soup shouldn't be missed.

FEBRUARY RECIPES

Onions

Spiced Leek Fritters
Miami Rolls
Homemade Onion Dip
Quick Onion Gravy
Roasted Onion Soup
Rustic Onion Tart
Smoky Stuffed Onions

Seasonal Extras

Rutabaga–Potato Soup
Citrus–Mint Fizz

Spiced Leek Fritters

MAKES 10 FRITTERS

Fritters are great for lunch on the run or as bite-sized appetizers. Here, thin leek slices make up the bulk of the fritter batter, which is punctuated by a traditional Indian spice mix of cinnamon, clove, and cumin; fresh chiles add heat and color. This recipe is special because of the care given to the batter—thick, flour-based batter is added to sautéed and spiced leeks, while a single whipped egg white is folded in for lift. The extra step produces a fat, fluffy fritter that holds its shape. Serve alongside chopped cilantro and use plain yogurt as a dipping sauce.

3 leeks, trimmed, washed well, and cut
    into thin rings
1 tablespoon butter
1 tablespoon olive oil, plus more for
    frying
1/2 teaspoon salt
1/8 teaspoon ground cloves
1/8 teaspoon ground cinnamon
1/8 teaspoon ground cumin
1/4 cup milk
1/2 cup all-purpose flour
1 teaspoon baking powder
1 egg
1/2 cup chopped fresh cilantro
1 small fresh red chile, cut into thin
    circles
1 egg white

Preheat the oven to 250 degrees F.

In a large sauté pan, set the leeks, butter, oil, and salt over medium heat. Cook and stir until the leeks are soft and cooked through completely, about 5 minutes. Remove from the heat and add the cloves, cinnamon, and cumin. Set aside in a large bowl to cool.

In a small bowl, combine the milk, flour, baking powder, and egg. Beat with a fork to mix thoroughly, making sure there are no lumps. When the batter is smooth and thick, pour it onto the cooled leeks and stir until well combined. Fold in the cilantro and chile.

Using the whisk attachment on an electric handheld or stand mixer, whip the egg white in a medium-sized bowl until soft peaks form and the volume has tripled. The egg whites will be fluffy, white, and foamy. Add a spoonful of the egg whites to the leek batter and stir gently to combine. Fold in the rest of the egg whites until just mixed.

In a large sauté pan, heat 1/4 inch of olive oil over medium-high heat. When the oil is hot, drop a spoonful of batter into the pan. The pool of batter should be about 3 inches wide. Repeat until the pan is full and cook each fritter until golden brown, about 2 to 3 minutes. Flip and continue cooking the other sides until golden brown, adding a bit of oil if your pan goes dry. When both sides of the fritters are browned, place them on a platter or roasting pan and hold them in the oven to finish cooking through, about 5 minutes more. Continue in this fashion until all fritters are browned.

Remove the platter of fritters from the oven and serve immediately.

PANTRY NOTE: Fritters can be cooked in advance and frozen, then warmed up in an oven before serving. Any leftovers may be wrapped loosely in plastic wrap and kept in the fridge, where they will last only a day or two. You cannot make the batter in advance, however, as it will not hold its volume.

Miami Rolls

MAKES 12 ROLLS

When I was fifteen, my sister and I worked weekends and some evenings at a Jewish bakery down the street from our house. The owners were strict but allowed us to eat anything for free while we worked. On Sundays, our busiest morning, I would go to great lengths to hide one of the quick-to-sell onion rolls from the customers so I could snack on it later during a lull. We called them Miami Rolls.

The memory of those perfect doughy rolls with their burned onion tops inspired this recipe, a simple yeast bread that you can put together and bake in less than two hours. Honey-sweetened onions and poppy seeds fill the centers of the rolls, which are baked into crisp domes. Fresh from the oven, these rolls and their sweet, onion-filled centers are perfect for a Sunday morning treat.

DOUGH
2 cups warm water
3 teaspoons active dry yeast
1 tablespoon honey
4 to 5 cups all-purpose flour, plus more
    for kneading
½ teaspoon salt

FILLING
2 tablespoons olive oil
2 tablespoons butter
1 large onion, finely chopped (about 1½
    cups)
1 tablespoon honey
1 tablespoon poppy seeds
Pinch of coarse salt

Measure out the water in a liquid measuring cup and add the yeast and honey. Set aside; the yeast and honey will dissolve, and the mixture will become foamy in about 5 minutes.

Put 4 cups of flour and ½ teaspoon of salt in the bowl of an electric mixer. Using the dough hook, mix to combine the salt and flour. When the yeast mixture is foamy, add it to the flour and mix on the lowest speed until all the liquid is incorporated. Slowly increase the speed (if you mix on high speed too quickly, the dough hook will spit out flour from the bowl) and continue mixing the dough on medium speed, about 5 minutes.

If the dough is sticky, add more flour in ¼-cup increments until it is no longer tacky. (Do not add more than 1 cup in total.) When the dough is

HANDY TIPS FOR STOPPING ONION-RELATED KITCHEN CONUNDRUMS

Onions get a bad rap because of their strong odor and residual scent left behind on hands and cooking surfaces—not to mention their tear-inducing nature. It's all worth it in the end, however—no other vegetable perfumes a dish like an allium. Garlic, shallots, and onions are pivotal flavor components of many savory meals, and without them, recipes would fall flat. Thankfully, I have a few tricks anyone can implement to stave off tears and cut down on odors.

Onions are full of sulfur, which is released when you slice an onion of any kind. This sulfur gas reacts with the water found naturally in your eyes, forming sulfuric acid. This acid burns your eyes slightly, causing them to attempt to wash the acid out by creating tears. Cooking onions actually deactivates this enzyme, which is why your eyes don't continue burning while you're cooking (or while you're eating!).

To eliminate fume-stimulated tears, immediately run a cut onion under cold water, which removes some of the sulfur. Refrigerating the onion in advance of chopping may also reduce the offensive vapors. If neither of these options appeals, try my sister's trick: she religiously sticks her tongue out while dicing, and swears she never cries anymore. A friend's Italian grandmother recommends holding a piece of bread in your mouth, which works like a charm. Both methods, of course, block the vapors from your eyes while you cut.

The potent scent of onions can linger on your hands and your cutting board. I find that the aroma of garlic, in particular, clings to my skin for hours. To rid your hands of the odor, rub them with a slice of lemon or a scrub of kosher salt and vinegar. *The Joy of Cooking* has a curious suggestion I've yet to try: rub your hands with mustard powder and then rinse. Follow the same set of guidelines to remove the smell of onions from pots or cooking surfaces. Cutting boards apparently do well with the mustard treatment after every few uses.

I would be doing a disservice if I offered tips on how to rid the onion flavor from pots, cutting boards, and hands without giving some advice on how to clear your breath of the dreaded raw onion smell. (My dentist, Dr. Sherman, refuses to eat raw onions for lunch!) Apples are thought to be palate cleansers, but I find them a weak solution. Better to chew on a potent raw herb, such as parsley.

no longer sticky, turn it out onto a lightly floured work surface and hand-knead for 3 minutes. The dough should not need more flour and should pull easily away from your work surface. Put the dough into a lightly oiled large bowl, covered loosely with plastic wrap and topped off with a clean dishtowel. Set it in a warm space to rise until the dough has doubled in size, about 45 minutes to an hour.

While the dough is rising, prepare the filling. In a large sauté pan, warm the olive oil and butter over medium-high heat. When the butter is melted and foaming, add the onion and cook, stirring occasionally, until it is browned and caramelized, about 25 minutes. Stir in the honey and poppy seeds and set aside to cool.

When the dough has doubled in size, move it back to your work space and punch it down, turning once or twice and kneading lightly. When most of the air has been removed, cut the dough into equal quarters. Then cut each quarter into three equal portions. Knead each dough portion on a countertop until smooth and then press down to form a disc about 5 inches wide. Hold the disc in the palm of one hand and, using your other hand, spoon a dollop of the onion–poppy seed mixture onto the center. Pinch the edges of the dough together, forming a smooth, round roll around the onion-filled center. Set, pinched side down, on a lightly greased sheet pan.

Continue forming rolls until you have twelve all together, and space them 3 to 4 inches apart on the sheet pan. (You may need two sheet pans,

depending on the pan size.) Cover the sheet pan with plastic wrap, topped off with a dish towel. Set in a warm space to rise for a second time, about 45 minutes.

Preheat the oven to 475 degrees F.

Remove the plastic wrap from the dough and sprinkle the rolls with a liberal pinch of coarse salt. Put the onion rolls in the oven and bake until golden brown, about 30 minutes. Remove from the oven and let cool slightly before serving.

PANTRY NOTE: These onion rolls will keep overnight if loosely wrapped in linen or parchment and kept on the countertop. Heat them up in the oven before serving. Alternatively, you can bake and freeze them immediately after they are cool, then warm the onion rolls in the oven before serving.

Homemade Onion Dip

MAKES 1½ CUPS

During any major holiday or birthday celebration, my sister will inevitably set out a bowl of onion dip alongside potato chips and celery sticks. It's her childhood favorite snack and now her kids love it as well. I typically steer clear of this dip, however, as my sister uses a dehydrated onion soup mix that is packed with sodium and preservatives. Here I offer a healthier version that is satisfying for all.

Caramelized onions, raw shallots, and a handful of chives season this dip with oniony tones, and balsamic vinegar gives it a bit of bite and that dark color you find in soup mixes. I switch up the dip's traditional base and use yogurt instead of mayonnaise—a much healthier option, particularly if you choose low-fat yogurt. The delicious flavor is spot on. My sister and the kids can't tell the difference.

1 tablespoon butter
1 tablespoon oil
1 cup finely chopped onion
Pinch of salt
1 tablespoon vermouth
1 cup plain yogurt
$\frac{1}{2}$ cup sour cream
1 tablespoon balsamic vinegar
$\frac{1}{8}$ teaspoon garlic powder
1 tablespoon finely chopped shallot
1 tablespoon finely chopped fresh
    chives

Set a medium sauté pan over medium-high heat and add the butter and oil. Once the butter has melted, add the onions and salt. Cook and stir until the onions are completely cooked through and brown, about 10 to 12 minutes. The pan will be dry and the onions will be starting to stick. Deglaze the pan with the vermouth, scraping up any brown bits, until the vermouth is evaporated, about 1 minute. Remove the pan from the heat and set aside to cool.

In a medium-sized bowl, combine the yogurt, sour cream, vinegar, garlic powder, shallot, chives, and cooled onions. Stir together until well combined and put in the fridge to chill until ready to use. Serve alongside crudité or potato chips.

PANTRY NOTE: This dip can be prepared ahead and held in the fridge, covered, for three days before serving. Leftovers will also last in the fridge, covered, for three days.

Quick Onion Gravy

MAKES ABOUT 1 CUP

Whenever I visit my best friend Michelle's family in Arizona, I take over cooking duty for the week to give her a break. Last time, her husband admitted he'd miss my cooking when I was gone. He was unable to articulate why, but I can sum it up in one simple word: *gravy.* Boys love sauces and gravies, so if I'm cooking for a dude, I'll make a sauce of some kind—anything from a thin pan juice to a thick, creamy gravy. Inevitably I look like a hero, and let's face it . . . gravy is *good.*

This onion gravy can be made in ten minutes from start to finish and is also flexible. You can use stock, booze, or milk as a base—or any combination of all three. Make this gravy in any pan that meat was just cooked in—the flavors from the pan juice will flavor the sauce. You can also work with a variety of onions to switch things up—red onion, shallots, green onions—anything will work.

2 tablespoons butter

1 shallot, minced

Pinch of salt

1 tablespoon all-purpose flour

1 tablespoon vermouth

1 cup milk

¼ teaspoon freshly grated nutmeg

In a large sauté pan, melt the butter over medium-high heat. Add the shallot and salt and stir continuously, until the shallots are translucent and the butter begins to brown, about 3 minutes. Sprinkle in the flour in a thin layer and, using a whisk, mix it into the butter. The mixture will be chalky and lumpy, but don't worry. Keep stirring continuously with the whisk so you don't burn the flour. Stir until the flour is golden brown and cooked through, about 3 minutes. Add the vermouth and whisk until combined, about 1 minute.

While whisking with one hand, use your other hand to slowly pour in the milk. Whisk constantly to avoid big clumps. When the desired consistency is reached, stir in the grated nutmeg and serve immediately.

PANTRY NOTE: Gravy can be stored in the fridge, covered, for three days. Use as a garnish for seared pork chops or steak. Any leftover gravy can be reheated in a small pan or poured over very hot meat, which will warm and soften it.

Roasted Onion Soup

MAKES 6 SERVINGS

Onions are a perfect pantry staple, as they are long-lasting and store well. When your cupboards are otherwise bare, you can rely on onions to make a meal. This is an ungraceful yet flavorful soup—perfect for anyone on a budget. Roasting the onions first brings out their sweeter quality and enriches the flavor. The onions are then puréed with stock, water, or milk—whichever you have on hand—and thickened with a slice of day-old bread. Cheap and delicious! Garnish with the accompanying melted-cheese croutons and a drizzle of olive oil, and this very humble soup becomes elegant.

SOUP

1-inch slice of day-old rustic bread

½ cup milk (or stock or water)

1 large yellow onion, chopped

1 small red onion, chopped

3 shallots, roughly chopped

2 cloves garlic, smashed

2 tablespoons olive oil

½ teaspoon salt

¼ teaspoon pepper

2 sprigs fresh rosemary, leaves finely chopped

CROUTONS

2 tablespoons freshly grated Parmesan

1-inch slice of day-old rustic bread

GARNISH
1 tablespoon finely chopped fresh chives
Olive oil

Preheat the oven to 425 degrees F.

Put the slice of bread and the milk in a blender and set aside to soak for about 20 minutes or more.

In a large roasting pan, put the onions, shallots, and garlic, tossing with the olive oil, salt, pepper, and rosemary. Put this in the oven and roast until the onions are crisping at the edges, about 40 minutes. Toss the onions occasionally while roasting. When the onions are just starting to crisp and are cooked through, remove from the oven and set aside.

Purée the soaked bread and its liquid on high until completely smooth, about 3 minutes. Add in the roasted onions, being sure to scrape all the browned bits from the bottom of the pan. Purée on high until the soup is very smooth. Transfer the puréed soup to a medium-sized saucepan and set over medium heat to keep hot.

Meanwhile, make the croutons. Sprinkle the Parmesan over the second piece of day-old bread. Place the bread in the oven and bake until the cheese is brown and bubbling, about 5 minutes. Cut the bread into a dozen big cubes.

In a shallow soup bowl, serve a ladleful of the onion soup. Top with two cheesy croutons and a sprinkle of chives. Drizzle with olive oil and serve immediately.

PANTRY NOTE: This soup will keep for three days in an airtight container in the fridge. Leftover soup may be added to stew or used as stock in gravy, as a thickener.

Rustic Onion Tart

MAKES 4 SERVINGS

I am not very good at making dough. To this day, I've only ever made one pie that I can recall. That explains why I was so captivated, many years ago, to learn about *pâte sablée*—a rustic, rough, meant-to-fall-apart dough. *Sablée,* which means "sandy" in French, takes well to imperfections. Roll out your dough between two layers of plastic, which guarantees no tears. Using the plastic wrap as transport makes it easy to move the rolled disc directly onto a baking sheet before filling.

Savory onion filling is paired with soft, whiskey-soaked raisins piled high in the center before the dough edges are inelegantly folded up and over the filling to create a free-form tart. You can use another dried fruit in place of the raisins (apricots and figs work well) or omit them altogether, if inclined. A stinky cheese is a lovely addition, helping to cut through the sweetness of the onion mixture. I prefer a soft goat cheese, but a pungent blue like Stilton or a sharp, hard cheese like Manchego would work equally well.

DOUGH

¾ cup all-purpose flour

½ cup whole wheat pastry flour

1 teaspoon sugar

½ teaspoon salt

6 tablespoons cold unsalted butter, cut
into small pieces

1 egg, beaten

1 teaspoon cold water

FILLING

½ cup raisins

2 tablespoons whiskey

1 tablespoon butter

1 tablespoon olive oil

1 pound onions, sliced

¼ cup chopped fresh thyme

Pinch of salt

2 ounces soft goat cheese

To make the dough, combine the flours, sugar, and salt in a medium-sized mixing bowl or a food processor. Add the pieces of butter and work in with your fingers, pinching the flour into the butter until small crumbs, like sand, are formed. (If you're using a food processor, blend until the mixture is sandy.)

When the butter is well incorporated, add the egg and water, mixing until just coming together. Turn the dough out on a counter and knead gently (only three to six times) to combine and push the dough together into a ball. It will be quite crumbly and uneven. Shape into a disc and flatten out. Cover well with plastic wrap and refrigerate for at least an hour.

While the dough is chilling, put the raisins in a small bowl and add the whiskey. Add enough water to the bowl so that the raisins are just covered. Set aside.

To make the filling, set the butter and olive oil over medium-high heat in a medium-sized saucepan. Once the butter has melted, add the onions, thyme, and pinch of salt. Cook and stir continuously, until the onions are starting to brown and the pan has gone dry. Once the onions are cooked through and brown, add the raisins, along with their liquid. Stir, scraping the bottom of the pan, and cook until most of the liquid has evaporated, about 2 minutes. The onions can be syrupy but should not be watery. Once the mixture is thick and jamlike, remove from the heat and set aside to cool.

Preheat the oven to 350 degrees F.

When the dough has chilled properly, remove it from the fridge and set it on the countertop. Layer the disc of dough between two long pieces of plastic wrap so that they are perpendicular to each other in the shape of a wide cross, with the dough securely in the center. Starting from the center and working out, roll out the dough to form a 10-inch circle, flipping over occasionally.

Once the tart crust is shaped, remove the top layer of plastic wrap and flip the dough onto a sheet pan or cookie sheet, centering it as best you can (it's okay if the edges overhang the sheet pan). The dough is very delicate and should not be handled with your hands, lest it fall apart.

Remove the plastic wrap and pile the onions into the center of the tart, leaving a 2-inch edge of tart dough. Dot on dollops of goat cheese. From there, fold the tart dough on top of the onions, creating a pentagon-shaped tart with an opening in the center.

Put the tart in the oven and bake for 30 to 40 minutes, until the tart shell is golden brown and crispy. Remove from the oven and let cool 10 minutes before serving in wedges.

PANTRY NOTE: This tart will hold at room temperature for two days. Try making it with all leeks, or mixing yellow onions, shallots, and garlic.

Smoky Stuffed Onions

MAKES 6 TO 8 SERVINGS

I recently visited my relatives in Croatia and was wildly impressed when my cousin's one-year-old, Ottilia, sat down to a dinner of puréed spinach and hake, a whitefish found in northern oceans. The adults were served a bowl of bean soup, but secretly I wanted nothing more than a spoonful of the baby's meal. Using her dinner as inspiration, I put together the recipe for these stuffed onions.

In many cultures it's very common to use mashed potatoes as some sort of filling. Here, whole onions are steamed until softened and then split on one side, making way for stuffing, which consists of near-equal parts cabbage,

potato, and smoked fish. Use any smoked fish you like—salt cod, salmon, trout, or haddock work equally well—and roast until the onions turn brown. This unpretentious dish smacks of country cooking—simple and hearty.

8 small yellow onions, tops and bottoms trimmed slightly
1½ pounds potatoes, cut into small pieces
½ teaspoon salt
About 10 ounces cabbage, cut into ½-inch ribbons
1 pound smoked fish
¼ teaspoon pepper
Olive oil for drizzling

Put the onions in a large pot and cover with water. Set the pot over high heat and bring to a boil. Reduce to a simmer and cook for 30 minutes, until the outer layer of the onions can be pierced with a knife. (The onions will still have some give.) Remove from the heat and strain, setting the onions aside to cool.

While the onions are cooling, in another large pot, set the potatoes and salt, in enough water to cover, over high heat and bring to a boil. Reduce to a low boil and cook until the potatoes are soft, about 25 minutes. Put all of the cabbage on top of the boiling potatoes and cover, cooking until the cabbage is completely soft, about 15 minutes more. Turn off the burner and strain the potatoes and cabbage, then place the pot back on the warm burner, uncovered, to evaporate any residual liquid. Stir often, so you don't burn the mixture. Eventually the burner

GROW YOUR OWN GREEN ONIONS

Most plants grown in a field or garden bed can withstand a bit of trimming without damaging the health of the plant. This means leaves from broccoli plants can be removed before broccoli is even formed, to be used in sautés, as you would spinach. This is also where foods like "garlic greens" come from—the soft greens growing on the garlic top are removed and used as a chive would be, while the garlic bulb still grows underground. This convenient gift from Mother Nature is particularly apropos where alliums and onion plants are concerned. Trimming some green from onion tops is a great way to introduce a gentle onion flavor to your meals and an excellent way to extend the harvest (see Homemade Onion Dip and Quick Onion Gravy).

For anyone without a growing garden, it's easy to implement this same idea with store-bought green onions. In a small glass or jar, put the white portion, along with the roots, of green onions. (You can do this after you've used the green parts for another recipe, like Butternut Squash & Shrimp Wontons in Green Onion Broth.) Be sure to leave the whole of the onion whites behind. Add water to the glass, just until the whites are partially submerged—only a half inch or so. Change out the water every two days; be sure that you don't overfill, which will cause the onions to decay.

Greens will start regrowing by the second day and can be harvested in a week's time. Cut back the greens, leaving the whites behind with the root structure, and the greens will continue to grow. Use onion greens in scrambled eggs, as garnish for tacos, or as a flavoring for soups (see Roasted Onion Soup).

will cool down and the potato-cabbage mixture will continue drying out.

Meanwhile, prepare the smoked fish by mashing or chopping it into small pieces. I like to tear it, using my fingers so there are some smaller bits as well as some larger chunks. Add the fish and pepper to the potato-cabbage mixture and stir to combine.

Preheat the oven to 375 degrees F.

Using a small paring knife, hold a cooled onion in the palm of your hand and carefully slice it lengthwise, cutting to the center of the onion. Continue like this until all of the onions are split. Then gently pry apart individual layers of the onion so you have several split layers. Cupping one individual layer in the palm of your hand, use a small spoon to add filling until the onion is just full but you can still overlap the seam slightly. Place the filled onion, seam side down, in a roasting pan. Continue in this fashion until all of the onions are full or you run out of filling.

Drizzle olive oil over the onions in a roasting pan and bake for 35 to 45 minutes, until the onion tops are golden brown and beginning to char. I like mine very charred, so I leave them in longer. Remove from the oven and let cool slightly before serving.

PANTRY NOTE: The potato-cabbage filling and the onions can be made a day in advance and held in the fridge. Any leftover filling can be used as a filling for bread or a savory pie. Leftovers can be held in the fridge for three days and reheated, but whole cooked onions do not freeze well, so plan to eat what you make.

Rutabaga–Potato Soup

MAKES 6 TO 8 SERVINGS AS A SOUP COURSE

This soup is so simple, I have a tendency to want to add more flavor—spices, milk, something to rich it up. But on its own, it is a true standout, owing in part to the subtle, earthy flavors of the vegetables. When left alone, they are truly delicious—no need for any more effort. However, this soup does make an excellent base for a heartier version—add pulled pieces of pork or short rib for garnish, or toss in some clams and clam juice for a different take on chowder.

Be sure that you don't overblend the soup when puréeing, lest you release too much potato starch and turn the soup gummy. You can substitute turnips for the rutabaga if that's what's available.

> 2 tablespoons olive oil
> 1 tablespoon butter
> 1 large leek, washed and chopped
>   (about 1½ cups)
> 1 teaspoon salt
> 1¼ pounds rutabagas, trimmed of roots
>   and tops, peeled and chopped
> 1 pound Yukon Gold potatoes, cleaned
>   and chopped
> 16 sage leaves
> 6 cups homemade chicken stock
> Salt

In a large pot set over medium-high heat, warm the olive oil and butter. When the butter has melted, add the leeks and salt, and sauté until the leeks are wilted and translucent, about 10 minutes. Add the rutabagas, potatoes, and sage, and let them sit on the heat without stirring, allowing them to brown slightly, about 5 minutes. Turn the veggies over and allow them to brown again, about 5 minutes. Add the remaining ingredients and turn up the heat, bringing the soup to a boil. Reduce to a simmer and cook until the rutabagas and potatoes are very tender and fall apart easily. Purée soup in a blender until smooth. Serve with a sprinkle of salt.

PANTRY NOTE: Extra soup holds well in the fridge, covered, for about three days. Any leftovers may also be frozen and eaten within a month.

Citrus–Mint Fizz

MAKES 4 DRINKS

At any party, I like to offer a non-alcoholic drink that is every bit as festive as a fancy cocktail or wine. I've been making this one for years after seeing a similar version in the *New York Times* holiday section. For this fizz-filled drink, a heavily spiced syrup is added to fresh orange juice, along with a drop of peppermint oil, to make a perfect savory, refreshing drink. You can substitute lemon juice for half of the lime juice, or use all lemon juice if so desired. The syrup can be flavored with many other spices— try allspice, fennel, or even a red chile for some heat. Make extra—most guests will choose this over Prosecco.

1½ cups sugar
½ cup water
2 tablespoons ground cloves
2 cinnamon sticks
2 whole star anise pods
3 thin slices fresh ginger
½ teaspoon peppermint extract
2 cups fresh-squeezed orange juice
½ cup fresh-squeezed lime juice

In a small saucepan over high heat, combine the sugar, water, cloves, cinnamon sticks, star anise, and ginger. Bring to a boil and stir to dissolve the sugar. Once all the sugar has dissolved, remove from heat and set aside to infuse and cool completely. Once it's cool, strain out the spices and stir in the peppermint extract.

In large pitcher, combine the orange juice, lime juice, and peppermint syrup. Stir vigorously until well incorporated. You will see little peppermint oil bubbles on the surface of the juice, so work to emulsify and whisk these in as best as you can. Serve immediately, pouring over ice, and stir well between pourings.

PANTRY NOTE: Leftover syrup (as if!) can be stored in a small glass jar in the fridge for many weeks or even several months. You can use this syrup in place of sweet vermouth in a manhattan, or try some with hot water and brandy for an updated version of a toddy.

SPRING

SPRING IS OFTEN A BUOYANT time of year. The sun shines a little longer every day, warm temperatures start to creep in, and early spring flowers can burst from the soil and light up the ground with a vibrancy that is welcomed with an exhale and a relaxing of the shoulders. As winter gradually departs, the lightness of spring cheers everyone up. Spring officially begins on March 21st and runs through June 21st.

But as flirtatious as spring feels, I find the whole season to be a big tease. It's true that the ground is ready to be seeded and many vegetables are beginning to pop up, but it can still be weeks until harvest. While all plants jump to life in the early days of spring, it is still an unpredictable time for seasonal food devotees. Late frosts or early thaws can wreak havoc on a farm's spring production—delaying beloved spring produce a few weeks, which can seem like months after the limited winter veggie selection, or speeding up the process entirely so that you have rhubarb in March and sweet peas in April. I've seen this happen again and again, causing chefs to scramble for anything—a color, a verdancy to replace heavy winter greens and potatoes. They force the season, bringing in produce from elsewhere, compelled to offer something new to eager mouths. But in truth, spring starts slow.

However, many wild edibles come in reliably early. Miners lettuce and watercress, for example, are typically available as early as late February. These potent, vitamin-rich wild greens are sometimes cultivated and available in groceries, and I've seen more and more foragers selling their fresh-picked wares at farmers markets. Spring mushrooms arrive just weeks later.

Herbs, too, can help us get a jump start on spring—they are fast growing and early budding. Many perennial herbs will overwinter and can start coming out of dormancy as early as late February. By April, herbs are filling in and will continue to prosper after early cuttings. Chervil, parsley, mint, tarragon, lovage, thyme, chives, and anise hyssop (among many others) all crop up early and add some verdancy and lightness to meals.

If you're patient enough, spring produce comes in waves, giving you plenty of time to gorge on one ingredient at a time. Just as you may be getting sick of eating rhubarb, a rainbow of spring lettuces will burst forth, closely followed by radishes, beets, and snap peas. While spring and winter crops can be somewhat repetitive (both carrots and beets, for instance, can be sown nearly year-round), there are actually different varieties for each season. Spring carrots are typically smaller, sweeter, and juicer than their fall counterparts. Winter-harvested carrot seed is bred to produce a carrot that is long lasting, while spring seeds are meant to grow roots that are succulent and sugary.

The final gift of spring comes with the arrival of berries starting in late May. Strawberries arrive first and last throughout summer, though the variety changes as the season wears on. Raspberries and blueberries soon follow suit, offering both savory and sweet recipe ideas.

It's true what they say about spring—in like a (variety-craving) lion, out like a (satisfied) lamb. There won't be much in those early days of March, but come May, your basket will be overflowing with options.

MARCH

CARROTS

TURNS OUT MARCH CAN BE a pretty dismal time for anything seasonal or local unless you live in southern environs. We rely heavily on storage vegetables, like carrots and potatoes, for early spring sustenance. As a gardener, I start loosening up my shoulders in March—the days are getting longer and even a few minutes of light in the morning sky help me adjust. But, really, everything is quiet and in the kitchen it's time to get creative.

When I told my friend Jason I was writing a carrot-centric chapter, he turned up his nose. Impossible! He just *thinks* he doesn't like carrots. I get it—they're not the sexiest ingredient on earth. We rarely see carrots center stage, so people don't often think of them as a delicious food. Instead, carrots are used primarily as a base layer, as building blocks in stocks and sauces—the foundation of many great recipes.

Me? I've always been a fan. My love affair with carrots started when I was a kid. I remember, at six or seven years old, sitting at the dining room table, happily dipping my carrot in a cup of water before eating it. I thought my secret technique sweetened them up. I'd delicately nibble off the outer meat, eventually exposing the sweet core and saving it for last, savoring every teensy bite.

As an adult committed to eating seasonally, I fell in love with carrots all over again several years ago after tiring of winter greens (which can be woody and bitter) and starchy root vegetables like potatoes. During the winter months, I find myself craving sunshine on a plate, and carrots fit the bill. Of course, they don't necessarily grow in winter—not much does—but they are root vegetables, like beets, and the cold ground acts as natural refrigeration over winter. Carrots are considered a winter-storage vegetable—one that holds well for a long time. My friend Lynda, a farmer, harvests her carrots in early November and stores them in a root cellar for winter eating. She plants enough so her supply lasts through early spring, when the first *spring* carrots can be sowed—March is about the time the two options meet! A short gap in time from running out of carrots until harvesting spring carrots is a welcome reprieve. Absence really does make the heart grow fonder.

Carrots come in a multitude of sizes and colors. Winter-storage carrots are a quintessential carrot—long and bright orange. Don't worry about knobby bits or turns in the surface, as most of this is removed by peeling (see the sidebar To Peel or Not to Peel). That thick skin protects the sweet inner core. In March, it's likely that you'll be eating storage carrots, which may taste slightly bitter, but no matter—all of the recipes included here improve upon the flavor significantly.

Come middle to late spring, the options increase. In recent years, more carrot varieties have become more widely available, particularly at farmers markets. Look for the stubby Thumbelina (so named for its diminutive round shape) and the sweet, thin-skinned Nantes. You may also find a carrot bunch in a rainbow of colors—purple, yellow, red, or white. (Though they are gorgeous in salads, I find the flavor of these a bit bitter and prefer regular-old orange carrots.)

In the kitchen, the beauty of cooking with carrots lies in their versatility. Carrots can be successfully prepared in many ways: raw, crisped up in oil, puréed into a velvety mash, roasted and charred to bring out their sweetness, or simply steamed. Using any combination of these techniques, you can incorporate carrots into almost any meal. They provide some relief from winter's other produce options, spanning both sweet and savory recipes, as they have a naturally high sugar content.

These recipes highlight the flexibility that carrots, as the main ingredient, can bring to a dish. Some quantities to keep in mind: one large carrot (with about a one-inch-wide circumference at the base), when peeled and trimmed, will equal about a cup of grated strands. Generally, 1 cup of grated carrots can feed two to three people—they are quite satiating! Carrot tops can also be used in many recipes. Substitute some chopped carrot leaves for fresh parsley, and the dish changes subtly. Be warned, though: not all carrot greens are created equal, and some may be too dense, furry, or bitter to be enjoyable.

Two additional benefits of carrots: they are super-affordable, and they pack a nutritional punch. One pound of carrots will easily provide a meal for four, so they make a great staple for any home on a budget. Among other health benefits, carrots are low in fat and sodium and high in fiber and vitamin A, which supports healthy eyes. Not bad for a vegetable you've been eating as far back as you can remember!

MARCH RECIPES

Carrots

Cardamom–Carrot Latkes
Roasted Carrots & Sesame Yogurt
Carrots & Eggs with Anchovy Crumbs
Steamed Clams in Lime–Carrot Juice
Carrot Quick Pickles
Carrot Peel Soup
Chard & Carrot Tart
Healthy Carrot Cake
Carrot Marmalade

Seasonal Extras

Warm Potatoes with Hazelnut–Mustard Vinaigrette
Sweet Potato & White Bean Soup

Cardamom–Carrot Latkes

MAKES 12 TO 16 LATKES

Pulling from traditional Jewish latkes, these savory pancakes are a cross between a latke and a fritter. Equal parts potato and carrot are mixed with an abundant dose of onion, then scented substantially with freshly ground cardamom. Prepare these for a festive weekend breakfast, when you have a little more time in the kitchen. Consider doubling the batch—I'd be lying if I didn't confess to eating them as a midnight snack, barefoot in the kitchen!

- 1 large russet potato (about 1 pound)
- 3 green onions
- 1 large carrot, peeled
- 1/2 medium red onion
- 2 eggs
- 3 tablespoons all-purpose flour
- 1/4 cup stout beer
- 1 teaspoon freshly ground cardamom
- 1/2 teaspoon salt
- 1/4 teaspoon pepper
- 1 to 2 cups vegetable oil

Using the largest grate on a box grater, grate the russet potato and immediately cover the pieces completely with water, allowing them to soak for about 15 minutes. Meanwhile, trim off the top 3 inches of the green onions and finely chop. (Reserve the remaining green onions for another use.) Put them in a large bowl. Using the largest setting of a box grater, grate the carrot and the red onion. Add both to the green onions.

In a small bowl, whisk together the eggs, flour, beer, cardamom, salt, and pepper until smooth. Add to the carrot-onion mixture and stir with a wooden spoon to combine.

To strain the grated potatoes, set a fine mesh strainer over a large bowl and line the strainer with cheesecloth or a thin linen towel. Using a slotted spoon, transfer the potatoes from the water to the strainer, reserving the water. Let the water sit, about 10 minutes, so the starch collects in the bottom of the bowl. When all the potatoes are transferred, pick up the cheesecloth or linen and squeeze well to remove the excess water. Really clamp down on the potatoes—you want them as dry as possible. Add 1 cup of the potatoes to the carrot mixture and stir to combine.

Slowly pour the water into the sink, being careful to leave behind the potato starch (this is the white paste that has collected in the bowl). Add the residual potato starch to the batter and stir to combine well.

Preheat the oven to 250 degrees F.

Set a large sauté pan over medium-high heat and add the vegetable oil until it's about a half inch deep. Using a large spoon, drop in 3-inch-wide rounds of batter, being sure not to overcrowd the pan. Stir the batter before shaping and frying each batch, as the liquid tends to pool at the bottom of the bowl. Cook the latkes until the bottoms are golden brown, about 4 minutes. Turn them over and cook the other side until golden brown, another 3 to 4 minutes.

TO PEEL OR NOT TO PEEL

Carrots, like most vegetables, come with an exterior skin meant to protect the flesh from the elements. Recipes often call for peeling carrots, but really . . . is it necessary? Nutritionally speaking, it's wise to leave the peels intact. Carrot skin cells contain strong plant cellulose, which is nutrient-dense and high in beneficial vitamins. Although there may be a health benefit to ingesting carrot skins, eating them may be another story, flavorwise.

Carrots are cultivated for a handful of attributes. Sweetness, days to maturation, storage capacity, and color vary across the spectrum of carrot varieties available to growers, who choose carrots because of these specific traits. Some farmers may elect sweet carrots over storage carrots, because they have a higher sugar content and are therefore more palatable. Because of their delicate skin, however, sweeter carrots tend to have a shorter shelf life; they'll go limp and soft in a matter of days post-harvest. Sweet carrots work for farmers with easy access to markets, but what if your farm is in the middle of nowhere?

Enter storage carrots, which are grown for longevity, not sweetness. Their thicker skin allows for a longer shelf life, which means they are not as fresh tasting. The thicker the skin, the more bitter the flavor profile due to the presence of tannins. As the vegetable ages and the sugars in the plant naturally convert to carbohydrates, the flavor in turn changes and becomes less sweet.

So, to peel or not to peel? There are far too many variables to provide a definitive answer. The flavor of a carrot varies regionally, depends on the time of year, and is dictated by its variety. At the end of the day, it boils down to the chef's choice. If you like the flavor with the peels on or you're using fresh-picked sweet carrots, why bother peeling? Just make sure you scrub the dirt out of the skins before eating. Aesthetically, if you prefer a bright orange carrot (cooked carrot skins tend to turn gray and pale, which may not be appealing to some) or don't like the taste of a particular carrot's peel, remove it. The good news is that you can use these peels in stock, as I do in my Carrot Peel Soup recipe.

Remove the latkes from the oil with a slotted spoon and place them on a layer of paper towels or a paper bag to drain. Once they're drained, arrange them on a platter and hold in the warmed oven. Continue cooking in this fashion until all the latkes are done. Serve immediately.

PANTRY NOTE: Any leftover batter will discolor and separate, so it's best to cook all of the latkes in one go. Leftover latkes can be held in the fridge for a few days, wrapped in parchment, or frozen and heated up in the oven when desired.

Roasted Carrots & Sesame Yogurt

MAKES 4 SERVINGS AS A SIDE DISH

Sweet carrots, tangy yogurt, and nutty sesame seeds make for a harmonious trio in this dish that everyone will ooh and ahh over. Carrots are left in long segments and roasted in a hot oven, allowed to char and burn slightly, then served in a cool pool of seasoned yogurt. Sesame and sunflower seeds add a nice crunch, in addition to a satisfying mouthfeel. This makes a great, nutritious side dish or a complete lunch for vegetarians.

4 medium carrots (about 1 pound), peeled and trimmed
2 tablespoons olive oil
1/4 teaspoon salt
1/4 teaspoon pepper
3/4 cup plain yogurt
1/4 teaspoon honey
1/4 teaspoon ground cumin
1 tablespoon sesame seeds, toasted
2 teaspoons sunflower seeds, roughly chopped
4 stems fresh cilantro

Preheat the oven to 475 degrees F.

Cut the carrots in half crosswise. Cut the thinner bottom portion of the carrot in half lengthwise; cut the larger top portion lengthwise into quarters—this should produce near-equal widths of carrot sticks. Put the carrots on a rimmed baking sheet and toss them with the olive oil, salt, and pepper until well coated. Spread the carrots so they are not touching, and roast for 20 minutes, turning once after 10 minutes, until they're cooked through and charred.

While the carrots are roasting, combine the yogurt, honey, and cumin in a small bowl and set aside. When the carrots are cooked through, remove them from the oven and let cool slightly.

Spoon equal amounts of the yogurt mixture on 4 small plates. Sprinkle the sesame seeds over each dollop of yogurt, covering the yogurt thickly. Place a few roasted carrot sticks across the yogurt, dividing them evenly among the 4 plates. Sprinkle equal amounts of the sunflower seeds over the carrots, then pick the leaves off the cilantro and add to each plate. Serve immediately.

PANTRY NOTE: This side salad will keep for a day in the fridge, covered. Brighten leftovers by adding a few more seeds and a handful of fresh cilantro.

Carrots & Eggs with Anchovy Crumbs

MAKES 4 SERVINGS AS A SIDE DISH

It's a challenge to improve upon a simple hard-boiled egg, but think of this recipe as a poor man's eggs and caviar. In recent years, eggs have moved from the cocktail plate to the breakfast plate and back. It's a pleasure to see them prominently displayed as snacks at restaurants and dinner parties. Here, hard-boiled eggs are cooked until the yolks are *just* set, preserving their brilliant-yellow hue and molten texture. Set on a bed of puréed carrots and topped with salty, anchovy-scented bread crumbs, these eggs are a lovely predinner treat—but would also make a hearty breakfast for any early riser in need of a kick start. Hard-boiled eggs can be cooked as loose or firm as you like. For a runnier yolk, cut the cooking time by two minutes.

- ¼ cup water
- 2 carrots, peeled, trimmed, and cut into small pieces
- 4 eggs
- 1 tablespoon butter
- 1 tablespoon olive oil
- 2 anchovy fillets
- ¼ cup bread crumbs

In a small saucepan over high heat, bring the water and the carrot pieces to a boil. Reduce to a simmer, cover, and cook until the carrots are soft and easily mashed with a fork, about 20 to 25 minutes. Strain the water (but reserve it) and put the carrots in a food processor. Purée the carrots until almost smooth (it's okay if some small bits of carrot are left behind). Add some of the reserved water, a little at a time, if needed to get carrots puréed. Set aside.

To make hard-boiled eggs, put the eggs in a small saucepan and cover with cold water. Bring to a boil over medium-high heat, then reduce to medium-low and simmer the eggs for 6 minutes. Discard the water and set the eggs aside to cool. (You can also plunge them into an ice-water bath to stop the cooking and speed up the cooling process, but this is not necessary.)

While the eggs are simmering (be sure to set your timer!), make the anchovy crumbs. Set a small frying pan over medium-high heat and add the butter and olive oil. When the butter is frothy, add the anchovy fillets, then cook and stir until the fillets fall apart easily.

When the anchovies have "dissolved" into the oil, add the bread crumbs, tossing until they are well coated. Cook until they're brown on one side before turning. Continue cooking in this fashion until the crumbs are a toasty golden brown. Remove from the heat and set aside.

To serve, put a dollop of the carrot purée on each of 4 small plates. Peel the eggs and cut them in half lengthwise. Place the egg halves in the middle of the carrot purée on each plate and sprinkle with anchovy crumbs. Serve immediately.

PANTRY NOTE: Leftover anchovy bread crumbs can be stored in an airtight container in the fridge for a week. These anchovy crumbs can add a pop of flavor to your meals. Try them in place of regular bread crumbs on gratins or to add flavorful texture to steamed fish or shellfish.

Steamed Clams in Lime–Carrot Juice

MAKES 2 SERVINGS AS A MAIN DISH, 4 AS AN APPETIZER

I landed my first restaurant job in the late nineties as a host. It was a hopping place, always packed to the gills, with an amazing applewood grill. Clams were a menu staple, and the broth changed almost daily. One of the clam preparations used carrot juice in place of the traditional butter, thyme, and white wine broth, and it has stayed with me all these years. For this simple dish, clams are steamed in a somewhat Asian-inspired broth with carrot juice as a base and lime, coconut milk, and galangal (a root in the ginger family that can be found in most Asian markets) as accents. If you can't find galangal, replace it with a few slices of fresh ginger and mint leaves—both available throughout the late days of winter.

1 tablespoon olive oil
1 shallot, cut into thin rings
1-inch piece of galangal root, cut into coins
1 cup carrot juice, store-bought or juiced at home
½ cup coconut milk
1 lime, sliced in half

1 pound clams, washed
1 cup fresh cilantro leaves

In a large saucepan, heat the olive oil over medium-high heat. Add the shallot and galangal and sauté until the shallots are beginning to crisp up and turn brown, about 6 minutes. Stir in the carrot juice, coconut milk, and lime halves.

Turn the heat to high and cover the saucepan, bringing the broth to a boil. Add the clams and cover. Turn the heat down to medium-high and cook until all the clams have opened and are fully cooked, about 5 to 8 minutes depending on the size of the clam.

Pour the clams and the broth into a large shallow serving bowl, and sprinkle the cilantro on top. Squeeze the juice from the softened and cooked limes over the clams. Serve immediately.

PANTRY NOTE: This broth also works nicely as a steaming bath for mussels or even whole pieces of fish. Reserve any leftover broth as a fish stock of sorts, adding potatoes and cabbage for a light soup.

WINTER PICKLES

Many summers ago, my friend Jimmy had a casual pool party that unexpectedly extended through dinnertime. The house wasn't stocked, and whipping up a meal for six on the fly resulted in a hodgepodge of offerings. My contribution was a big plate of pickled carrots, and everyone loved them! For months after, Jimmy and Rusty called me for the "recipe"—in truth I had made up the dish in the moment.

This recipe for quick winter pickles originally appeared in *Urban Pantry: Tips & Recipes for a Thrifty, Sustainable & Seasonal Kitchen,* but it is worth the mention here. For firm produce such as carrots, quick pickles work best if the pickling liquid is heated and thereby actually cooks the veggies a bit. These pickled carrots are a perfect side dish in winter, when our plates are otherwise bogged down in onions and potatoes, as they offer a crisp and refreshing flavor note. This same process can be used for other winter vegetables, like celery, fennel, or beets.

CARROT QUICK PICKLES

MAKES 4 TO 6 SERVINGS AS A SIDE DISH

4 carrots, peeled, trimmed, and thinly sliced
1½ cups apple cider vinegar
2 tablespoons sugar
3-inch piece fresh ginger, peeled and cut into coins
2 whole star anise pods
1 cinnamon stick
1 teaspoon whole black peppercorns
1 teaspoon coriander seeds
Pinch of salt

Put the carrots in a nonreactive mixing bowl (one that is not metal) and set aside. In a medium-sized saucepan, heat the vinegar, sugar, ginger, star anise, cinnamon, peppercorns, coriander seeds, and salt over medium heat until simmering. When the liquid is near boiling, pour it over the carrots and let the mixture sit on the counter until cool, stirring occasionally.

Serve the carrots in the brine. Store any leftovers in an airtight container in the fridge.

Carrot Peel Soup

MAKES 2 SERVINGS AS A MAIN DISH

The beauty of this soup lies in its use of kitchen scraps. Save your carrot peels for this fragrant broth, and add in any leftover meat. Here, small pulls of short ribs deepen the soup's satisfying nature. Carrot peels are cooked in a broth along with a few slices of onion and a stalk of celery, if you have them on hand. If not, skip them and toss in another vegetable to flavor the broth—scraps of fennel frond, parsley stalks, anything. To intensify the flavor, this stock is heavily scented with whole spices like cinnamon stick and star anise. While not absolutely necessarily, these spices most definitely take the soup to another level.

1 teaspoon olive oil
½ yellow onion, sliced
½ teaspoon salt
1 celery stalk, chopped
Peels from 4 or 5 carrots
2 tablespoons white vermouth
1 cinnamon stick
10 whole allspice berries
1 whole clove
½-inch piece ginger, cut into coins
2 whole star anise pods
2 large carrots, peeled and cut into thin matchsticks
1 cup leftover beef short rib pieces
Salt and pepper

Heat the olive oil in a large stockpot set over medium-high heat. Add the onion and salt, cooking and stirring until the onion softens and starts to brown, about 6 to 8 minutes. Add the celery and carrot peels and let sit, without stirring, for 2 minutes to brown. Deglaze the stockpot with the white vermouth, scraping up the bits.

Add water to the stockpot, high enough to just cover the peels. Bring to a boil, then reduce to a simmer. Cover and cook for 1 hour, then remove from the heat. Strain out the vegetables, reserving the broth.

Return the broth to the stockpot and add the aromatics—the cinnamon stick, allspice berries, clove, ginger, and star anise. Cook over low heat, covered, for 20 minutes to allow the spices to infuse. Add the carrot matchsticks and short rib pieces, and cook until the carrots are al dente, about 20 minutes. Season with salt and pepper to taste.

Divide the soup evenly into 2 bowls and serve immediately.

PANTRY NOTE: Leftover soup holds in the fridge for about three days. You can also use leftover roasted chicken or even fish in this soup, making sure to adjust the cooking time. (Add the fish only in the last minute of cooking, to just warm through.)

Chard & Carrot Tart

MAKES 6 SERVINGS AS A MAIN DISH

I love tarts for their stress-free nature—easily assembled ingredients that bake up into a gorgeous centerpiece for the table. Skipping a few steps, I use store-bought puff pastry as the dough layer for this recipe. If you're up for the extra effort, though, a simple tart dough (see Rustic Onion Tart in February: Onions) works beautifully. Here, puff pastry is rolled slightly and left in its rectangular shape, a perfect base for spreading a savory carrot purée. The thick layer of spiced purée is topped with blanched chard and a béchamel sauce spiked with nutmeg.

½ cup water

4 carrots, peeled, trimmed, and cut into
   1-inch pieces

½ teaspoon curry powder

½ teaspoon salt

3 tablespoons olive oil

15 stalks chard (or 1 bunch)

2 tablespoons butter

2 tablespoons all-purpose flour

1 cup milk

1 teaspoon ground nutmeg

½ teaspoon lemon zest

Salt and pepper

1 sheet frozen puff pastry, defrosted

Preheat the oven to 350 degrees F.

In a small saucepan, heat the water and carrot pieces over high heat and bring to a boil. Reduce to a simmer and cook until the carrots are soft and easily mashed with a fork, about 20 to 25 minutes. Drain off the water and put the carrots in a blender or food processor. Add the curry powder, salt, and olive oil and purée the mixture to a smooth paste. Set aside.

Fill a large saucepan with water and salt liberally. Set the saucepan over high heat, cover, and bring to a boil. Slice the stem of each chard stalk vertically down the middle. Stack the halved leaves and slice into 1- to 2-inch ribbons, including the stems.

When the water is boiling, add the chard stems and blanch for 1 minute. Then add the chard leaves and blanch 3 minutes more to cook them briefly. Strain the chard, pressing down with the back of a spoon to squeeze out all of the water. Set aside.

In a large sauté pan, heat the butter over medium-high heat. When the butter is foamy, sprinkle the flour over the surface and use a whisk to blend the flour and butter into a thick paste. Cook, whisking constantly, until the flour begins to change color, about 4 minutes.

Still whisking the flour paste, slowly pour in the milk. This will help to reduce lumps. When all of the milk is incorporated, whisk continuously until the sauce begins to thicken and easily coats the back of a spoon, about 4 to 5 minutes. Remove the mixture from the heat and stir in the nutmeg, lemon zest, and salt and pepper to taste. Add the chard leaves to the sauce, stirring to coat evenly. Set aside.

Lightly dust your work surface with flour and roll out the puff pastry to about a third of an inch thick, keeping its rectangular shape. Place the dough on a baking sheet. Evenly spread the carrot purée in the center of the dough, leaving a 2-inch allowance around the edges. Place the chard leaf mixture directly over the carrot purée, distributing evenly. Fold the 2-inch allowance up and over the edges of the tart filling, pinching at the corners to seal.

Bake the tart for 30 to 40 minutes, until the puff pastry is a deep golden brown. Remove from the oven and let cool slightly before serving.

PANTRY NOTE: This tart stores well on the countertop for a day, loosely covered with parchment. For longer storage, wrap in aluminum foil and store in the fridge. Heat a few minutes under the broiler before serving, to help crisp up the dough. You can also substitute any leafy green of your choosing for the chard here—try kale or radicchio.

Healthy Carrot Cake

MAKES 1 SINGLE-LAYER 9-INCH CAKE (6 SERVINGS)

Yes, I know. You don't need another carrot cake recipe. But this one is worth a try! For this dense cake, grated carrot is combined with carrot purée, removing the need for the added fats found in most carrot cake recipes. Pair that with some carrot juice and it's a healthy(ish) crowd favorite.

Of course, the strong carrot flavor is best topped with an indulgent cream cheese icing.

CAKE

1 cup sugar

½ cup brown sugar

1 stick butter, at room temperature

½ cup puréed carrots*

3 eggs

4 large carrots (about 1½ pounds), peeled, trimmed, and grated

1 tablespoon vanilla extract

1 tablespoon freshly grated ginger

2 cups all-purpose flour

1 teaspoon baking powder

1 teaspoon baking soda

1 teaspoon salt

1 teaspoon ground cinnamon

ICING

8 ounces cream cheese, at room temperature

½ cup powdered sugar

½ cup plain yogurt

Zest from 1 orange

Zest from 1 lime

* Prepare 2 carrots as described in Carrots & Eggs with Anchovy Crumbs in this chapter.

Preheat the oven to 350 degrees F. Grease a 9-inch cake pan with a removable bottom and line the bottom with a parchment circle.

In the bowl of an electric mixer, blend the sugars and butter on medium-high speed until well incorporated, about 5 minutes. The sugar–butter combination should be light, nearly white, and fluffy. Add the puréed carrots and blend until just mixed. Add the eggs one at a time, mixing until well incorporated; be sure to scrape down the sides of the bowl. Add the grated carrots, vanilla extract, and ginger, stirring to combine.

In a medium-sized bowl, whisk the flour, baking powder, baking soda, salt, and cinnamon. Carefully add the dry ingredients to the butter mixture and blend until just combined.

Pour the batter into the prepared cake pan and place it in the center of the oven. Bake for 50 to 60 minutes. To test for doneness, insert a butter knife into the center—if it comes out free of crumbs, the cake is done. Remove the cake from the oven and set aside to cool completely before icing.

While the cake is baking, you can make the icing. Put the cream cheese in a medium-sized bowl and beat it to soften. Sift the powdered sugar over the cream cheese, then stir with a flat rubber spatula to incorporate it completely. Stir in the yogurt, orange zest, and lime zest until the icing has no lumps. Keep cool in the fridge until ready to use.

Just before serving, allow the frosting to warm up a little, so you can spread it easily. Add a generous dollop of the icing to the center of the cake and, using an offset spatula or butter knife, spread the icing over the cake and along the sides. Keep in the fridge until ready to serve, removing 30 minutes before serving.

PANTRY NOTE: The unfrosted carrot cake can be made a day or two ahead and kept in the fridge, wrapped very well with tight-fitting plastic wrap. Be sure the cake is cooled completely before wrapping. You can substitute applesauce for the carrot purée, if you like.

Carrot Marmalade

MAKES 2 PINTS

This carrot jam recipe was inspired by my favorite carrot cake ingredients (see Healthy Carrot Cake). The jam is so close to a citrus marmalade, you may not be able to tell the difference. Because carrots are low in pectin, this recipe takes some time. To help activate the pectin, the jam is cooked for a short time and then left overnight to "infuse." Try this marmalade as a marinade for baked chicken (for a honey–orange chicken vibe) or as a side with roasted pork. Serve with cheese and crackers, or use it as a filling between layers of carrot cake or coconut cake. You can add cinnamon or cardamom to this marmalade with excellent results. The final product will be sweeter and makes a delicious dessert relish or filling.

> 1½ pounds carrots, peeled, trimmed, and finely grated (about 6 cups)
> 3½ cups sugar

3 limes, juiced (about ½ cup juice),
   2 half-rinds reserved
2 oranges, juiced (about ¾ cup juice),
   2 half-rinds reserved
2 tablespoons freshly grated ginger
1 cup water

In a large saucepan, set the carrots, sugar, lime and orange juices, ginger, and water over medium heat. Add the reserved lime and orange rinds. Cook the mixture until the carrots are just softened and the sugar is dissolved, about 20 to 30 minutes. Remove from the heat and cover. Put the covered saucepan in the refrigerator overnight.

The next morning, return the saucepan to medium-high heat and cook until the marmalade is just set, about 45 minutes to 1 hour. It will be a loose set, just on the side of thick syrup. Remove the orange and lime rinds and discard. Scoop the marmalade into clean preserving jars and store in the fridge.

PANTRY NOTE: Carrot marmalade will keep in the fridge for about eight weeks.

Warm Potatoes with Hazelnut–Mustard Vinaigrette

MAKES 4 SERVINGS

This potato salad veers from a traditional American version into a more French-influenced salad made with thin mustard and vinegar, as opposed to a cream-based version with mayo. Fit for a dinner side dish or perfect for a light lunch, warm potatoes are tossed in a tangy vinaigrette while toasted hazelnuts are added for crunch. Try to purchase potatoes that are about the same size so the final plating is uniform and elegant.

½ pound waxy potatoes, such as round
   yellow, Yukon Gold, or Red Bliss
2 tablespoons salt
2 tablespoons minced shallot
1 tablespoon red wine vinegar
1 tablespoon Dijon mustard
3 tablespoons olive oil
¼ teaspoon pepper
More salt and pepper
¼ cup chopped toasted hazelnuts
Flat-leaf Italian parsley leaves, for garnish (optional)

Peel the potatoes and submerge them immediately in a bowl of cool water. Once all the potatoes are peeled, move them to a large pot and cover them with cold water. Add the salt and bring the potatoes to boil over high heat. Reduce the heat slightly, and cook until potatoes are just tender, about 15 to 20 minutes.

While the potatoes are cooking, put the shallots and red wine vinegar in a large salad bowl and let it sit for 5 mintues to macerate. Add the Dijon mustard, olive oil, and ¼ teaspoon of pepper to the bowl, and stir well with a fork to emulsify the oil with the vinegar and mustard.

Once the potatoes are tender, drain them, reserving ¼ cup of the boiling liquid. Add the potatoes and reserved liquid to the salad bowl

HOW TO GROW CARROTS

True confession—the act of growing carrots is one rife with frustration for me. I don't know what it is about these colorful roots that vexes me so, but I have a challenging time growing them. Fortunately, my garden clients don't let me indulge in my anti-carrot temper tantrums—everyone loves carrots, so I have to plant them all year long.

Carrots are finicky vegetables and demand certain conditions be met before they'll produce their long, sweet roots. Soil preparation is the first line of defense in successful carrot growing. Any clumps in the soil or rocks will cause the root to split, resulting in oddly shaped carrots and forked roots. Carrot seeds are also weak, so will not push through compacted soil. Before seeding a bed for carrots, it is wise to till and sift through the soil, removing all debris like rocks, pebbles, and root hairs, and pulverize any sod clumps you encounter.

Once the soil is clear and loamy, carrots should be seeded in shallow trenches, just barely under the surface of the soil. I trace a line in the soil with my fingertip to sow carrot seeds and very lightly sprinkle soil over them by the handful. Carrots take several days to germinate—up to two weeks—so be patient and keep the seed beds moist. In order for any seed to germinate, it needs moisture. If seeding carrots in hot, dry weather, consider blanketing the rows with a thin sheet of spun cloth called floating row cover. This cover allows water and sunlight in, and holds water (including morning dew) against the seeds.

Carrots can be planted nearly all year long, starting with early spring just after the frosts are over. This is typically in the first weeks of April for milder climates, but planting also must be planned around soil moisture—anything too wet will compact the soil and the seeds will not do well. Carrots can be planted from spring through August in most areas, though this will depend on your choice of seed varieties.

Spring carrots are typically sweet and crispy, perfect for eating fresh out of the garden. Seeds sown in late summer for winter eating, however, are storage carrots and have more starch to their makeup, leaving them somewhat bitter as they age. To help winter carrots along, mulch the rows with a layer of straw for insulation. The ground acts as storage, and hay will protect your produce until you're ready to harvest.

Carrots come in a variety of colors, compliments of eager breeders and gardeners everywhere. Choose from a rainbow of white, orange, yellow, red, and purple, or sow

→

multiple varieties side by side. If you have dense or clay-rich soil, opt for a shorter, rounder variety like the Thumbelina, which is also a decent choice for anyone trying to grow carrots in a container. The shorter and broader Chantenays also work well. For winter carrots (which are sown in the summer months), be sure to choose a proper storage carrot.

The only other rule for growing carrots is to actively thin them. Carrot seeds are small and, inevitably, you will plant too many too close together. Thinning is the process of removing some of these plants so that others have space enough to grow. Thin without guilt and remind yourself that you're making way for more full-grown carrots—too often new gardeners suffer from pruning guilt, which is futile. Once they're thinned to one plant every three inches or so, you can leave carrots alone to grow, harvesting them when ready.

and, using a large spoon, fold gently to combine. Taste for seasoning and sprinkle the hazelnuts and a generous handful of parsley on top, if using, and leave covered on the countertop until ready to serve.

PANTRY NOTE: This salad keeps well up to three days in the fridge. You can embellish this salad by adding a hard-boiled egg for each person, along with a slab of preserved tuna.

Sweet Potato & White Bean Soup

MAKES 6 SERVINGS

This soup cooks up thick, more like a fragrant bowl of beans than a soup. Simple ingredients cook for hours over low heat, resulting in a hearty, filling stew that can be served for

lunch or dinner. Sweet potatoes and ginger give each bowl a subtle flavor kick. I like mine with a spoonful of plain yogurt and some pickled or fermented carrots or cabbage kraut as garnish.

2 tablespoons olive oil
1 large onion, chopped (about 2 cups)
1½ teaspoons salt
½ teaspoon pepper
2 tablespoons finely diced fresh ginger
1 teaspoon ground cumin
1 cup large dried Corona beans or other broad bean, soaked overnight
4 cups chicken or vegetable stock
1 sweet potato, peeled and cut into ½-inch dice

In a large pot, warm the olive oil over medium-high heat. Add the onion, salt, and pepper, and cook until the onion starts to color, about 5 minutes. Add the ginger and cumin and cook another 2 minutes, until the mixture is fragrant and beginning to stick to the bottom of the pan slightly. Add the beans and stock and bring to a boil. Reduce the heat to low and simmer until the beans are cooked through and easily mashed with the back of a fork. This can take anywhere from 2 to 5 hours, so keep stirring occasionally and monitor the progress. Add a cup or two of water or stock as needed.

When the beans are cooked through, add the diced sweet potato to the stew and turn under.

Cook until the sweet potato is just cooked through and tender, about 15 to 20 minutes, and serve.

PANTRY NOTE: This soup holds in the fridge, covered, for about five days. Reheat before serving, and if it's too thick add a cupful of water to loosen the broth. Any legume can be used for this stew, though larger beans hold together better and won't break down as quickly as smaller soup beans.

APRIL

RHUBARB

RHUBARB IS ONE OF THOSE plants that everyone loves, at least in theory. It has an old-timey feel to it, as our grandmothers used to cook rhubarb pies. Rhubarb's history is indeed long—it's popular in many cultures across the world and has been used as a medicinal plant in Asia and as a wedding dowry for Norwegian brides. And recently rhubarb has come back into fashion, culinarily speaking.

Rhubarb is a perennial vegetable, which means it comes back year after year, and the root can be split to increase the harvest (see the sidebar How to Grow Rhubarb). Much of the commercial rhubarb sold is hothouse rhubarb. These stalks tend to be redder, thinner, and often sweeter, and they are available in late winter. Garden-grown rhubarb comes into season right as April rolls around in temperate climates—my own rhubarb plant, thanks to a moderate Seattle winter, sprouted up in early February this year. As rhubarb is one of the first true spring vegetables to appear in markets, people tend to go gaga for it. After a long winter of root vegetables and cabbages, it's refreshing to see another option—and a brilliant red one at that.

Rhubarb has a reasonably long season. If harvested regularly, the plant may produce from spring through summer, allowing a lot of opportunities for kitchen experiments. While it is a natural choice for desserts, like pie or tarts or the molded Rhubarb Jelly with Sweet Rose Cream included here, rhubarb can also be used in savory dishes. But this vegetable isn't a total culinary slam dunk. Let's face it: rhubarb is crazy tart. Have you ever eaten a stalk of raw rhubarb? Your face will pucker in seconds. It's not that the astringency of this plant is offensive, but it is incredibly strong. This tart flavor may appeal to some, but I admit to needing a liberal dose of sugar or honey where rhubarb is concerned. Adding a touch of sweetness to rhubarb recipes soothes the sour flavor, allowing for a more pleasurable experience. If you're into tart foods, however, omit the honey or sugar from any recipe here and see what you think.

Rhubarb is not the easiest ingredient in the world to work with—it's acidic, falls apart easily, and needs some coaxing to become palatable. But I'm happy to share that cooking with rhubarb has been an awesome exercise. It's actually quite versatile and can be eaten raw, pickled, roasted, cooked down into a mash, juiced, and stewed. Using these cooking techniques, I've come up with seven tasty recipes, including a few for breakfast, starters, salads, main courses, and desserts. As a bonus, I threw in a zinger of a preservation recipe (Rosemary-Rhubarb Drinking Vinegar).

I recently spent some time in the UK (my boyfriend lives in Scotland), and there are some definite British influences in these rhubarb recipes. It's fitting, as Britain is one of the first documented places to grow rhubarb out of season in forcing sheds (see Varying Shades of Red). While the traditional cuisine in the UK is different from that of the States, it has been an adventure for me to try new (and old) things there. I've taken some traditional ideas and shaken them up. I've also been influenced by the sweet-sour focus often found in Persian foods. And of course, straight-up American dishes always inspire. For example, I've included a recipe for a take on traditional breakfast sausage, Rhubarb-Tarragon Sausage. What you won't find here, however, is strawberry rhubarb pie. Dig in!

APRIL RECIPES

Rhubarb

Rhubarb–Tarragon Sausage
Smoked Trout Brandade with Pickled Rhubarb
Rhubarb & Celery Salad with Toasted Hazelnuts
Coriander Ribs with Rhubarb BBQ Sauce
Oatmeal-Brittle Cranachan with Poached Rhubarb
Rhubarb Jelly with Sweet Rose Cream
Rosemary–Rhubarb Drinking Vinegar

Seasonal Extras

Molten Egg with Chervil & Tarragon
Seared Chicken with Scallion Butter

Rhubarb–Tarragon Sausage

MAKES 8 PATTIES

These delicious and vibrant breakfast sausages go with any breakfast food—serve alongside a fried egg, crumble into an egg scramble, or cook up as a protein side for pancakes. Tarragon is a tender spring herb with a delicate licorice note. With mild ground pork and tangy bits of rhubarb, this combination offers a tart, crisp flavor against a traditionally seasoned sausage patty. Maple syrup or honey add a bit of sweetness to the mix, but omit if you prefer the strong tang of rhubarb.

> ½ pound ground pork
> 4 ounces rhubarb (about half a thick
>   stalk), trimmed and finely chopped
> 1 clove garlic, grated
> 1 tablespoon chopped fresh tarragon
> 1 tablespoon maple syrup or honey
> ¼ teaspoon salt
> ⅛ teaspoon pepper
> 2 tablespoons bacon fat or olive oil

Combine the ground pork, rhubarb, garlic, tarragon, maple syrup or honey, salt, and pepper in a medium-sized bowl. Using a wooden spoon, mix all the ingredients well. Make sure the herbs are evenly distributed throughout the pork. Using your hands, shape the mixture into 4-inch-wide patties and set aside.

In a large sauté pan, heat the bacon fat or oil over medium heat. Place the sausage patties in the pan in a single layer, taking care not to over-crowd. Cook until golden brown on the first side, about 4 to 5 minutes. Flip the patties over and heat until cooked through and golden brown, another 4 minutes or so.

Serve immediately.

PANTRY NOTE: Any leftover patties can be frozen or kept in the fridge, covered, for up to three days. This recipe can be doubled and also makes a great meatball.

Smoked Trout Brandade with Pickled Rhubarb

MAKES 1 CUP PICKLED RHUBARB; SMOKED TROUT BRANDADE MAKES 4 TO 6 SERVINGS AS A STARTER

Pickled rhubarb is crisp and tangy—a nice change of pace from pickled cucumbers or cornichons. It offers an acidic bite to rich and heavy meals and pairs well with roasted beef or duck. Try it alongside a big slice of paté, served with a spoonful of mustard and a crunchy baguette. Here, Smoked Trout Brandade takes the place of paté, making for a lighter, springlike nosh that may be served hot or cold. I love smoked fish for its ease of preparation and its strong flavor profile. These are my favorite pickling aromatics, but you can vary the spices to suit your own palate. In summer, add a sliced jalapeño or a handful of basil. The combination of potatoes and fish extends the meal, making this an affordable starter when you want to serve something elegant yet cost-effective.

PICKLED RHUBARB

½ pound rhubarb, trimmed and cut into
    thin slices

1½ cups apple cider vinegar

½ cup sugar

3-inch piece fresh ginger, peeled and
    cut into thin coins

2 whole star anise pods

1 cinnamon stick

15 whole cloves

1 tablespoon whole coriander seeds

1 tablespoon red chile flakes

Pinch of salt

SMOKED TROUT BRANDADE

4 ounces smoked trout

1 large Yukon potato (about ½ pound),
    peeled and boiled until soft

1 teaspoon chopped fresh tarragon

1 teaspoon grated lemon rind

¼ teaspoon salt

⅛ teaspoon pepper

4 to 6 tablespoons heavy cream

To prepare the pickled rhubarb, put the rhubarb in a nonreactive mixing bowl (one that is not metal) and set aside.

In a medium-sized saucepan, heat the vinegar, sugar, ginger, star anise, cinnamon, cloves, coriander seeds, red chile flakes, and salt over high heat until simmering, about 10 minutes.

When the liquid is near boiling, remove from the heat and pour it over the rhubarb. Let the mixture sit on the countertop until cool, stirring occasionally. Once the pickled rhubarb has cooled, refrigerate in a covered glass jar until ready to use.

To prepare the trout, break it into pieces in a medium-sized mixing bowl. Add the potato, tarragon, lemon rind, salt, and pepper, and mash together using the tines of a fork until it becomes a thick paste. It's okay to leave larger pieces of fish for texture. Pour in half of the heavy cream and stir well to combine.

If you would like a thinner spread, add more heavy cream until the desired consistency is reached. Season to taste with more salt and pepper, if desired.

Put the brandade in a small bowl or ramekin and serve alongside crostini or crackers and a small bowl (about ¼ cup) of the pickled rhubarb, allowing people to build their own appetizers.

PANTRY NOTE: Pickled rhubarb is high in acidity and will therefore keep for many weeks, covered, in the fridge. Once you've eaten it all, do not discard the brine—you can reheat it and make another batch of pickled rhubarb or use as a seasoned rhubarb vinegar on green salads or legumes. The Smoked Trout Brandade can be made ahead and held in the fridge for up to two days before serving. If made in advance, remove from the fridge and let it warm to room temperature before serving.

HOW TO GROW RHUBARB

Rhubarb is a perennial plant that comes up early in spring and produces edible stalks through early summer. A cool-season plant, rhubarb needs a winter freeze and cooler growing temperatures to thrive, so it grows well in cool and temperate climates.

Most rhubarb plants are started through propagation, a process of splitting the root cluster into several viable plants. This is done easily but should happen in early spring before the plant puts on too much growth, or just before winter, giving the plant time to be dormant before spring bloom. A winter freeze is necessary, as it stimulates spring growth. Growth is slower in these seasons, and transplanting at this time is less likely to stress the plant.

A rhubarb plant is composed of several easily identifiable features. There is the "crown" (the stalky bit that breaks through the soil), the main root (a massive root called a rhizome), and then the "roots" (the branches of root growing directly off the rhizome). To propagate the plant through root division, dig up the entire plant. Do this carefully, starting a good foot out from the center of the crown before breaking the soil with a spade. Working in a circle, loosen the soil around the rhubarb, eventually working up to the roots. Rhubarb root systems are large and deep, so it's inevitable that you'll break through a lot of the root structure. Don't worry—focus on getting the crown out in one piece, along with a good portion of the rhizome. These are necessary for the success of any future growth.

When the crown and rhizome are dug up, divide the plant into several segments. Do this by identifying the buds in the crown—they are the beginning of the rhubarb stalks, sometimes called "eyes" (I assume because of their circular shape). Cut between the buds so that each new plant has a bud or two, in addition to a piece of rhizome. Make sure each segment has both healthy roots and at least one bud. The smaller the cut piece, the smaller the rhubarb plant will be the first year. If you're splitting and transplanting in your own yard, experiment by cutting them into different sizes and comparing growth over the years.

Once you have the rhubarb separated, plant the segments in well-composted soil. Make sure the entire root fits in the hole—you don't want any roots bending up or weaving into the top layer of soil, so make sure to dig deep if it's a big segment. Water well and be sure to keep the plants watered until they catch on and begin to put out new growth. You don't want to stress the plant from lack of water. A bit of straw around the transplanted crown acts as a nice mulch to hold in moisture.

Right after transplanting, remove any large leaves and stalks from the plant. This allows the rhubarb to put its energy into growing a strong root system. You may get a few thin stalks of rhubarb the first year. In August cut all the stalks and greens from the stem, preparing it for winter dormancy, and by spring the next year you should have a healthy, strong plant. To harvest, hold stalks around their base, as close to the soil as possible, and turn them slightly, wiggling back and forth. You can also cut rhubarb at the base with a sharp knife.

Rhubarb & Celery Salad with Toasted Hazelnuts

MAKES 4 SERVINGS

Rhubarb is incredibly tart and usually not eaten raw, but this salad makes an exception. Thinly sliced rhubarb pairs beautifully with celery and avocados, and hazelnuts add some tasty fat. And when I say "thinly sliced rhubarb," I mean featherlight and see-through. Use a mandoline if you have one (with the guard on!). If you don't have a mandoline, use a sharp knife and (very important) take your time. Work slowly, and you'll be rewarded with a fantastic and refreshing salad.

1 tablespoon finely diced shallot
1 tablespoon apple cider vinegar
1/2 teaspoon salt
1/4 teaspoon pepper
1/4 cup olive oil
1/2 teaspoon Dijon mustard
1 tablespoon honey
1/2 teaspoon grated fresh ginger
2 celery stalks plus leaves, cut very thin
4 ounces rhubarb (about half a thick stalk), trimmed, quartered, and cut very thin
1/2 avocado, cut into a large dice
1/2 cup toasted hazelnuts, chopped

Put the shallot, vinegar, salt, and pepper in a medium-sized bowl. Set aside for 10 minutes. (Allowing the shallot to sit for a short time in vinegar pickles it slightly while also mellowing its flavor, removing the oniony bite.)

Next, add the olive oil, Dijon mustard, honey, and ginger to the shallot-vinegar mixture. Whisk to emulsify and combine. When everything is well incorporated, add the celery, rhubarb, and avocado, and fold all of the ingredients together, coating evenly in the vinaigrette.

Sprinkle the hazelnuts over all and serve immediately.

PANTRY NOTE: Because both celery and rhubarb are sturdy vegetables, this salad will hold in the fridge overnight if you have any leftovers. Store tightly covered, and make sure to eat leftovers the next day while they are still crispy. Refresh with some celery leaves or fresh avocado.

Coriander Ribs with Rhubarb BBQ Sauce

MAKES 4 SERVINGS

This recipe has become a household favorite. Regionally, the ratio of tart to sweet varies greatly in traditional barbecue sauces, but I prefer a less sweet version. Here, rhubarb takes the place of vinegar in the sauce, enhancing the tart-sweet balance. The sauce can double as a side once the ribs are cooked and served, allowing an extra little something for dipping. The pork ribs are first dry-rubbed and then slow-roasted in a low oven, which makes for succulent, fall-off-the-bone meat. In the final minutes of cooking, the ribs are doused with the rhubarb sauce (made from burned sugar and rhubarb mash) and allowed to caramelize slightly before serving. Although the recipe uses an oven, you can just as easily grill these ribs when the weather permits.

RIBS
3 to 4 pounds pork ribs, racked or
    precut
1 tablespoon ground cumin
1 tablespoon coriander seeds, crushed
1/4 teaspoon ground cinnamon
1 tablespoon ground fennel
1 teaspoon salt
1/2 teaspoon pepper

SAUCE
1/2 cup sugar
1 cup warm water
1 pound rhubarb (about 3 to 4 stalks),
    trimmed and cut into 2-inch pieces

Place the ribs in a large baking pan. Sprinkle the cumin, coriander seeds, cinnamon, fennel, salt, and pepper over the ribs. Using your hands, press to coat the ribs, working the spices evenly across each rib until most of the spices are absorbed. Set aside at room temperature for 30 minutes.

Preheat the oven to 300 degrees F. Roast the ribs for 2 to 2½ hours, until the meat is tender and easily comes away from the bone.

While the ribs are roasting, make the sauce. In a small saucepan, pour in the sugar and shake gently, so it forms an even layer along the bottom of the pan. Set this over medium-high heat—the sugar will start melting after a few minutes. Do not stir the sugar, but monitor it closely. It will begin to brown at the edges. Swirl the pan slightly to distribute the heat and hot caramel, making sure to keep the sugar level so it does not coat the sides of the saucepan. The caramel will turn dark brown and amber at the edges. Continue swirling gently until all of the sugar is dark amber, about 5 to 7 minutes, and smells of burned sugar. Pour in the warm water and stir.

VARYING SHADES OF RED

Rhubarb, like many other plants, is available in several varieties, each boasting varying shades of red. There are three types of rhubarb—red rhubarb, which is deep crimson and may have an interior pink stalk; speckled rhubarb, where a pink to red stalk bottom tapers to speckled pink and green toward the top of the stalk; and green rhubarb, where the bulk of the stalk is lime green. Rhubarb grown outdoors, without any coverage during its growth cycle, typically has strong green leaves and tougher speckled stems. The shade of red varies across varieties, but a lot of garden-grown rhubarb is lighter in color. Some commercial rhubarb may be bred for long, tender, deep-red stalks.

In the early twentieth century, the region around Yorkshire, UK, was dubbed the Rhubarb Triangle for its mass production, and it supplied much of the world's rhubarb. Farmers would "force" rhubarb earlier than the season would allow by using forcing sheds. In winter, after the first freeze (rhubarb crowns must experience a freeze in order to produce), farmers would move low sheds over their rhubarb plants. These sheds were warmed slowly, tricking the rhubarb with springlike conditions to make them produce. Because the sheds also kept light off of the rhubarb, the plants tended to stay red throughout and are thought of as more tender and more sweet than field rhubarb. This area is still a large producer of rhubarb and is now a Protected Designation of Origin (PDO), which specifically protects the area's Forced Yorkshire Rhubarb.

If you come across a particularly green batch of rhubarb this season, it will probably cook up into a slightly muddy color. To help keep jams and sauces pink, steep a few hibiscus flowers or some beets in the liquid while cooking. This ensures a rosy hue.

Be careful: The caramelized sugar will sputter and pop. Cook until the caramelized sugar has dissolved.

Add the rhubarb and bring to a boil. Then reduce the heat to low and allow the rhubarb to simmer 10 minutes. Remove from the heat and let the mixture cool slightly, about 20 minutes. Once it's cooled, add the rhubarb sauce to a blender and purée until perfectly smooth. Pour the rhubarb sauce into a small bowl and set aside.

When the ribs are cooked through, remove them from the oven and set aside. Increase the oven temperature to 425 degrees F. Brush the ribs with half of the rhubarb sauce. Return to the oven and let the sauce caramelize and bubble, about 10 to 12 minutes. Remove the ribs from the oven and let cool slightly. Serve the ribs alongside a small bowl of the remaining rhubarb sauce.

PANTRY NOTE: Any leftover sauce or ribs (although I doubt you'll have any) can be covered and held in the fridge for up to three days. The rhubarb sauce recipe can be doubled and the ribs basted twice for extra-rich flavor, if you like.

Oatmeal-Brittle Cranachan with Poached Rhubarb

MAKES 6 SERVINGS

Cranachan (CRAN-ah-ken) is a traditional Scottish dessert that combines toasted oats, whipped cream, and fruit in a fluffy, folded mass. Although I love oats, leaving them unadorned doesn't feel very special, so I decided to make a crisp oatmeal "brittle." A simple version—here a clumpy mass of butter, sugar, and oats—is baked, allowing the sugar to melt and spread, resulting in a thin sheet of oatmeal brittle. Cracked into pieces, this layer adds crispiness to a fruit and whipped cream parfait. The sweetness of the brittle is the perfect counterpoint to the tart, poached rhubarb.

4 ounces butter (8 tablespoons, or 1 stick)
½ cup brown sugar
1 tablespoon vanilla extract
1½ cups rolled oats
1 teaspoon ground cinnamon
⅛ teaspoon salt
1 cup sugar
½ cup water
1 pound rhubarb (about 3 to 4 stalks), trimmed and cut into 3-inch pieces, then cut into quarters
1½ cups heavy cream
1 tablespoon bourbon, brandy, or whiskey

Preheat the oven to 350 degrees F.

Melt the butter in a small saucepan set over medium heat. Stir often and make sure you don't brown the butter. Once all the butter has melted, stir in the brown sugar and vanilla extract. Remove from the heat and set aside.

In a large mixing bowl, stir together the rolled oats, cinnamon, and salt, mixing well to combine. Pour the butter, vanilla, and brown sugar mixture over the rolled oats and fold, using a rubber spatula. The mixture will be gummy, not smooth and liquid-like, so you'll need to press and mash the brown sugar clumps into the oats until evenly distributed.

Pour the oat mixture onto a parchment-lined baking pan, pressing into a thin flat layer across the entire pan. Bake it in the oven for 25 to 30 minutes, until the oats are starting to brown and caramel is bubbling at the edges. Remove the baking pan from the oven and set aside to cool.

Meanwhile, in a small saucepan, set the sugar and water over high heat. Bring to a boil and then remove from the heat, setting aside. Add the rhubarb to the hot syrup and let cool. It will cook in the hot syrup; removing it from direct

TOP Smoked Trout Brandade with
Pickled Rhubarb, p. 106
BOTTOM Rhubarb & Celery Salad with
Toasted Hazelnuts, p. 109

OPPOSITE
TOP Rhubarb–Tarragon Sausage, p. 106
BOTTOM Coriander Ribs with Rhubarb
BBQ Sauce, p. 110

TOP Rosemary–Rhubarb Drinking Vinegar, p. 114
BOTTOM Rhubarb Jelly with Sweet Rose Cream, p. 113

OPPOSITE
Oatmeal-Brittle Cranachan with Poached Rhubarb, p. 112

OPPOSITE
TOP Lettuce Wedge with
Herbed Yogurt, p. 122
BOTTOM Stir-Fried Escarole,
p. 122

TOP Blueberry–Oregano Turkey Meatballs, p. 145
BOTTOM Lemon Beef with Raspberry Dipping Sauce, p. 144

TOP Strawberry Mousse, p. 146
BOTTOM Raspberry Vinegar, p. 148

TOP Basil & Pine Nut Salad with Zucchini Ribbons, p. 162
BOTTOM Roasted Summer Squash with Cilantro Vinaigrette, p. 163

TOP Upside-Down Corn Bread with Summer
Squash, p. 164
BOTTOM LEFT Zucchini–Coconut
Cupcakes, p. 170
BOTTOM RIGHT Ricotta–Squash
Dumpling Soup, p. 166

heat prevents the fruit from breaking down into a mash.

Once the oatmeal brittle and the rhubarb-syrup mixture are cool, assemble the cranachan. In a large mixing bowl, whip together the heavy cream and bourbon using an electric mixer on high speed (or whisk quickly by hand), until firm peaks form.

Drain the rhubarb from the syrup (saving the syrup) and fold the fruit into the bourbon whipped cream. Put a spoonful of fruit-cream mixture in the bottom of 6 individual glasses—I like to use glass lowballs. Crumble in some oatmeal brittle, creating another layer. Top with the remainder of the fruit-cream mixture and another layer of crumbled oatmeal brittle. Serve immediately.

PANTRY NOTE: Oatmeal brittle can be made up to two days ahead and kept out on the counter-top until ready to use. You can boil down the residual rhubarb poaching liquid and use it for dessert syrup or as an addition to beverages. Rhubarb syrup will hold in the fridge, in a covered container, for about three weeks.

Rhubarb Jelly with Sweet Rose Cream

MAKES 6 SERVINGS

When we were growing up, my mom often made my sister and me chocolate pudding or Jell-O for dessert. I was always a chocolate pudding kid, but my sister preferred Jell-O, and the fridge shelves were full with both options—it is the one thing we never fought over! Not a thing has changed with age, and while I still prefer the pudding, my sister often makes up a batch of gelatin for my nieces and nephews—a pleasant reminder of our youth. I've grown to love the texture and light flavor of jelly molds. Here, I turn loads of rhubarb into an earthy pink juice and combine it with powdered gelatin until set. Served with a fluffy mound of rose-infused whipped cream, this is a delightful, light dessert. Rose water can be found in the Mediterranean food section of most grocery stores.

1 pound rhubarb (about 3 to 4 stalks),
    trimmed and cut into 1-inch pieces
3 cups water
½ cup sugar
2 tablespoons powdered gelatin
1 cup heavy cream
1 tablespoon caster sugar
1 tablespoon rose water

In a large saucepan, bring the rhubarb, water, and ½ cup of sugar to a boil. Reduce to a simmer and cook until the rhubarb completely breaks down, about 20 minutes. Remove from the heat and let cool completely, stirring occasionally.

Once the rhubarb is cool, strain the pulp from the liquid by using a fine mesh strainer suspended over a large mixing bowl. Use a rubber spatula to gently press on the fruit solids and expel all of the juice. Reserve the juice and save the rhubarb mash for another recipe (perhaps Coriander Ribs with Rhubarb BBQ Sauce).

Measure out 2 cups of rhubarb juice. Reserve any extra for another use. In a small saucepan, warm 1 cup of the measured juice over medium heat. Once the juice is warm, remove the saucepan from the heat and sprinkle in the powdered gelatin. Let sit for 5 minutes. Stir to dissolve all of the gelatin, then add the reserved cup of rhubarb juice to the pan and stir to combine well.

Lightly grease a 4-cup capacity jelly mold by moistening a paper towel with vegetable oil and wiping the inside of the mold. You may also use large muffin tins, if you wish to make individual servings. Do not allow the oil to pool—you just want to lightly coat the pan so the jelly unmolds easily. Pour the rhubarb-gelatin liquid into the mold and skim off any bubbles that form on the surface. Cover tightly with plastic wrap and place it in the fridge. Leave the mold undisturbed until completely set, about 6 hours or overnight.

To prepare the Sweet Rose Cream, whip together the heavy cream, caster sugar, and rose water with an electric mixer until soft peaks form.

To unmold the gelatin, fill a large bowl with warm water and submerge the outside of the mold briefly. Set a large plate on the bottom of the mold and quickly flip them over. Jiggle the mold slightly to loosen. The gelatin should release easily from the mold and should retain the mold's shape. Serve the plated jelly mold with a bowl of the Sweet Rose Cream, and allow guests to portion out for themselves.

PANTRY NOTE: Leftover gelatin or rose cream can be stored in the fridge, covered, for up to three days. You can easily add other aromatics to this recipe by infusing the rhubarb juice while it's cooking. Try adding a cinnamon stick, a vanilla bean, or any other flavor you prefer.

Rosemary–Rhubarb Drinking Vinegar

MAKES ABOUT 4 CUPS

Drinking vinegars are known as "shrubs" and have recently been cropping up on bar menus across the country—and the world! A shrub is an excellent and refreshing way to preserve the flavors of a season and makes good use of a glut of any ingredient. Come late May, when I've had my fill of rhubarb, I turn to this recipe for pantry stocking and making the most of the harvest. Rhubarb is cooked down with apple cider vinegar and sugar, then strained to create a pungent and nasal-clearing syrup. I pair my shrubs with fizzy water for a bracing, nonalcoholic aperitif, but this one also works well with herbaceous gin.

    4 large rhubarb stalks, trimmed and
        diced (about 2 cups)
    4 cups apple cider vinegar
    3 sprigs fresh rosemary
    1½ cups sugar

In a medium-sized saucepan, heat the rhubarb, vinegar, and rosemary sprigs over medium-high heat. Bring to a gentle boil and cook another 10 minutes. Add the sugar and stir until dissolved. Remove the saucepan from the heat and let cool to room temperature.

Meanwhile, wash and dry a quart-sized glass canning jar or other glass jar with a lid. When the rhubarb mixture is cool, strain all solids from the vinegar and pour into the jar and cover. Put the drinking vinegar in the fridge, where it will keep for several months.

To serve, add approximately 2 tablespoons of Rosemary-Rhubarb Drinking Vinegar to an ice-filled glass. Fill with seltzer water and garnish with a sprig of rosemary.

PANTRY NOTE: Shrubs are awesome drinking tonics, but they also work well in vinaigrettes or as a gastrique for cooking sauces.

Molten Egg with Chervil & Tarragon

MAKES 4 SERVINGS

This softly cooked egg hovers between hard-boiled and underdone, producing a creamy, bright orange yolk soft enough to dip a fork in. Eggs and tender herbs make excellent companions and go well together in any form. Chervil is a spring herb that is best grown in small pots or garden beds. One of the first herbs up in spring, it has a delicate leaf packed with a soft anise flavor. Here, boiled eggs are paired with soft-whipped cream infused with herbs and served alongside toast—an easy and elegant breakfast or brunch.

4 eggs
½ cup heavy cream
2 tablespoons chopped fresh chervil
2 tablespoons chopped fresh tarragon
¼ teaspoon salt
¼ teaspoon pepper

Place the eggs in a medium-sized pot and add cold water just until the eggs are fully submerged. Set over medium-high heat and bring to a low boil. Once the water begins to boil, drop the heat to medium and set the timer for 3 minutes. After 3 minutes, remove the eggs from the water and place them in a bowl full of ice-cold water, or run the eggs under cold water for several minutes to halt the cooking. Set aside and let cool for 10 minutes.

While the eggs are cooling, put the heavy cream in a large mixing bowl. Turn the bowl at an angle and whip, using a whisk, for 1 to 2 minutes, until the cream holds soft peaks. Do not overwhip—firm peaks will be too thick. If you do overwhip, add a small spoonful of cream to the mixture and fold it in to loosen. Fold the herbs into the cream, turning only until just combined.

Peel the eggs and slice them in half lenghtwise, placing one egg on each of 4 plates. Spoon a small amount of herbed cream over each egg and sprinkle with salt and pepper. Serve immediately.

PANTRY NOTE: For a harder-cooked yolk, leave the eggs in the water for 6 minutes before draining and plunging into cold water. Leftover soft-whipped cream can be added to beaten eggs for an omelette or used for another savory dish. It will hold in the fridge, covered, up to two days.

Seared Chicken with Scallion Butter

MAKES 4 SERVINGS

Green onions can be planted and grown all year long—if not in the ground, then in a glass of water on a windowsill. They make an excellent addition to meals and cook down into a succulent pile of delicate onion flavor. Here, green onions are wilted in butter alongside a thin chicken breast, making for an effortless lunch or quick mid-week dinner. You can also use green garlic in this recipe, or use the tender tops of young leeks or sprouting onions.

   1 tablespoon olive oil
   2 tablespoons butter
   2 boneless, skinless chicken breasts, cut
      in half lengthwise and pounded thin
   2 bunches green onions (about 12),
      chopped (about 1½ cups)
   ¼ cup vermouth or dry white wine
   ¼ cup chicken or vegetable stock
   Salt and pepper
   1 tablespoon heavy cream (optional)

In a large sauté pan, warm the olive oil and butter over medium-high heat. When the butter has melted and the pan is hot, add the chicken pieces and cook until golden brown, about 2 to 3 minutes. Turn them over and brown the other side, about 2 to 3 minutes more.

Remove the chicken from the pan and turn to high. When the pan is hot, add the green onions and stir constantly, until they're wilted and soft, about 1 to 2 minutes. Add vermouth to deglaze the pan and scrape up any brown bits, cooking until the liquid is reduced by half, about another minute. Add the stock and bring to a boil. Reduce the heat to medium-low and add the chicken back to the pan. Cook until the chicken is just cooked through, about 8 minutes. Add salt and pepper to taste. Remove the pan from the heat and set the chicken pieces on individual plates. Add the cream to the pan, if desired, and swirl to combine. Pour equal portions of sauce over each chicken breast and serve immediately.

PANTRY NOTE: This recipe holds well in the fridge for about three days—reheat slightly before serving or let it warm to room temperature, which will help loosen the sauce. I am not a fan of using only the chicken breast, so I purchase a whole bird (which is less expensive) and trim the breasts off. Reserve the bones for stock and use the dark meat for roasting.

Smoked Trout Brandade
with Pickled Rhubarb

LETTUCE

LETTUCE AVAILABILITY EBBS AND FLOWS throughout the year. Lettuce is one of the first spring greens to pop up in the garden. Sown from March on, this quick-growing crop can be seeded and harvested through fall. Tender, sweet greens are available during spring and summer. Spring offers tender, leafy greens and eventually larger Bibb lettuces. In summer, long-to-mature romaines come in, and winter greens like endive and radicchio are planted, some of which will overwinter well and offer welcome greenery during an otherwise dismal season. As a general rule, bitter greens are available in late autumn and mid-spring. Lettuce turns bitter with age, so when in doubt, rip off a small piece of the leaf and see if the flavor agrees with you.

Lettuces are most commonly used in salads, but they can also be cooked, roasted, and steamed. These less traditional preparations take care of seasonal garden gluts and allow for gorging on lettuces when they are fresh, plentiful, and inexpensive. Commercially grown lettuces are widely available in grocery stores, but when homegrown, these somewhat mundane leafy greens take on extraordinary flavor and textures. Generally speaking, lettuces fall under several categories defined by their type and growing disposition: butterheads, Batavians, looseleafs, icebergs, romaines, and chicories. I like to grow a little from each group in my gardens. When shopping at the farmers market, I prefer buying two or three different heads to ensure variety of texture, color, and flavor in my dishes. Here's a short and casual description of each group, as they are sold at the grocery store and farmers markets:

Butterheads. Bibb and Boston lettuces are both butterhead varieties. This type of lettuce is known for its tender and somewhat sweet flavor. Butterheads grow in delicate, thin leaves, with a loose head that allows the leaves to fall freely from the core.

Batavians. Labeled as "greenleaf" in the grocery store, these lettuces are a flavor marriage of tall, green romaines and crispy, white icebergs. These lettuces have a strong green flavor and a firm leaf and rib.

Looseleafs. Often called spring salad mixes at the grocery store, looseleafs are widely available. Arugula, oakleaf, mâche, and miner's lettuce are all considered looseleafs; they're often cut at the stem and eaten as one whole leaf—hence the name (they are also called cutting lettuces). Use looseleafs in salads or as a slightly wilted green, as in Wilted Lettuce & Herb-y Pasta.

Icebergs. These thick, uniform mounds of closely fitted lettuce leaves, often white and full of water, are low in nutritional value. They are better when homegrown so the darker outer leaves can be eaten—these provide more fiber. Garden-grown icebergs often have dark green leaf layers encasing an inner core of white. Icebergs are sometimes smaller than other varieties and make lovely, compact salads when served in wedges (see Lettuce Wedge with Herbed Yogurt).

Romaines. These tall, upright lettuces have thick ribs and crinkled leaves. Romaines take the longest to come to maturity—from sixty to seventy days. Spring romaines are grown in California (which has a warm spring season and is home to huge commercial farms) or seeded early under a cloche. Because of their thick ribs, romaines are a perfect choice for adding texture to recipes like Lettuce Bowl with Pickled Beets & Honey-Lime Chicken.

Chicories. This popular group of lettuces includes broad-leaved escaroles, curly-leaved frisée, radicchio, endive, and (commercial) dandelion greens. Radicchio usually grows in a tight ball of leaves, red- and white-ribbed and bitter tasting, whereas Treviso (a radicchio variety) has conical heads ranging from white to green to red-tipped and speckled. Endives (escarole and frisée are both endives) are equally bitter-tasting but have a thicker, larger leaf structure. Dandelion greens are sold in bunches and often have red-veined leaves. Spring chicories are regrowth from winter that sweeten up after frosts. Chicories seeded and grown in spring tend to be more bitter and benefit from roasting or sautéing.

I've included recipes for all types of lettuces in this book: large, strong leaves, bitter-tasting greens, and delicate cups. Whether chopped for traditional salads, steamed for a hot meal, or lightly dressed for breakfast, lettuces can be used in many inventive ways beyond the usual bowl of tossed greens. Break out of your comfort zone and try a few new dishes! Lettuce begin . . .

MAY RECIPES

Lettuce

Lettuce Wedge with Herbed Yogurt
Stir-Fried Escarole
Lettuce Bowl with Pickled Beets & Honey–Lime Chicken
Wilted Lettuce & Herb-y Pasta
Mustard-Braised Pork Chops & Lettuce

Seasonal Extras

Spring Carrots with Hummus & Salted Dates
Snap Peas & Baby Potatoes with Chive Blossoms

Lettuce Wedge with Herbed Yogurt

MAKES 4 SERVINGS

Having grown up on Long Island, I can tell you: there was no shortage of seafood restaurants and clam shacks. These hot spots often served nothing more than steamed shellfish and fries along with chilled lettuce drenched in a thick blue cheese dressing. Every once in a blue moon, I crave that crispy crunch of white iceberg drizzled with luscious homemade dressing, although I like mine with a touch of heat.

> 1 cup plain nonfat yogurt
> 1/4 cup crumbled blue cheese
> 2 to 4 tablespoons milk
> 1/4 cup finely chopped fresh mint
> 1/4 cup finely chopped fresh dill
> 1/4 teaspoon red chile flakes
> 1/8 teaspoon salt
> 1 medium head iceberg or Bibb lettuce, quartered and held in the fridge until ready to use

To make the dressing, use the back of a spoon to mash the yogurt and blue cheese together in a medium-sized bowl, making an almost-smooth paste. Use a few spoonfuls of milk to thin the yogurt–blue cheese mixture to a pourable consistency. Add the mint, dill, red chile flakes, and salt, and stir well to combine.

To serve, place a quartered lettuce wedge on each salad plate and top with equal portions of the herbed yogurt.

PANTRY NOTE: Leftover dressing will hold in the fridge, covered, for up to two days. Refresh the texture and flavor by adding a small amount of chopped fresh herbs.

Stir-Fried Escarole

MAKES 4 SERVINGS AS A SIDE

Because most lettuce leaves are thin and composed mostly of water, they cook up quickly (this recipe takes less than ten minutes from start to finish) and take on flavor with ease. Sautéing greens is a common preparation, but sautéing *lettuce* results in a more subtle flavor and texture, making this a light side dish. Escarole works well as its strong flavor sweetens with heat, but any thick-ribbed lettuce will work. Try romaine or even older Buttercrunch from the garden.

> 2 tablespoons olive oil
> 3 cloves garlic, smashed
> 1/2 teaspoon salt
> 1 head escarole, cored, leaves washed and chopped into 1-inch pieces
> 2 tablespoons rice wine, Chinese cooking wine, or vermouth

In a large sauté pan, set the olive oil over medium-high heat. Add the garlic and salt and stir frequently, making sure the garlic doesn't stick and burn, about 3 to 4 minutes. When the garlic begins to brown, add the escarole to the pan and stir to wilt. (You may have to add it in increments—as the first batch wilts, quickly add another until all the escarole is in the pan.)

HOW TO GROW LETTUCES IN POTS

Lettuces are a very smart crop to grow at home. Many lettuces grow to full heads in forty to sixty days, so I opt for a smattering of maturing times, which ensures that as one is finishing, another is just coming in. As lettuces have a shallow root system, they can be grown in the smallest of pots and don't take up much space (perfect for balconies, patios, and porches). Lettuce can be harvested over the course of several weeks by trimming off only the outer leaves of the plant. They quickly fill back in.

Growing lettuce at home is made all the more appealing by the vast selection available from seed, in a range of shapes, sizes, colors, flavors, and textures. Some are sweet, some are frilly, some are bitter, and some are speckled. Order a variety you've never heard of and give it a go. Variety is important with any edible plant, as it keeps your palate interested and engaged. You can mix soft, crispy, sweet, and bitter in one juicy forkful. Try this diverse assortment in your garden: Forellenschluss (heirloom speckled romaine), Lollo Rosso (frizzy red looseleaf), and Buttercrunch (green Bibb).

Whether you opt for butterheads, romaines, crispheads, or looseleafs, lettuce is one of the quickest and easiest plants to grow. Direct-sow lettuce from seed. If you'd like a summer lettuce, choose a heat-tolerant variety. Little Gem (a romaine variety), Rouge d'Hiver (a cross between romaine and butterhead), and oakleaf lettuce (a looseleaf variety) are all great choices. If you know you'll be planting in fall, a cool-season lettuce is in order—arugula and miner's lettuce are cool-season greens. To ensure flexibility, purchase a range of seeds for different lettuce types at the beginning of the year and sow according to the season.

When & Where to Plant. Lettuces can be sown in early spring and throughout summer and fall. Frequent sowings guarantee a constant supply. Lettuce needs sun but can do with as little as six hours of direct sunlight a day. Sow six inches apart to allow room for heads to develop. You'll need to thin any lettuces that grow too close, so that the remaining plant or plants can come to maturity. Thinning is a natural process, and you actually do more damage by leaving plants to grow too close together than you do by removing one early on. Sow arugula seeds in the top layer of potting soil in March or April. Sow again in late summer and early fall—late August and anytime through October. Plant miner's lettuce in early spring. You can seed directly into pots from February through early April and again in fall.

→

> **Pot Size.** After years of experimenting, I have found the perfect lettuce pot to be long, shallow, and narrow (the pot need only be four inches wide). Both terra-cotta and plastic pots come in this size, and they fit well butted up against the edges of a deck or tied to a railing or windowsill. Make sure the soil depth is six to eight inches. Get the length of pot that works best in your space. For me, the longer, the better (to fit in more lettuces).
>
> **How to Harvest.** As the lettuce heads grow, snap off the large outer leaves at the stem. The lettuce will fill in and continue producing new leaves. Loose lettuces may be cut at the base of the stem when they reach three to four inches tall (for baby lettuce mix). Ultimately, you can decide for yourself when the leaf is big enough to cut and harvest. If you leave your lettuces unharvested for too long, they'll turn bitter in the heat. If this happens, harvest the entire head and hold it in a damp paper towel in your fridge's crisper for two days. The leaves should sweeten up.

Pour in the rice wine and turn the heat to high. Cover the sauté pan and steam until the lettuce is cooked through, about 3 minutes. Remove the cover and cook, stirring frequently, until most of the liquid is evaporated. Remove from the heat and place the stir-fried lettuce in a serving bowl. Serve immediately.

PANTRY NOTE: Any leftover lettuces or escarole can be held in the fridge for a day. Warm leftovers up to room temperature before eating, which brings out the flavors, or toss into a pan quickly to reheat.

Lettuce Bowl with Pickled Beets & Honey–Lime Chicken

MAKES 4 SERVINGS

This busy yet healthful dish bursts with flavor. A lean bowl of rice noodles incorporates a hearty portion of lettuce alongside a heaping amount of tender herbs. You can omit the rice noodles entirely and make this a Vietnamese-inspired salad. The addition of pickled beets and carrots spices things up, while quick-charred chicken adds some protein. Burned shallots contribute a depth of flavor. Don't be intimidated by the length of this recipe—despite the extensive instructions, the dish is easy to make.

PICKLED BEETS AND CARROTS

1 cup apple cider vinegar

½ cup sugar

1 medium red beet, peeled and cut into matchsticks

1 carrot, peeled and cut into matchsticks

1 bay leaf

½ cinnamon stick

10 cloves

1 tablespoon red chile flakes

BURNED SHALLOTS

2 tablespoons olive oil

2 shallots, peeled and thinly sliced

¼ teaspoon salt

HONEY-LIME CHICKEN

1 tablespoon honey

1 tablespoon fresh-squeezed lime juice

4 boneless chicken thighs, skins
    removed

LETTUCE BOWL

8 ounces rice noodles

4 cups chopped romaine (about half a
    head)

1 cup fresh mint leaves

1 cup fresh cilantro leaves

VINAIGRETTE

½ cup fresh-squeezed lime juice

4 tablespoons fish sauce

6 tablespoons brown sugar

1 teaspoon red chile flakes

To make the pickled beets and carrots, heat the vinegar and sugar in a small saucepan over high heat and bring to a boil. Put the beets, carrots, and all of the aromatics (bay leaf, cinnamon, cloves, and red chile flakes) in a medium-sized glass bowl and set aside. Once the vinegar is just boiling and all of the sugar is dissolved, pour the mixture over the beets and carrots and set aside until ready to use, allowing them to quick-pickle.

To make the burned shallots, heat the olive oil in a small sauté pan over medium-high heat (the oil should cover the bottom of the pan; add more if needed). Once the oil is heated, add the shallots

and salt, stirring to coat evenly. Cook and stir the shallots until they begin to soften, about 3 to 4 minutes or until they are slightly brown. You want them to develop a rich brown color and get crispy, so let them sit on the heat without disturbing for another 4 to 6 minutes. Once the shallots are deeply browned and crispy, remove them from the sauté pan, place on a small plate, and set aside to cool.

To prepare for the noodles, set a large saucepan full of water over high heat and bring to a boil. While waiting for the water to boil, turn on the broiler to high.

To make the honey-lime chicken, combine the honey and lime juice in a small bowl and stir until incorporated. Pound out the chicken thighs slightly until uniform in thickness, about ¼-inch thick. Place the chicken on a lightly greased baking sheet and brush on a thin coating of the honey-lime juice. Cook under the broiler until just beginning to brown, about 2 minutes. Remove the baking sheet from the oven, turn the chicken thighs over, and baste the other side with a coating of honey-lime juice. Place the baking sheet back under the broiler and cook until just beginning to brown, about 2 minutes. Continue basting and flipping until all the honey-lime juice is used and the chicken is charred and crispy. Remove from the oven and set aside to cool. From start to finish, this process takes only 8 to 10 minutes, so work quickly. When the chicken thighs are cool enough to handle, cut each into thin ribbons, about ¼-inch thick.

Once the water is boiling, remove the saucepan from the heat, drop in the rice noodles, and cook according to instructions on the package—about 5 minutes for most thin rice noodles—until just soft. Drain and rinse the noodles under cool water, which helps prevent them from sticking.

To make the vinaigrette, combine the lime juice, fish sauce, brown sugar, and red chile flakes in a small bowl and stir until the brown sugar is dissolved. Pour four equal portions into small bowls or jars.

To compose the lettuce bowls, put equal portions of the rice noodles into 4 bowls. Add 1 cup of the chopped romaine lettuce and ¼ cup each of the fresh mint and cilantro to each bowl. Place a forkful of pickled beets and carrots and a pinch of burned shallots on top. Finally, place one fourth of the sliced chicken meat in each bowl. Serve with the vinaigrette on the side.

PANTRY NOTE: Most of these components can be made ahead of time and held until ready to serve. If you make the rice noodles ahead, toss with a small spoonful of sesame oil or vegetable oil to prevent sticking. All components of this salad hold well in the fridge for about five days, stored individually in airtight containers.

Wilted Lettuce & Herb-y Pasta

MAKES 4 SERVINGS

This is one of my all-time favorite dishes, and I've been making it for years. It is a quintessentially springtime dish—light and fragrant—due in large part to the fresh ingredients. Local lettuces, asparagus, and morels come in right about the same time in May. Here, pasta cooks in one pot, while the morels and asparagus brown in a sauté pan. The lettuce leaves are added in the last moment, along with the pasta and some pasta water.

3 tablespoons olive oil
1 tablespoon butter
5 cloves garlic, thinly sliced
1 shallot, peeled and thinly sliced
12 morel mushrooms, washed and thinly
   sliced
4 slices prosciutto, torn into pieces
8 spears asparagus, woody ends
   trimmed, cut into 2- to 3-inch pieces
1 tablespoon dry vermouth
4 cups penne or other short, shaped
   pasta
4 cups mixed lettuce greens
½ cup mixed fresh herbs (such as parsley, mint, basil, lovage)
Parmesan, for shaving (optional)

Set a pot of salted water to boil for the pasta.

In a large sauté pan with high sides, heat the olive oil and butter over medium-high heat. When the butter is melted and starting to bubble, add the garlic, shallot, and morels. Cook and stir until the shallots are starting to brown at the edges, about 8 minutes. Add the prosciutto and let sit, stirring only occasionally, allowing it to get brown and crispy, about 4 minutes.

When the mixture starts to stick to the bottom of the sauté pan, add the asparagus and deglaze the pan with the vermouth, scraping up any brown bits. Cook the vermouth down for 1 minute, then remove the sauté pan from the heat.

Drop the pasta into the boiling water and cook until just al dente, 8 to 10 minutes for penne pasta. A minute before the pasta is ready, put the sauté pan back over high heat. It will start to sizzle almost immediately. Pour a cup of the pasta water into the sauté pan and stir continuously.

When the pasta is al dente, drain and add it to the sauté pan. Cook until the pasta water starts to evaporate and bubble at the bottom of the pan, about 3 minutes. Add the lettuce greens and fresh herbs, one handful at a time, and toss the mixture to wilt. Remove from the heat and spoon four equal portions into shallow bowls; shave Parmesan over the top, if desired, and serve immediately.

PANTRY NOTE: Use whatever lettuces and fresh herbs you have on hand—Bibb lettuce, romaine, radicchio, arugula, marjoram, dill, cilantro, and so on. This is a great way to use up any lettuce that may be starting to turn bitter or has begun to wilt with age. Leftover pasta does not hold well, so plan to eat it all when you make it.

Mustard–Braised Pork Chops & Lettuce

MAKES 4 SERVINGS

Braised lettuce is surprisingly rich and works especially well in this slightly creamy, mustard-infused sauce. Here, thick, bone-in pork chops are seasoned and seared. A generous portion of chopped lettuce is added to the pan, in addition to a spoonful of mustard and a splash of heavy cream. All of this cooks down quickly into an intense and flavorful sauce that feels luxurious but is actually light and healthy. All sorts of lettuces work in this dish—romaine, Bibb, looseleafs, arugula, dandelion greens, and so on. Mix and match or try them all, depending on what you have around.

    4 thick bone-in pork chops
    ¼ teaspoon salt
    ¼ teaspoon pepper
    1 tablespoon butter
    2 tablespoons olive oil
    1 cup chopped yellow onion
    ½ teaspoon Dijon mustard
    ½ cup chicken stock
    4 cups lettuce, cut into 1-inch ribbons
    ¼ cup chopped fresh parsley
    1 tablespoon heavy cream or
        half-and-half

Season both sides of the pork chops with the salt and pepper and set aside. In a large sauté pan, heat the butter and olive oil over medium-high heat. Once the oil is heated and the butter melted, add the onion and cook and stir until soft, about 3 minutes. Push the onions to the edges of the pan and add the pork chops, cooking about 4 minutes. Don't move the pork chops around—you want them to caramelize and brown—but stir the onions occasionally to prevent burning.

Turn the pork chops and cook on the other side, 4 minutes more, stirring only the onions as needed. Stir the Dijon mustard into the onions (the mustard may be a bit chunky at first). Pour in the chicken stock and add the lettuce and parsley to the sauté pan, sprinkling them over the pork chops. Cover and cook for 4 minutes, until the lettuce is mostly wilted but still vibrant green. Take off the cover and remove the pan from the heat. Stir in the heavy cream until well combined.

To serve, place one pork chop on each plate with equal portions of greens and sauce. Serve immediately.

PANTRY NOTE: Any leftovers hold very well in the fridge, covered, and should be eaten within two days. Try slicing the pork thin and making a pressed griddle sandwich—the braised greens are a perfect garnish.

Spring Carrots with Hummus & Salted Dates

MAKES 4 SERVINGS

I made this salad course for my friend Nga's fortieth birthday several years back, and it was a hit with everyone. Not quite a salad, but not quite a main dish, this plated morsel falls somewhere in between. A dollop of mashed chickpeas is served alongside harissa-coated carrots (spicy, but sweet) and warm dates cooked in butter and salt. It's one of those dishes that's universally appealing because it hits every flavor note we crave. Try it—you and your friends will love it.

2 bunches spring carrots (about 12),
    4 to 6 inches long, peeled
2 to 4 tablespoons olive oil
2 tablespoons harissa
1½ cups cooked chickpeas
1 teaspoon salt
1 teaspoon ground cumin
1 teaspoon ground coriander
¼ teaspoon smoked paprika
1½ tablespoons butter
8 dates, pitted
1 teaspoon coarse salt

Preheat the oven to 425 degrees F.

Spread the carrots on a large, rimmed sheet pan. Drizzle 1 tablespoon of the olive oil over the carrots and, using your hands, toss to combine. Spread the carrots out evenly and roast in the oven for 10 minutes. Remove from the oven and add harissa to the pan. Toss to coat the carrots well and return them to the oven. Cook until the carrots are charred and al dente and you are just able to pierce them, about 5 to 7 minutes more. Check occasionally to be sure the harissa isn't burning. Remove from the oven and set aside to cool.

In a small bowl, combine the chickpeas, salt, cumin, coriander, smoked paprika, and 2 tablespoons of the olive oil. Using the tines of a fork, mash the chickpeas to evenly distribute the spices, until the chickpeas are almost totally smooth and thick. You want the chickpea mash to be the consistency of thick peanut butter, so add a little oil at a time if need be, to achieve that. When it's the proper consistency, taste for seasoning, adjust if necessary, and set aside.

In a small sauté pan, melt the butter over medium heat. Add the dates and cook until just warmed through and hot, about 4 minutes. Remove from the heat and set aside.

To serve, spread equal portions of mashed chickpeas on four plates, using the back of a spoon. Fan out a few carrots on top. Tuck the dates around the edges of the carrots and sprinkle everything with coarse sea salt. Serve immediately.

PANTRY NOTE: All of these components can be broken down and used as individual recipes. Mashed chickpeas can be puréed with water into a smooth hummus. Roasted carrots can be used as a side dish for most meals. Any leftovers can be held in the fridge for up to three days.

Snap Peas & Baby Potatoes with Chive Blossoms

MAKES 4 SERVINGS

Teeny-tiny spring potatoes can be ready as early as May and make a lovely addition to this salad. Here, cooked potatoes are tossed with chopped snap peas and spring chive blossoms, which are plump and blooming in May. This fresh-tasting, crisp salad is excellent served with a sweet grilled sausage for dinner, or a hard-boiled egg and some olives for a healthy lunch. You may alter the flavor by varying the herbs or the vinegar you use.

1 pound spring potatoes, cleaned
2 tablespoons salt
2 tablespoons minced shallot
1 tablespoon red wine vinegar
½ pound snap peas, ends trimmed
1 tablespoon Dijon mustard
3 tablespoons olive oil
¼ teaspoon pepper
3 tablespoons chive blossom petals
Salt and pepper
Mixed herb leaves, for garnish
  (optional)

Set a large pot of water over high heat, add the potatoes and salt, and cover. Bring the potatoes to boil over high heat. Reduce heat slightly and cook until potatoes are just tender, about 20 to 25 minutes.

While the potatoes are cooking, put the shallots and vinegar in a large salad bowl and let them sit for 5 minutes to macerate. After 5 minutes, add the snap peas, Dijon mustard, oil, and pepper to the bowl, and stir well with a fork to emulsify the oil with the vinegar and mustard and coat the peas.

Once the potatoes are tender, drain and add the still-warm potatoes to the salad bowl. Using a large spoon, fold gently to combine. Taste for seasoning and add in the chive blossoms and any other herbs you choose to include. Serve immediately.

PANTRY NOTE: This salad keeps well enough overnight in the fridge, but you will need to revive it with fresh herbs and a handful of pea pods.

SUMMER

SENDING THANKS FOR ALL THINGS sunny and lush—summer is here! The summer solstice falls on June 21st and the season runs through August, and, in many places, well into September. The months leading into summer feel like a slow incline up a long, sloping mountain trail. You know it's worth the effort, and you know you'll be handsomely rewarded at the end, but good lord, could it take any longer?

Happily, now is the time to wait no more, but rather kick back and rejoice in all that summer has to offer. Farmers are in their second crop rotation of the year, and fields are often overflowing with fruits and vegetables. Many spring crops are re-sown and available all summer long, and summer crops start coming into the markets in June and July. You don't really need a strategy for summer shopping, eating, and cooking, as the selection of fruits and vegetables is abundant—so abundant, in fact, that it's easy to overshop and get overwhelmed. If you find yourself in this position (as I often do), don't worry. You can blanch, freeze, or quick-pickle many vegetables, and juice, freeze, or can any turning fruits—all to make summer last.

There are several fruits and vegetables that are summer-only, and therefore need to be used in bulk now. Zucchinis and cucumbers don't stay around too long—by August, their production dwindles and they won't make it through those cool September nights. Green beans, too, come in during July and last just a few weeks before growing too big and starchy—they're best harvested and eaten as tender young pods. With fruits, cherry and peach seasons are often short-lived, here and gone within a handful of weeks. Grapes, too, are gone in a blink during the transition between summer and fall.

Where you do need to strategize is in making sure to eat all that the season has to offer. In summer, fruits and vegetable selections abound, so it's hard to keep up and easy to let entire selections pass you by. This last summer I didn't eat one single cherry! Total bummer. Summer allows for an incredibly varied diet—one where cooking is often optional. Because so many fruits and vegetables are fresh and seasonal, I switch my buying habits and pick up only what I can eat in one meal. Purchasing in smaller quantities ensures you can work through your pantry quickly and also forces a multifarious diet, helping to break cooks out of recipe repetition. There is no need to eat the same caprese salad or strawberry shortcake all summer. Instead try herbed yogurt with tomatoes or a savory dipping sauce (see Lemon Beef with Raspberry Dipping Sauce in June: Berries). It's the time of year to take advantage of all of your options.

While this book focuses on cooking from a fresh pantry, I'd be regretful if I didn't remind you that summer is also an excellent season for preserving. As good practice, a few times a month while at the farmers market, purchase four to five pounds extra of something to blanch, freeze, or can. For example, I make a habit of buying extra ears of corn when they are sweet, and then I trim off the kernels and blanch them, freezing them for later winter cooking. Corncobs can be boiled into stock and the strained broth frozen for future soup recipes. Buying in small quantities keeps kitchen projects manageable and fills the pantry slowly. By early autumn, the cupboard shelves should be buckling from the weight of winter supplies.

For home gardeners, summer is a time for attentiveness. Monitoring water levels on plants will spare your garden from disease and stressed plants, assuring they are as prolific as possible.

And while summer's longer days tend to fill up and be busy, I urge you to slow down this summer and relish every prolonged ray of sun. Get in your kitchen and cook, invite friends over for a slow meal. On quiet nights, take advantage of pink evening skies and ambient light to put up a few jars of something delicious for winter—crushed tomatoes are a must. You will never regret making the extra effort when you had the extra energy.

Crushed Tomatoes

JUNE

BERRIES

EVERYONE LOVES BERRIES! HOW DO I know this? I took a poll of eight people with moderate to expert cooking ability, asking what they would prefer—a chapter on snap peas or a chapter on berries? Only one person chose peas (sorry, Katie O!). Juicy, sweet, and encapsulating all that is good about summer, berries are undeniably sexy. And they are ridiculously accessible—who hasn't grabbed a handful of blackberries from prickly vines, tearing up their forearms in the process, while out on a summer stroll?

Berries come from reasonably easy-to-grow perennial plants that require little maintenance. They tend to produce over the course of many weeks, and, if cared for properly, these plants can turn out pounds of fruit in a small growing space like a patio (see the sidebar How to Grow Strawberries, Raspberries & Blueberries for details). Berries come into season right about mid-May to June, depending on your location and climate. California-grown strawberries are available in grocery stores starting in early May, but it's best to purchase locally grown berries, which are sweetest immediately after harvesting and rarely require additional sweeteners. The acidity of an individual berry varies according to age and sun exposure. Sun converts starches in plants to sugar, so the longer a berry sits in the sun, the sweeter it gets. Berry season lasts through early fall, as plants have a range of maturing times. I suggest buying berries all summer long and exhausting your palate while the getting is good.

This chapter highlights three of the most popular and early-ripening berries—raspberries, blueberries, and strawberries. The recipes offer fresh ideas and new methods for introducing berries into your daily meals. Rather than focusing on desserts, as we all have our favorite berry dessert recipes, these recipes emphasize the savory properties of each fruit. (Still, I couldn't resist including one for strawberry mousse here.) You can use fresh and frozen berries interchangeably in any of the cooked dishes, unless otherwise specifically noted.

Strawberries have similar characteristics to tomatoes—they are sweet but slightly acidic and thus perfect in salads or crushed, as in Arugula with Strawberry-Caraway Vinaigrette & Toasted

Goat Cheese. They are also heavy and meaty for a fruit, which makes for a perfect texture in a thick purée.

Raspberries have a sweet tendency as well, but they are more acidic than strawberries and lend a subtle floral note to dishes. If the seeds are strained, raspberry purée makes an excellent sauce—as a coulis for a dessert or as a savory dip (see Lemon Beef with Raspberry Dipping Sauce).

Blueberries are sweet and juicy, their acidity coming mostly from their thick, tannin-rich skin. They are terrific roasted, which allows their flavor to be concentrated in small doses (you'll love Blueberry-Oregano Turkey Meatballs).

When purchasing or harvesting berries, choose firmer and younger berries for cooking or preserving. Save the perfectly sweet and juicy ones for eating fresh. Fresh berries start to mold very quickly, so you have to work fast to store, cook, preserve, or eat them. To store fresh berries, remove them from their containers and pick out rotten berries or debris from the field. Raspberries and blueberries do not require washing (unless you purchase from an area known for pesticide use), but because strawberries grow low to the ground, you may need to soak off some soil, mud, or dust. (Be sure to do this especially if you're harvesting from an area that has recently flooded, as floodwaters can leave behind harmful bacteria.)

To clean strawberries, half-fill a large bowl with water and gently roll the berries into it. Do not dump them into the bowl—they bruise easily! Swish gently in the water and rub lightly to remove any soil stuck between the seeds. You may need to change the water a few times. Strain the berries and set out to air-dry on a cooling rack. Once they are clean and dry, stack the strawberries in layers (no more than three or four deep) in a shallow baking dish and store in the fridge. They keep longer if a linen kitchen towel, paper towel, or length of parchment is placed between the stacks of berries (direct contact instigates decay).

For preserving berries, one excellent method is freezing. Practice what is known as IQF—individually quick frozen. Lay clean, dry berries in a single layer, spaced so they don't touch one another, on a rimmed baking sheet, and put the entire thing in the freezer. They freeze quickly (in about an hour) and are easy to handle. Store frozen berries in a resealable plastic bag, pressing out all of the air before sealing it. Secure the berry bag in an additional plastic bag to minimize freezer burn. Freezing and storing berries in this way allows for easy use later—you can grab them by the handful instead of dealing with a juicy clump.

There is one bummer about berries—they are expensive! I often find them at anywhere from three to five dollars a pint. A pint! That's about two or three cups of fresh berries, never mind if you cook them down. Because of the expense, I suggest going berry-picking. At many U-pick farms, the more you buy, the less expensive the berries are. Get out into the berry fields with friends! Plan ahead and pick up twenty pounds of berries to stock both your pantry and your fridge. At the very least, buy berries in flats from the farmers market, which is less expensive than buying individual pints. Whatever you do, eat these berries by the handful. It's summer, baby!

JUNE RECIPES

Berries

Buckwheat Crêpes with Blueberry Syrup
Arugula with Strawberry–Caraway Vinaigrette & Toasted Goat Cheese
Raspberry-Mole Baked Chicken
Lemon Beef with Raspberry Dipping Sauce
Blueberry–Oregano Turkey Meatballs
Strawberry Mousse
Blueberry–Cardamom Drop Donuts
Raspberry Vinegar
Orange-Flower & Raspberry Jelly
Whole Strawberry & Vanilla Jam

Seasonal Extras

Mom's Stuffed Artichokes
Charred Broccoli Rabe with Herbed Quinoa

Buckwheat Crêpes with Blueberry Syrup

MAKES 4 SERVINGS

Hearty and earthy buckwheat flour makes super thin and healthy crêpes. Buckwheat is a flower seed, so this flour is gluten-free. In this recipe, the crêpes are paired with summer fruits, but they easily pull double duty and can be used with a savory filling—try them stuffed and rolled with the Zucchini Breakfast Sammie filling. A spoonful of honey sweetens the blueberries and creates a thick breakfast syrup, accented with a bit of lime zest.

  ½ cup buckwheat flour
  1 cup milk
  2 large eggs
  1 tablespoon melted butter, plus more
     for the skillet
  2 tablespoons honey, divided
  ¼ teaspoon ground cinnamon
  2 cups fresh blueberries
  1 tablespoon vanilla extract
  1 teaspoon lime zest
  Almond butter (optional)

In a medium-sized bowl, whisk together the buckwheat flour, milk, eggs, melted butter, 1 tablespoon of the honey, and the cinnamon until all lumps are gone and the batter is smooth. Set aside for at least 20 to 30 minutes.

While the crêpe batter is resting, make the syrup. In a small saucepan, set the blueberries, the remaining tablespoon of honey, and the vanilla extract over medium heat until the blueberries start to release their juice. Continue stirring until the berries are thick and syrup-like, about 4 minutes. Remove the saucepan from the heat and stir in the lime zest. Set aside to cool slightly.

When the crêpe batter is ready, set a medium-sized skillet (about 6 to 8 inches in diameter) over medium-high heat until hot. A drop of water splashed in the skillet should sizzle and evaporate immediately. Add a bit of butter (about ¼ teaspoon) to the skillet and wipe out the excess with a paper towel, working to coat all sides.

Ladle a small amount of crêpe batter (about ⅛ to ¼ cup) into the skillet. Lift the skillet slightly, swirling to evenly coat it with a very thin layer of batter. If the batter does not coat the skillet evenly, add another spoonful or two of milk to the bowl of batter and stir well. When the crêpe is lightly browned, use an offset spatula or small kitchen spatula to pick up the edges and flip over the crêpe (use your hands to lift and turn it). Cook the second side until lightly browned, about another minute more. Continue working in this fashion, stacking cooked crêpes on a plate, until all the batter has been used.

To serve, fold 2 or 3 buckwheat crêpes in quarters and lay them on a plate, spooning a portion of the blueberry-lime syrup on top. You can also serve the crêpes family-style with a side of almond butter, for people to build their own crêpes at the table.

PANTRY NOTE: Buckwheat crêpes are easy to make and they freeze well, so double the batch if you like. Layer cooked crêpes in a single stack, placing a piece of parchment between each one, and wrap tightly in plastic wrap before freezing.

Arugula with Strawberry–Caraway Vinaigrette & Toasted Goat Cheese

MAKES 4 SERVINGS

Strawberry and arugula are the perfect pair—one is sweet, the other spicy. Instead of simply being tossed with the arugula, here strawberries are mashed to make a thick dressing for these robust greens. Crushed caraway seeds lend an herbaceous note, and a baked disc of goat cheese gives a bit of fattiness. Arugula works well, but you can use any salad green—the real star in this appetizer is the spiced strawberry vinaigrette.

- ¼ cup bread crumbs
- 4 ounces chèvre, cut into 4 discs
- 1 tablespoon olive oil, plus ¼ cup for the vinaigrette
- 1 tablespoon caraway seeds
- ½ cup chopped fresh strawberries
- 2 tablespoons apple cider vinegar
- 4 cups arugula
- Salt and pepper

Preheat the oven to 375 degrees F.

Put the bread crumbs on a small plate. Working with one disc of chèvre at a time, press it firmly into the bread crumbs without breaking the

shape. Turn over and press the other side into the bread crumbs. Put the bread crumb-coated disc onto a small, parchment-lined baking pan. Continue working this way until all four discs are well coated. Drizzle 1 tablespoon of olive oil over the tops of the discs and put the baking pan in the oven. Bake until golden brown, about 20 to 25 minutes.

Using a mortar and pestle, crush the caraway seeds until they are broken down into coarse pieces. (If you don't have a mortar and pestle, use a spice grinder or chop finely with a sharp knife.) In a small bowl, muddle the strawberries until well broken down and juicy. It's okay if fleshy bits remain, but you don't want any large chunks. Add the crushed caraway seeds and the vinegar and stir well to combine.

Pour the mixture into a glass jar, add the remaining ¼ cup olive oil, and screw on the top. To emulsify, shake the jar vigorously for 1 to 2 minutes. When the vinaigrette is thick and creamy looking, set it aside until ready to use.

To make the salad, put the arugula leaves in a large bowl and pour the strawberry-caraway vinaigrette over all. Toss to combine well—make sure all of the leaves are coated. Season to taste with salt and pepper. Portion the salad out onto 4 small plates and place one warm goat cheese disc on top of each. Serve immediately.

PANTRY NOTE: Leftover salad does not store well, but you can double the batch of vinaigrette. It will hold in the fridge in a small jar for one to two days (it may discolor slightly).

HOW TO GROW STRAWBERRIES, RASPBERRIES & BLUEBERRIES

Perennial strawberry, raspberry, and blueberry plants produce fruit year after year. They are fabulous investments and great plants to have around, particularly if you have kids. From toddlers to grandparents, who doesn't love fresh-picked berries? There's no greater taste than a sun-kissed berry eaten out of the palm of your hand.

Each fruit has a different growing pattern and demands different planting strategies in the landscape. Blueberries are planted and left alone for years. Raspberries need a dedicated bed with easy access, as they require annual maintenance to secure fruit production from their tall canes. Strawberries need consistent cultivation as the season progresses, so they are best left in rows or in a tiered and elevated structure, like the strawberry towers you may have seen at a nursery. All berries prefer a slightly acidic soil. Have your soil tested and adjust by adding lime and/or phosphorus prior to planting, matching the cultivar you choose.

Following is a brief introduction to the natural dispositions of the berry plants, along with some notes on how to grow and care for each type. The berries have a variety of maturation times—some bear fruit early and only once, others bear a little bit of fruit all summer. Choose a good cultivar for your region, climate, and needs. For instance, I prefer a fall-bearing raspberry, as I'm too busy in summer to appreciate the bounty coming in during those months. Picking raspberries in late fall is a bonus at the end of a busy summer in the garden. Check your local nursery or, better yet, your university (or county) extension programs—they are an excellent source of nonbiased information.

Strawberries. Strawberries are a perennial plant, which makes them a great investment. Each plant will send out runners, a means for propagation. Strawberries are formed from a flower on the plant and take about a month from flower opening to a ripe strawberry for harvest. Fruit is produced off of the main stalk (or terminal) of the plant, as that is the first flower to form. From there, subsequent stems and flowers will produce throughout the season. The first flower and strawberry fruit will be the largest, and as the season progresses, the fruits grow smaller.

Strawberry plants produce good-sized berries for about three to four years before you'll need to replace the plant. You can do this by removing old plants and replanting the runners in tidy rows or within your planting structure. One strawberry plant in a pot is a lonely one that won't produce much fruit. If pots are your only option, use a strawberry pot, which has several openings for plants and allows for runners to grow in soil. First-year plants should be planted in early April; they prefer a loose and loamy soil that doesn't hold too much water. Most berry plants are shallow rooted, but none prefer "wet feet," so make sure your planting medium drains well. Space plants about eighteen inches apart, allowing for runners to produce and root down. After fruit production, keep rows tidy by thinning your beds and leaving one plant about every five inches. You must leave space for strawberries to produce, so don't allow the plants to grow thick with a glossy canopy. Remember to remove the mother plant after three or four years.

Raspberries. Raspberries (aka brambles) grow from the flowers of tall, sturdy canes and produce fruit in early to late summer. Fruits grow only on second-year canes, so a root cluster planted in summer will produce fruit the following year. This means that both new and second-year canes will be growing in the same patch simultaneously. No matter, they are easily identifiable by the color of their canes—new growth is succulent, green, and shorter than second-year canes, which are tall and develop flower buds in spring. Spent cane—those that have fruited already and will no longer produce—turn brown and dry from age and must be pruned out of the raspberry patch in late fall or through winter.

Plant raspberry rootstock in early spring. These can be taken from a neighboring garden, as raspberries are prolific and often produce more cane than a small patch can handle. Dig rootstock or new growth into well-amended soil; adding a bag or two of manure prior to planting, and every spring thereafter, is an excellent practice. In a perfect world, you'll have one long row of raspberries, about four feet wide at minimum. One side of the row should house second-year canes and the other, a place for new growth. Keep canes in tidy rows through physical training, replanting, and manipulation. This way, you have organized sections of the bramble patch and good air circulation. Build a trellis by digging in a sturdy post at both ends of the row—stanchions, rebar, or any weight-bearing material is best. The posts should be about 6 feet long, which allows for a foot of depth to secure them. Run thin wire or heavy twine between the posts at several different heights, starting about three feet off the ground and spaced every foot above that. Tie and train the raspberry canes directly to the wire, twisting them over the top as they grow.

At the end of the season (from November through March in most areas), remove all dead canes and thin your beds to about a foot. Anything wider prohibits sun from

→

reaching the canes and minimizes air circulation—both of which can result in disease. In each bed leave one cane every four to six inches and either replant or give away the extra. Any tall first-year canes can be "tipped" in late fall by pruning the tops off so they stand about four feet tall. There is more to learn about successful raspberry maintenance (my tips will just get you started), so be sure to do a little homework in the years to come.

Blueberries. Reasonably low maintenance, blueberry plants are some of my favorites to grow. Once planted in well-prepared beds, they are pretty much left alone to do their thing—grow, flower, and produce fruit. These plants are sensitive to acidity levels of soil, however, so you'll want to have your soil tested before planting. Blueberries can be propagated from softwood (new growth) cuttings, but it's best to start out with a two-year-old plant (or older) purchased from a reputable local nursery. Plant blueberries in well-drained soil, hilling them up a bit if need be, as they do not take well to wet roots or vastly fluctuating degrees of moisture. Remove all of the flowers the first year, allowing plants to establish a strong root system. This may seem wasteful, but it is necessary for the plant's vigor in coming years. You'll also need to prune about half of the wood the first year, allowing the plant to become established.

In order to produce berries, blueberry plants need cross-pollination with another cultivar. Be sure to choose at least two varieties for this when planting. Typically I pick an early-bearing, a midsummer ripening, and a fall-bearing plant, which keeps the garden in a small and steady supply of berries all summer long. Plant blueberry bushes at least four to five feet apart for a successful harvest. Many bush out or grow tall—you'll need to accommodate that growth for years to come. Once established, blueberry plants go dormant over winter, but if evergreen, they'll hang on to their red-tipped leaves. This makes them lovely landscape plants, if you need filler in your yard.

As the plants age, blueberry bushes do well with pruning to rid the plant of older, less productive canes (branches). Blueberry canes are usually most productive between three and six years of age. To stay organized, mark new branches with a small colored tag labeled with the pruning year. As the years roll on, you'll establish your own rhythm and likely won't need the visual indicators to prune correctly. Prune only while the plant is dormant—late winter is a great time.

New blueberry cultivars for container growing have recently become popular. If you choose dwarf varieties (perfect for patios), make sure you select those that are suited to your region and commit to a consistent watering schedule. Follow the rules I've outlined above for nutrients and pruning.

Raspberry–Mole Baked Chicken

MAKES 6 SERVINGS

Mole, a sauce traditionally used in Mexican cuisine, uses charred and roasted peppers as a base. I have taken liberties in this mole recipe and instead rely on raspberries for their acidity and on toasted seeds and spices for their earthy flavor. The raspberries cook down into a thick paste that is then slathered over the chicken. The resulting dish is hearty and flavorful, though I'll be the first to admit it's not the prettiest. Serve this dish alongside Spanish rice or simple roasted vegetables.

- ½ cup toasted whole almonds
- 1 cup hot water
- 2 tablespoons olive oil
- 1 cup chopped onion (about half a medium onion)
- Pinch of salt
- 2 cups fresh raspberries
- ⅓ cup whole sunflower seeds
- 1 tablespoon whole fennel seeds
- 1 tablespoon whole cumin seeds
- 1 tablespoon whole brown mustard seeds
- 1 tablespoon smoked paprika
- 1 teaspoon salt
- ½ teaspoon pepper
- 4 tablespoons butter, melted
- 1 whole chicken, cut into 8 pieces, skinned

Preheat the oven to 375 degrees F.

Put the almonds in the hot water and set them aside to soak.

In a medium-sized sauté pan, set the olive oil over medium heat. Add the onions and pinch of salt, cooking (without stirring) until the onions begin to soften. When the first side of the onions is just brown, toss and stir well, redistributing them to cook for another 2 minutes without stirring. This process darkens the onions quickly and adds a nice depth of flavor.

Add the raspberries to the sauté pan, stirring until they start to break down and release their juice. Cook until the raspberries are falling apart and cooked through, about 4 to 5 minutes more. Remove from the heat and put the mixture in a blender (don't purée just yet).

Set a small sauté pan over medium-high heat. When it's hot, heat the sunflower seeds until toasted and slightly brown, stirring often, about 3 minutes. Add the toasted sunflower seeds to the blender.

Return the small sauté pan to the heat and add the fennel, cumin, and brown mustard seeds, stirring often. Cook until the mustard seeds begin to pop, about 2 minutes. Stirring continuously, cook until the seeds are fragrant and toasted. Remove from the heat and use a mortar and pestle or a spice grinder to smash (or grind) the seeds until just coarse, then put the toasted-seed mixture in the blender.

Pour the almonds and their water into the blender and add the smoked paprika, salt, pepper, and the melted butter. Blend on high until the mixture is well combined and becomes a thick paste, about 2 to 3 minutes.

Pour the mole into a large bowl. Toss in the chicken pieces and mix to coat well. Place the chicken on a large rimmed baking sheet, leaving a bit of space in between each piece. Spread any remaining mole over the chicken so the pieces are completely covered. (You may have some mole left over.)

Cover the baking sheet with a loose layer of aluminum foil and put it in the oven. Bake for 40 minutes and then remove the foil. Continue baking another 15 to 20 minutes, until the mole is crispy and brown. Remove the baking sheet from the oven and set aside to cool slightly before serving.

PANTRY NOTE: Any leftover chicken can be stored in the fridge, covered, for up to three days. Leftover mole can be stored in the fridge in a small jar and will keep for five days. Use left-over mole as a spread for sandwiches, a dip for crudité, or a garnish for roasted or cured meats.

Lemon Beef with Raspberry Dipping Sauce

MAKES 4 SERVINGS

This fragrant beef and lively dipping sauce can be served as a main dish alongside rice and steamed bok choy, or on its own as a filling appetizer. Strips of sirloin marinate in a potent mix of lemon juice, garlic, and honey before charring under the broiler. An Asian-style sauce made from raspberries complements the lemon beef. The sauce is a bit of work, as you want to strain out all of the raspberry seeds, but the reward of a super-smooth sauce is worth the effort.

LEMON BEEF
2 pounds top sirloin steak, cut into thin
    strips
Juice of 1 lemon
3 cloves garlic, smashed
1 teaspoon red chile flakes
1 tablespoon honey
Olive oil, for drizzling

RASPBERRY SAUCE
1 teaspoon olive oil
1 cup chopped onion (about half a
    medium onion)
Pinch of salt
2 cups fresh raspberries
1/3 cup rice wine vinegar
1/2 cup water
1 tablespoon soy sauce
1 1/2 tablespoons peeled and grated fresh
    ginger

To make the lemon beef, put the steak strips into a medium-sized bowl along with the lemon juice, garlic, red chile flakes, and honey. Stir to combine so that all the steak pieces are coated. Submerge as much steak as you can in the marinade and cover the bowl with plastic wrap. Set aside to marinate for at least one hour, or put it in the fridge and marinate overnight.

To make the raspberry sauce, heat the olive oil in a medium-sized sauté pan over medium heat. Add the onion and a pinch of salt and cook until the onions begin to soften, about 3 to 4 minutes. Without stirring, cook the onions until the undersides are just brown, another 4 minutes or so. Toss and stir well, redistributing the onions, then cook for another 2 minutes without stirring. This process caramelizes the onions and adds a nice depth of flavor.

Put the raspberries, rice wine vinegar, water, soy sauce, and ginger in the sauté pan and cook until the raspberries are falling apart and cooked through, about 15 minutes. Remove from the heat and put the raspberry mixture in a blender.

Purée the mixture until super smooth, then pour into a fine-mesh strainer set over a medium-sized bowl. Using a rubber spatula, stir and push the raspberry sauce through the strainer, working to reserve the raspberry seeds. It takes some time and muscle to get all the sauce through the strainer while leaving the seeds behind, about 5 minutes total. Taste the sauce and add more ginger if desired. Put the raspberry sauce in a small bowl and set aside.

To cook the lemon beef, preheat the broiler to high. Remove the steak pieces from the marinade and place them on a parchment-lined sheet pan. Drizzle the olive oil over the steak and place the sheet pan under the broiler. Cook until the steak is caramelizing and brown, about 8 to 10 minutes. Remove from the heat. Place the steak and the dipping sauce on a platter and serve immediately.

PANTRY NOTE: Leftover raspberry sauce can be stored in a small jar in the fridge for up to one month. Thin the sauce with water or oil for a salad dressing, or spoon a portion over grilled fish as garnish. This sauce also works well as a taco sauce—go figure!

Blueberry–Oregano Turkey Meatballs

MAKES 4 SERVINGS

Yes, *blueberries* in meatballs! The roasted-down juiciness of blueberries does wonders for otherwise lean ground turkey in this harmonious blend of flavors. A generous dose of fresh oregano spices up the mix and lends a balanced, savory note. This recipe comes together easily and is great for a crowd. Eat the meatballs on their own or add them to a big bowl of broth and greens (like escarole) for a light and healthy dinner.

    1 cup fresh blueberries
    4 tablespoons olive oil, divided
    1 pound lean ground turkey
    ½ cup pine nuts, toasted and chopped
    2 green onions, chopped
    2 tablespoons chopped fresh oregano
    ¼ teaspoon salt
    ¼ teaspoon pepper

Preheat the oven to 450 degrees F.

On a small sheet pan, toss the blueberries in about 1 tablespoon of the olive oil. Roast them in the oven for 10 minutes, until the blueberries burst and release their juices. Remove the pan from the oven and set aside to cool.

In a large mixing bowl, stir together the ground turkey, pine nuts, green onions, oregano, salt, and pepper. Use your hands to combine until the ingredients are uniformly distributed. Using a rubber spatula, fold in the roasted blueberries and all of their juices. Form the mixture into medium-sized meatballs, about 2 inches in diameter.

In a large sauté pan, heat the remaining 3 tablespoons olive oil over medium heat (the oil should just cover the bottom of the pan). Once the oil is hot, add the meatballs and let the bottoms turn golden brown, about 3 minutes. Turn the meatballs to brown another side, about 2 to 3 minutes. Continue working in this way until all sides of the meatballs are brown. Remove the meatballs from the heat and set them on a paper bag to drain them of any excess oil before serving.

PANTRY NOTE: Leftover turkey meatballs can be held in the fridge, covered, for up to three days, or they may be frozen and warmed up before serving at another time.

Strawberry Mousse

MAKES 6 SERVINGS

Mousse is sort of an old-fashioned dessert, but I've always loved the silkiness of puddings and custards. For a recent Sunday dinner, my boyfriend's mother made a strawberry charlotte (a molded dessert made with ladyfingers and filled with a whipped, gelatin-based cream) and so inspired this dessert. Here, instead of gelatin, a proper custard is made by cooking egg yolks with strawberry purée. From there, it's a straightforward mousse recipe—half whipped cream and half whipped egg whites, allowing for a light-as-air dessert that can be made ahead and held in the fridge until serving. Add strawberry slices as a garnish, or serve alongside small cookies. You can easily switch the fruit in this recipe (try blackberries); just keep the same proportions.

1 pound fresh strawberries, chopped
   (about 3 cups)
½ cup sugar
1 tablespoon lemon juice
1 tablespoon vanilla extract
3 eggs, separated
1 cup heavy cream

In a medium-sized bowl, combine the strawberries, sugar, lemon juice, and vanilla extract. Set aside to macerate for at least 30 minutes.

Once the sugar has dissolved and the strawberries have released their juices, pour the mixture into a blender and purée until perfectly smooth. Pour the puréed mixture into a medium-sized saucepan. Whip the 3 egg yolks into the purée until completely combined. Set the saucepan over medium heat and cook, stirring often, until the mixture thickens into a custard and increases in volume, about 5 to 7 minutes. The custard is done when it lightly coats the back of a spoon. Pour into a large mixing bowl and set in the fridge to cool completely, about an hour.

When the custard has completely cooled, remove from the fridge and set aside. Using an electric mixer, beat the 3 egg whites until soft peaks form. Add a third of the whites to the strawberry custard and stir to combine. This lightens the custard slightly. Fold in the remaining egg whites and set aside.

Working quickly, add the heavy cream to the mixer bowl and beat until soft peaks form. Fold the heavy cream into the strawberry custard until just incorporated. Don't beat vigorously! Fold in gently with a rubber spatula.

Pour equal amounts of the strawberry mousse into dessert cups or small bowls. Set in the fridge to chill for at least 1 hour before serving. If making well in advance, cover the tops of the dessert cups with plastic wrap.

PANTRY NOTE: Strawberry mousse holds in the fridge for up to three days, covered with plastic wrap. You may also freeze mousse in large muffin tins for a refreshing summer treat.

Blueberry–Cardamom Drop Donuts

MAKES 24 DONUTS

When I was a kid, my mom used to buy a roll of premade dinner rolls at the grocery store and fry them up in small pieces. Before serving, she'd shake them in a bag full of powdered sugar, just like an Italian *zeppole*. This donut recipe is about that simple and steers clear of the time investment required for yeasted donuts. A quick batter is made from yogurt and flour, then spiked with a heavy dose of cardamom and a handful of fresh blueberries. Toss the hot donuts in powdered sugar, roll them in granulated sugar, or serve them plain—any way, they are delicious!

2 cups all-purpose flour
1 teaspoon baking soda
1 teaspoon baking powder
½ cup sugar
1½ tablespoons ground cardamom
1 cup plain yogurt
1 egg
Zest from 1 lemon
3 tablespoons lemon juice
1 tablespoon vanilla extract
1 tablespoon coconut oil (melted and cooled) or vegetable oil
1 cup fresh blueberries
1 cup vegetable oil, for frying
½ to 1 cup powdered or granulated sugar, for dusting

In a large mixing bowl, stir together the flour, baking soda, baking powder, sugar, and cardamom. In a separate bowl, whisk together the yogurt, egg, lemon zest and juice, vanilla extract, and coconut oil. Fold the wet ingredients into the dry ingredients until well combined. Fold the blueberries into the batter until just combined. Refrigerate for at least 30 minutes.

To fry up the donuts, set the vegetable oil in a medium-sized saucepan over medium heat. The oil is ready when it hits 375 degrees F, or when a small bit of batter dropped into it bubbles quickly and floats. Using a dessert-sized spoon, drop the batter into the hot oil (be careful not to overcrowd the pan) and cook on one side until golden brown, about 2 to 3 minutes, then turn over. Cook the other side until golden brown, another 2 minutes or so.

When the donuts are brown, drain any excess oil by setting the donuts on a paper bag, and let them cool slightly. Once the donuts are cool enough to handle, put them inside another bag, add sugar, shake, and serve while still warm.

PANTRY NOTE: Leftover donut dough can be covered and held in the fridge for up to three days. Leftover donuts (as if you'll have any!) can be held at room temperature for about a day before going soggy, wrapped loosely in a paper bag or parchment paper.

Raspberry Vinegar

MAKES 1 TO 2 CUPS

Preserve the sweet flavor of summer by preparing this simple raspberry-infused vinegar. A fantastic addition to salads and meals, infused vinegar can also be added to a chilled glass of fizzy water as a drinking vinegar. You can make fruit vinegar two ways: the easy way (cover the berries in vinegar and call it done) or the labor-intensive way. I opt for the latter because the extra effort produces a stellar product with an undeniable raspberry taste.

> 4 cups fresh raspberries (about 1 quart)
> 1 cup red wine vinegar
> ½ cup sugar

In a medium-sized shallow bowl, stir together the raspberries and vinegar. Cover with plastic wrap, setting the wrap directly on the surface to help keep the berries submerged. Set aside on the countertop for two days.

After two days, purée the raspberry mixture in a blender until smooth. Set a fine-mesh strainer over a medium-sized bowl. Using a rubber spatula, stir and push the mixture through the strainer, working to reserve the raspberry seeds. It takes about 5 minutes to get all the raspberry mixture through while leaving the seeds behind.

Put the berry purée and the sugar in a medium-sized saucepan and set over medium heat. Bring to a low boil and cook, stirring often, until all of the sugar has dissolved. Taste and add more sugar, if desired. Pour the raspberry-infused vinegar into a small glass bottle or jar and cool (uncovered at this point). Once the vinegar has cooled, cover and store in the fridge.

PANTRY NOTE: This raspberry vinegar keeps well in the fridge for many months, thanks to the high acidity of both the fruit and the vinegar. This same process can be used for any fruit—try strawberries or blackberries!

Orange-Flower & Raspberry Jelly

MAKES 2 TO 3 PINTS

Given the time involved in making raspberry jelly, it is a labor of love. And a big bowl of berries offers only a few small jars of preserves. The flavor, however, will not disappoint. This recipe calls for a minimum of sugar and is punctuated with the sweet citrus from oranges. The addition of orange-flower water (an old-fashioned ingredient but still found in most grocery stores) adds a subtle floral note, punching up the natural acidity of the berries and rounding out the sweetness of the preserve. But you can omit the ingredient if you don't have it in your pantry. For a step-by-step guide to canning at home, check out Water-Bath Canning 101 in this chapter.

1 large orange
2 pounds fresh raspberries
3 cups sugar
1 tablespoon orange-flower water

Zest the orange, reserving 1 tablespoon of the zest. Halve and juice the orange (you should get about 1/4 cup of juice), reserving the halves. In a large saucepan, heat the raspberries, sugar, the tablespoon of zest, the orange juice, and the orange halves over medium heat. Bring to a boil and stir until all the sugar has dissolved, about 15 minutes. Remove the saucepan from the heat and let it cool. When the mixture has cooled, cover and move to the refrigerator to chill overnight. (By heating the fruit first, you are releasing the natural pectin and then letting it macerate overnight. Raspberries are naturally low in pectin and are helped in this recipe by the addition of the higher-pectin orange.)

The next morning, put a small plate in your freezer. You will use this later to check the set of the jelly. Remove the saucepan from the fridge and set it over medium heat. Cook the mixture until it is warmed through and the berries are soft, about 30 minutes. Remove the raspberry mixture from the saucepan and run it through a food mill, reserving only the pulp and juice and holding back the seeds. Return the pulp and juice back to the saucepan and place over medium-low heat.

Cook, stirring often, making sure the jelly does not burn. Skim off and discard any foam that forms on the jelly's surface. After 15 minutes, check the set of the jelly by placing a small spoonful on your cold plate and letting it sit for 30 seconds. If the jelly wrinkles when pushed with your fingertip, it is set. If it does not wrinkle, continue cooking until the desired consistency is reached, another 15 to 20 minutes max. Check the set again.

Pull the saucepan from the heat and stir in the orange-flower water. Pour the jelly into sterilized pint jars and process in a water bath for 5 minutes.

Remove the jars with tongs and let them cool on the countertop. When they're cool, check each for proper seals and label with the date and contents.

PANTRY NOTE: Store in a cool, dark cupboard until ready to use, for up to a year, and refrigerate after opening. Once opened, the jelly will keep for many weeks in the fridge.

Whole Strawberry & Vanilla Jam

MAKES ABOUT 6 PINTS

When I was young, my mom almost always had Neapolitan ice cream in the freezer. As homage to that creamy strawberry-vanilla flavor, here I infuse strawberry preserves with vanilla bean. The heavy perfume of the vanilla subtly flavors the jam, making it the perfect topping for crêpes or gussied-up morning toast. For preserving, choose firm fruits, which hold their shape longer than overripe fruits. Strawberries don't contain much natural pectin, so pectin must be added for the jam to set properly. Instead of adding powdered pectin, however, I use a whole lemon. For a step-by-step guide to canning at home, check out Water-Bath Canning 101 in this chapter.

6 cups small fresh strawberries, hulled but whole
4 cups sugar
1 cup water
1 lemon, cut in half, with each half wrapped in muslin or 4 layers of cheesecloth, tied
3 vanilla beans, cut in half

Put the strawberries, sugar, water, and lemon parcels into a large bowl and let them macerate at room temperature for 1 hour. Pour all into a large saucepan set over medium heat, cooking until the berries release their juices, about 15 minutes. Skim off and discard any foam that forms. Pull the saucepan from the heat and put it in the refrigerator to cool down. When it's cooled, cover the saucepan and let the mixture sit overnight. Make sure your lemon parcels sit in the liquid as well. (Strawberries are a low-pectin fruit and will benefit from the extra pectin in the lemon membrane and seeds.)

The next morning, put a small plate in your freezer. You'll use this later to check the set of the jam. Prepare six or seven pint-sized jars for canning; they must be sterilized for this recipe. Remove the saucepan from the refrigerator and set it over medium heat. Add the vanilla beans.

When the strawberry preserves are just warm, about 5 minutes, use a slotted spoon to strain out the fruit solids and vanilla beans. Reserve these for later. Remove the lemon halves and discard. Stir the jam continuously, holding it at a constant simmer—be careful not to burn the bottom of the saucepan. After 15 minutes,

WATER-BATH CANNING 101

This is a step-by-step guide to water-bath canning at home. There are a few options to choose from, but all work well. Be sure to set up your jars and workspace beforehand so you can establish a rhythm. Also, be mindful of the processing times given in each recipe.

Cleaning the Jars. Wash your jars and lids in hot, soapy water and set them to dry completely on a rack or on a clean dish towel.

Preparing the Jars. Glass jars and lids do not need to be sterilized before use if your food will be processed more than 10 minutes in a boiling water bath or pressure canner. If jar-processing time is 10 minutes or less, jars must be sterilized before filling. Do this by placing jars in a canning pot; fill with water and bring to simmer. Hold jars in water until ready to use. Alternatively, I hold just-washed jars in a 225-degree oven until ready to use. This is *not* recommended by the USDA, but I'm still alive to give you the option.

Filling the Jars. All canned goods will need headspace to allow for expansion of the food and to create a vacuum in cooling jars. As a general rule, leave ¼ inch of headspace on all the jams and jellies and ½ inch of headspace on all whole fruits. When using whole fruits, release any air bubbles in the just-filled jars by tapping the jar on the counter or by inserting a wooden chopstick or skewer into the jar and gently stirring the fruit. When placing lids and rings on canning jars, do not overtighten the rings. Secure just until rings have tension and feel snug. Overtightening will not allow air to vent from the jars—a crucial step in canning.

Heating the Canning Pot. Fill your canning pot or a deep stockpot half full of water and heat to a low boil. Hold the liquid on a very low boil until ready to use.

Filling the Canning Pot. If using a canning pot, place prepared jars of food on the rack in the canner. Do not stack, as you need to allow for circulation of water for proper sealing. Lower jars into the canning pot, and add enough water to cover the jar tops by an inch or more. Cover the pot and return to a boil. *Processing times begin once the canning-pot water is brought back up to a boil.* This can take as long as 15 minutes, so be sure to keep an eye on your pot and have a timer nearby. You may also use a deep stockpot (best only in small-batch preserving) by lining the bottom of the pot with a dish towel and placing jars on top. This helps keep jars from clanging around on the bottom of the pot or tumbling over onto their sides. This form of canning is not universally recommended or endorsed by the USDA. I have seen plenty of farmers and European country folk use this old-school technique, and I've adapted their laissez-faire ways.

check your jam set by placing a small spoonful on your cold plate and letting it sit for 30 seconds. If the preserves wrinkle when pushed with your fingertip, the jam is set. If the preserves do not wrinkle, continue cooking and checking the set every few minutes, up to a maximum of 15 minutes, stirring occasionally. When the jam is set, add the reserved solids (the strawberry fruit and the vanilla beans) back to the saucepan and stir until combined and heated through.

Put the strawberry preserves into the sterilized jars, making sure each jar has a piece of vanilla bean in it. Gently tap the bottom of each jar on the countertop to release any air bubbles. Using a damp clean towel, wipe the rims of the jars and put on the lids and rings as directed. Process the jars in a water bath for 5 minutes.

Remove the jars with tongs and let them cool on the countertop. When they're cool, check each for proper seals and label with the date and contents.

PANTRY NOTE: Store jam in a cool, dark cupboard for up to a year, and refrigerate after opening. You can also store this jam in the fridge, without sealing in a water bath, for several months.

Mom's Stuffed Artichokes

MAKES 4 SERVINGS

Visiting Long Island, where I grew up, is like going back in time. Not a lot has changed in many towns I knew as a kid—everyone still goes to the bakery for daily bread and hits the bagel place next door for a mixed dozen. You still find specialized Italian butchers in small brick buildings along the main drags—it's undeniably charming, and I love going home.

In Seattle, it's impossible to find some of the delicacies known as everyday food in Long Island, and so I often cook them for myself and friends. My mom's stuffed artichoke dish is exactly this sort of meal. You can walk into any pub on Long Island, and they'll have a thick, hearty stuffed artichoke. Here on the West Coast? Nothing. These filled artichokes are rich and indulgent, easily served as a main course.

4 large globe artichokes
3 tablespoons olive oil
½ large onion, diced
10 button mushrooms, diced
3 tablespoons fresh thyme, finely chopped
¼ cup crushed tomatoes
½ cup homemade bread crumbs
¼ cup grated Pecorino or Parmesan
½ cup fresh parsley, chopped
¼ teaspoon red chile flakes

Set up a large bowl of acidulated water. To clean the artichokes, cut off the bottom stems, leaving about 1 inch. Cut off the top ½ inch or so of the artichoke, trimming off most of the spiky leaf tips. Use scissors to trim off any remaining pointed tips, which will be on the lower part of the artichoke. Using a vegetable peeler, peel off the first few fibrous layers of the stem, removing any small dark leaves as you work. Pull the center leaves out to expose the thin inner leaves and the fuzzy heart (which is tinged purple). Using a small spoon, scrape out the small leaves and fine hairs to expose the flat, firm heart at the bottom. This is arduous and takes practice, so work meticulously but quickly, so you don't leave behind many fine hairs, which are inedible and bothersome. Drop the artichokes into the acidulated water, which will help prevent browning from oxidation, until ready to use. Continue in this fashion until all artichokes are clean.

To make the filling, put the olive oil in a large sauté pan set over medium-high heat. Cook the onion until soft and beginning to brown, about 10 minutes. Add the mushrooms and thyme and cook, stirring constantly, until the mushrooms release their juice and start to stick to the bottom of the pan, about 10 to 12 minutes more. Add the crushed tomatoes and bread crumbs to the pan, and stir to combine. Remove from the heat. The filling will be slightly pasty and thick. Stir in the Pecorino or Parmesan cheese, parsley, and red chile flakes, and set aside to cool.

Preheat the oven to 400 degrees F.

To fill the artichokes, remove the cleaned artichokes from the water and drain them upside-down on a kitchen towel or paper cloth for about 10 minutes.

Using both hands, cup an artichoke in your palms and, using your thumbs, spread the leaves of the artichoke open, pulling firmly to create space. Starting with the exterior leaves, use a small teaspoon to scoop in a small amount of stuffing in front of every other leaf. Press down on the stuffing slightly so it's lodged firmly and won't fall out. Work this way until most of the outer leaves are filled. Add another few spoonfuls to the center of the artichoke and set aside.

Place the four artichokes snugly in a shallow baking dish and fill the bottom with about 1 inch of water. Cover the artichokes with aluminum foil and bake for 30 minutes, replacing the water in the bottom of the baking dish as needed. Remove the foil and continue baking until the stems are easily pierced and the stuffing is brown and crispy, another 20 to 30 minutes. Remove from the oven and let rest and cool 10 minutes before serving.

PANTRY NOTE: These artichokes hold well in the fridge, covered, for about two days. Reheat by steaming on the stovetop, or eat slightly chilled. You can embellish the stuffing with crumbled sausage, or add a mix of vegetables instead of using bread crumbs—it is easily adaptable.

Charred Broccoli Rabe with Herbed Quinoa

MAKES 4 SERVINGS

This recipe is a super healthy, filling, and sustaining lunch to pack any day of the week. Protein-packed quinoa, toasted almonds, and olive oil work together to provide both good nutrients and the beneficial fat necessary in a vegetarian meal. The olive oil should well coat the broccoli rabe (or regular broccoli if you can't find it)—but don't be alarmed at the amount! The oil plus a super hot oven help the greens turn crispy and charred—an awesome combination of flavor and texture. You can vary the spices in the quinoa to your liking, but the sweet-sour marriage of lime juice and honey is a crowd pleaser. Throughout the year, you can replace the broccoli rabe with kale flowers, purple sprouting broccoli or any roasted cruciferous vegetable—such as florets of broccoli or cauliflower in autumn.

2 cups water
Pinch of salt
1 cup quinoa, rinsed and drained
1 bunch broccoli rabe
10 cloves garlic, peeled and smashed
5 tablespoons olive oil
Salt and pepper
½ carrot, sliced thinly and cut into
    matchsticks
¼ cup almonds, toasted and chopped
Handful of dried currants or raisins
½ cup fresh herbs, chopped—any combination of mint, parsley, cilantro, dill

¼ teaspoon ground cumin
1 tablespoon honey
1 lime, juiced

Preheat the oven to 450 degrees F.

While the oven is heating, bring the water to a boil in a medium saucepan. Once it's boiling, add a generous pinch of salt and the quinoa to the water. Reduce the heat to medium-low, cover, and let it steam for 12 minutes. Remove the pan from the heat and set aside, leaving the cover in place to continue cooking the quinoa.

On a large baking sheet, place the broccoli rabe and the smashed garlic. Cover with 3 tablespoons of the olive oil, turning with your hands to coat thoroughly and evenly. Season liberally with salt and pepper and spread into a single layer on the baking sheet. Set this in the oven. Cook the broccoli rabe until it's charred and tender, about 20 to 25 minutes, turning it once. Remove from the oven and set aside to cool.

Put the cooked quinoa in a medium-sized glass bowl and add the carrots, almonds, currants or raisins, herbs, cumin, honey, lime juice, and remaining 2 tablespoons of olive oil. Stir to combine. Taste for salt and pepper and adjust seasonings to your liking. Serve at room temperature, topped with a pile of the roasted broccoli rabe.

PANTRY NOTE: Leftovers hold well in the fridge, covered, for about two days.

Blueberry–Cardamom Drop Donuts

JULY

SUMMER SQUASH

IF EVER THERE WERE A "most frequently requested recipes" vegetable, it would be zucchini. This quintessential summer ingredient is easy to grow, and new gardeners often make the mistake of planting too much. The plants are so prolific and adept at developing and ripening squash that a single plant produces nearly enough for a family of four. I recall walking around our neighborhood as a kid, peddling too-big squashes from my family's backyard vegetable garden. My dad had the habit of letting them go too long—a habit he was rather proud of. However, although many people brag about the size of their squashes, overgrown squash is tasteless. For peak flavor, summer squash should be harvested when smaller.

Summer squash is a member of the Cucurbitaceae family of flowering plants (they're commonly called cucurbits), which also includes melons, cucumbers, pumpkins, and winter squashes like butternut and acorn. Unlike hard-shelled winter squashes, however, the skin on summer squashes is edible—you can even eat the stem. Green summer squash, or zucchini, is everywhere, but in recent years speckled and yellow squashes have been showing up at the market.

Yellow squash comes in several shapes and sizes: the most popular are crookneck squash (the long, horn-shaped variety most often available in grocery stores), and pattypan squash (round and squat with scalloped edges). Pattypans have a firm exterior flesh and tend to have a larger seed basket inside. I cook with these only occasionally, when I want to highlight their unique shape. My personal preference is for the traditional green zucchini, harvested when they're medium in size—about six to eight inches long. Seeds are also available for round, green, speckled squashes—I've seen these called 8-Ball (or Ronde de Nice or Goldball) squash—and they are best when harvested young. In most recipes, summer squash varieties can be used interchangeably, so buy your favorite or pick the least expensive of the lot—you'll barely notice a difference in flavor.

Summer squash is an incredibly flexible ingredient. I've seen one too many recipes for squash bread in my day, but I have included an irresistible recipe here (Upside-Down Corn Bread with Summer Squash) that is an updated spin on a classic. When grated, zucchini is an excellent addition in many recipes, as the innocuous flavor allows you to sneak in a full serving of vegetables where you would otherwise not expect it. See, for example, Ricotta-Squash Dumpling Soup (where extra squash is added to the steamed dumpling for lightness) or Zucchini-Coconut Cupcakes with chocolate icing—a great recipe for children's parties because it uses minimal amounts of sugar and maximum amounts of "invisible" vegetable.

For recipes that demand a (relatively) strong zucchini flavor, grated or sliced zucchini can be roasted at very high heat. This water-dense vegetable cooks quickly as the water evaporates, allowing for a concentrated and distinct zucchini flavor.

Summer squash is also delicious when served raw, as in Basil & Pine Nut Salad with Zucchini Ribbons, an excellent recipe for raw-food first-timers. When sliced very thin, zucchini has a delicate flavor and pleasurable texture that you'll flip over. Leave the edible stems intact—be sure to slice them thin, as they add a gorgeous visual component (as in Zucchini & Olive Salad with Licorice-Mint Vinaigrette).

After all this hype, there is a sad truth about zucchini: what little flavor it *does* offer is not very strong, and most of the flavor is lost when you cook it. Composed mostly of water, zucchini provides a crisp, fresh flavor to any dish when used raw. But when heated, zucchini goes from firm to flimsy in a matter of minutes, so the secret is to cook it quickly (lest you end up with limp and soggy squash) and cook it well.

I've included a handful of simple and delicious recipes for summer squash here—breakfast through dessert—that are seasonal from top to bottom, using fresh ingredients from crops ready right about the same time (like Summer Squash & Corn Fritters with Lox). Enjoy!

JULY RECIPES

Summer Squash

Zucchini Breakfast Sammie
Summer Squash & Corn Fritters with Lox
Basil & Pine Nut Salad with Zucchini Ribbons
Zucchini & Olive Salad with Licorice–Mint Vinaigrette
Roasted Summer Squash with Cilantro Vinaigrette
Upside-Down Corn Bread with Summer Squash
Ricotta–Squash Dumpling Soup
Creamy Parsley Risotto with Zucchini
Zucchini–Coconut Cupcakes

Seasonal Extras

Sugar-Cured Cucumber & Onion Salad
Pork Loin with Bing Cherries & Charred Onions

Zucchini Breakfast Sammie

MAKES 4 SERVINGS

This breakfast sandwich takes a bit of effort, but it's worth the extra ten minutes to add a bite of fresh veg to your morning meal. Zucchini pieces are left over high heat to crisp up the edges and cook quickly, leaving their centers al dente and crunchy. With bacon, a creamy mustard dressing, and some refreshing parsley, this sammie offers an irresistible combination. You can easily improvise on this recipe: add a handful of arugula or a slice of melted cheese (try Gruyère) over the egg.

4 slices bacon

1 tablespoon olive oil, plus more for sautéing

½ tablespoon butter

½ small shallot, minced (about 2 tablespoons)

½ medium zucchini, diced (about 1½ cups)

2 tablespoons mayonnaise

1 teaspoon whole-grain mustard

2 tablespoons chopped fresh parsley

4 eggs

4 English muffins, or 8 slices bread

Cook the bacon in a medium-sized sauté pan over medium heat, turning occasionally, until crispy, about 10 minutes. Put the cooked bacon on paper towels to drain the excess oil. Cover to keep warm and set aside.

While the bacon is cooking, heat the tablespoon of olive oil and the butter in a medium-sized sauté pan over medium heat. When the butter is melted, add the shallot and cook until softened and translucent, about 3 to 5 minutes. Add the zucchini and cook until just cooked through, about another 3 minutes. Increase the heat to high and, without moving the zucchini-shallot mixture, continue to cook until the mixture is brown on one side, about 2 more minutes. (Do not be tempted to stir the vegetables. This will allow the ingredients to brown nicely without getting too soft.) Remove from the heat and set aside.

To make the sandwich sauce, combine the mayonnaise, mustard, and parsley in a small bowl and mix well. Set aside.

To cook the eggs, put some olive oil in a sauté pan over medium-high heat. When the olive oil is hot, carefully crack in the eggs. Cook 3 to 4 minutes, until the outer edges of the egg whites are crispy and brown. Use a spatula to flip the eggs yolk side down and cook for another 2 minutes, making sure to leave the yolks runny. Remove from the heat. While the eggs are cooking, toast the English muffins or bread.

To assemble the sandwiches, lay out 4 of the English muffin halves or 4 slices of bread. Spread them with the sandwich sauce. Break the bacon slices in half and layer them on top, then slide one egg onto each sandwich and add a spoonful of the zucchini-shallot mixture. Place the remaining muffin halves or bread slices on top of the 4 sandwiches and serve immediately.

PANTRY NOTE: Breakfast sandwiches are meant to be cooked and eaten right away.

Summer Squash & Corn Fritters with Lox

MAKES 4 SERVINGS

Corn and squash go hand in hand, both in meals and in the garden (along with beans, this trio makes up what is commonly referred to as "the three sisters"). Here, sweet corn complements the clean taste of summer squash for an amazingly effortless breakfast. For garnish, horseradish is combined with sour cream and served alongside lox—a very traditional pairing.

1 tablespoon freshly grated horseradish
¼ cup sour cream
2 to 3 medium zucchinis, grated (about 2 cups)
1 teaspoon salt
1 ear raw corn, kernels cut off
2 green onions, chopped
¼ cup finely chopped fresh parsley
2 eggs, beaten
1 teaspoon all-purpose flour
3 tablespoons grapeseed oil or vegetable oil
4 ounces lox (thinly sliced smoked salmon), cut into ribbons

Stir together the horseradish and sour cream in a small mixing bowl and set aside.

In a large bowl, gently toss the zucchini and salt. The salt will bring out excess moisture in the squash. Transfer the zucchini to a colander and set it over the sink. Let the zucchini drain for about 30 minutes.

Using your hands, gently squeeze any remaining liquid from the zucchini, then put it in a large mixing bowl. Add the corn, green onions, parsley, and eggs, stirring to combine. Sprinkle the all-purpose flour over the mixture and lightly fold all of the ingredients together until the flour is just incorporated.

Set a medium-sized sauté pan over medium-high heat. Heat the oil until it is hot but not smoking. Scoop and drop small spoonfuls of the fritter batter into the hot oil. The batter will be slightly loose. Do not overcrowd the sauté pan—leave sufficient room between each fritter to ensure they do not stick together or become soggy.

Cook the fritters on the first side for about 3 minutes or until golden brown. Using a small spatula, turn them over and continue to cook for another minute or so. (Adjust the heat down a bit if they are browning too quickly.) Remove the fritters from the sauté pan and let them rest on a paper bag for a few minutes to absorb any excess oil.

To serve, arrange the fritters on a platter and top each with a dollop of horseradish sour cream and a ribbon of smoked salmon. Serve immediately.

PANTRY NOTE: Leftover fritters hold well in the fridge for up to four days. Keep them stored in a single layer, with a piece of parchment in between each fritter to minimize sogginess. Fritters are excellent cold but can be reheated under the broiler for 3 minutes to warm them through.

Basil & Pine Nut Salad with Zucchini Ribbons

MAKES 4 SERVINGS

A few summers ago, I had this salad at one of my favorite Seattle restaurants (Tavolàta), and it quickly became my seasonal standard. Here, zucchini ribbons are cut using a mandoline run the entire length of the squash—stems too! These feather-thin, raw slices are tossed in lemon juice with an abundant portion of basil and mint leaves. Toasted pine nuts add an earthy flavor that can't be beat.

> 1/4 cup pine nuts
> 1 teaspoon lemon zest
> 1 tablespoon fresh lemon juice
> 3 tablespoons olive oil
> 1 pound zucchini (2 to 3 medium zucchinis)
> 1/2 teaspoon salt
> 1 tablespoon chopped fresh mint
> 2 tablespoons chopped fresh basil
> 3 ounces feta, crumbled

Set a medium-sized sauté pan over medium-high heat. When the sauté pan is hot, add the pine nuts and stir continuously until they are golden on all sides and you can smell them toasting, about 3 to 5 minutes. Remove the pine nuts from the heat and place them on a small plate to cool. Set aside until ready to use.

In a medium-sized salad bowl, stir together the lemon zest, lemon juice, and olive oil. Set aside. Wash and dry the zucchinis and trim the ends to remove any discolored portions, but keep as much of the stem intact as possible. Using a mandoline set on a very thin setting, cut the zucchinis into long ribbons, about 2 millimeters thick. You should be able to almost see through the slices. If you don't have a mandoline, use a very sharp knife and cut the zucchini ribbons as thin as possible.

Gently place the ribbons in the salad bowl and fold to coat in the vinaigrette, turning carefully so you do not break the ribbons. Work quickly, as this dressing helps the zucchini from turning brown prior to serving.

Add the salt, mint, basil, and reserved pine nuts to the salad bowl. Fold once or twice until just combined. Transfer the salad to a serving platter or a large shallow bowl and sprinkle the feta on top. Serve immediately.

PANTRY NOTE: This salad holds okay in the fridge for up to one day, but it is best eaten day-of. You can substitute toasted almonds or walnuts for the pine nuts.

Zucchini & Olive Salad with Licorice-Mint Vinaigrette

MAKES 4 SERVINGS

This easy-prep salad stands out because of its strong and innovative flavors. The meaty fattiness from cured Kalamata olives pairs well with raw zucchini and fresh mint leaves as well as a bold dose of sambuca-infused vinaigrette. Sambuca is an anise-flavored Italian liqueur. When used sparingly, it emphasizes the flavors in this salad while simultaneously refreshing the palate. If you can't find sambuca, try Pernod as a substitute—or grow licorice-flavored mint instead! The addition of shaved fennel bulb or chopped wild fennel fronds will accomplish the same sort of flavor combination. If nothing else, grind a few anise seeds with a mortar and pestle and add them to the salad bowl.

> 1 tablespoon minced shallot
> 2 tablespoons apple cider vinegar
> 1 tablespoon sambuca
> 3 tablespoons olive oil
> ½ cup torn fresh mint leaves
> ½ cup cured Kalamata olives
> 1 medium zucchini, cut into thin half moons (about 1½ cups)
> Salt and pepper

Put the shallots and apple cider vinegar in a small jar with a lid and let macerate for 10 minutes. Add the sambuca and olive oil and cover. Shake the jar to emulsify, about 1 minute. Set aside until ready to use.

Put the mint, olives, and zucchini in a large salad bowl and toss to combine evenly. Pour in the vinaigrette and toss until the zucchini-olive mixture is glossy and well coated. Season with salt and pepper to taste. Serve immediately.

PANTRY NOTE: This salad does not hold well in the fridge. Leftover vinaigrette can be stored in a glass jar for up to five days.

Roasted Summer Squash with Cilantro Vinaigrette

MAKES 4 SERVINGS

I love this combination of aromatics—the spices and fresh herbs make a pungent and flavorful vinaigrette for roasted summer squash. High oven heat is necessary so that the squash browns quickly before cooking through completely. The summer squash will continue to cook in the marinade once it's out of the oven—you're going for al dente. Serve this salad alongside grilled meat at a summer barbecue and you have al fresco dining perfection. (The marinated beef from the recipe for Lemon Beef with Raspberry Dipping Sauce in June: Berries would work beautifully!)

> 1 pound summer squash (2 to 3 medium)
> 1 tablespoon olive oil
> 2 tablespoons minced shallots
> 2 tablespoons chopped fresh cilantro
> 2 green onions, thinly sliced
> 3 tablespoons fish sauce

3 tablespoons fresh-squeezed lime
juice (from about 1 lime)
1 tablespoon sugar
2 teaspoons red chile flakes

Preheat the oven to 475 degrees F.

Wash and dry the squash and trim off the stems. Cut each squash in quarters lengthwise, then cut each quarter into 4-inch-long pieces. Put the squash in a large mixing bowl and drizzle with the olive oil, mixing well to coat each piece.

On a parchment-lined baking sheet, place the squash cut side down and roast in the oven for about 10 to 15 minutes, or until the squash is deep brown on one side. Be careful not to over-cook it! You want the squash al dente.

While the squash is roasting, prepare the dressing. In a large mixing bowl, combine the shallots, cilantro, green onions, fish sauce, lime juice, sugar, and red chile flakes. Use a whisk to dissolve the sugar.

When the squash is nicely brown, remove it from the oven and add it immediately to the dressing. Using a spatula, gently fold the squash into the dressing, so all the pieces are evenly coated. Set aside for 10 minutes before serving. This allows the flavors to infuse and develop.

PANTRY NOTE: Summer squash breaks down quickly when cooked, so this salad holds for only one day and may turn a bit mushy. If you have a grill, try grilling the squash over high heat until just charred before adding it to the vinaigrette.

Upside-Down Corn Bread with Summer Squash

MAKES 6 TO 8 SERVINGS

This upside-down squash corn bread is meant to be savory (served alongside a fried chicken dinner perhaps), but it can also be eaten as a sweet breakfast bread. The corn bread is dense with coarse cornmeal and turns slightly custard-like with the addition of both milk and sour cream. Warning: The resulting treat is not for calorie counters!

4 tablespoons butter (1/2 stick)
1/4 cup brown sugar
1 1/2 cups cornmeal
1/2 cup all-purpose flour
1 1/2 teaspoons baking powder
1 teaspoon salt
2 eggs
1 cup milk
1/2 cup sour cream
1 medium summer squash (about
1/2 pound), cut into thin slices

Preheat the oven to 375 degrees F.

Put the butter and brown sugar in a 9-inch, round cast-iron skillet or square cake pan. Put the skillet in the oven for about 5 minutes to melt the butter and brown sugar.

Combine the cornmeal, flour, baking powder, and salt in a small bowl. Set aside. In a large mixing bowl, crack in the eggs and whisk well. Add the milk and sour cream, beating well to

HOW TO GROW SUMMER SQUASH

Summer squashes are the plants that keep on giving. They are prolific, and you don't need many to keep you in a productive crop most of the season. Summer squashes can be harvested when small or left alone to get big and fat—just remember that the longer you leave the squash on a plant, the less the plant will produce. The more you harvest, the more the plant will work to continue producing seed, which means more zucchini! Also, the larger the squash, the bigger the seeds and the seed membranes—these are often fibrous and not very tasty, so I prefer to harvest when the squash is small to medium in size.

When & Where to Plant. Sow zucchini in May through early June, or when temperatures are consistently in the sixties. In cooler climates, you may need to do this under a cloche or tunnel. You can also sow seeds in late June or even early July for some late-season crops, but if it is a cool summer where you live, this may not work.

To sow squash seeds, mound up the soil (about eight to twelve inches in diameter) so it sits about four inches higher than the soil line. Mounding the soil allows for drainage and for warmer soil temperatures. As the sun hits the side of the mound, it will warm up the soil faster than if you were sowing directly into the ground. Position your mounds about eighteen inches apart in the bed—this leaves enough room for the plants to grow and the leaves to have space. If you plant them too densely, the plants will compete and grow into each other. Zucchini plants have thin, spiky hairs on their stems that pierce your skin when touched, so leaving more space between them makes for easier harvesting.

Poke three holes about an inch deep, in a triangular pattern, on top of the soil mound and drop in one seed per hole. Only one! Eventually you'll have more than one plant germinate and you'll need to thin them out—remember, one zucchini plant per mound. But don't throw out your seedlings! Pass them on to a friend or move them to a container.

If you're using a pot to grow your summer squash, select a large pot and sow three seeds per pot at the farthest edges from each other. Zucchini roots spread out shallowly. They tend to be fat and fleshy for about seven or eight inches of depth, then fan out into root hairs. For this reason, zucchini is well suited to container growing. Thin any vines that are being dwarfed after six weeks.

→

How to Harvest. When your zucchinis are a nice size (about six to eight inches long), snap the zucchini straight from the stem, or cut using a straight-edged knife. You can harvest zucchinis when they are young or wait until they are older and riper. Younger squashes are quite firm and will hold their shape in sautés or on the grill. A more mature fruit has a softer flesh and larger seeds. It is a personal preference for when to harvest. (Baby squashes or courgettes are generally about three to five inches long and thin. Medium-sized squashes range from six to twelve inches long and about two inches in diameter.)

incorporate. Slowly add the cornmeal mixture to the egg mixture and stir until just combined. Do not overmix.

Pull the skillet with the melted butter and brown sugar from the oven and, using the back of a spoon, swirl to combine. Place the zucchini in a decorative pattern across the bottom of the skillet; a wagon-wheel pattern is pretty (and easy), or simply line up the zucchini slices in tidy rows. Gently pour the batter into the skillet over the zucchini slices. Tap the skillet on the counter a few times to level out the batter, then set the skillet on the center rack in the oven.

Bake for 35 to 45 minutes, or until the edges and the top are golden brown and the sides are bubbling from the butter mixture. Remove the skillet from the oven and cool on a rack for just 10 minutes, as the corn bread will need to be removed from the skillet while it's still warm. Place a serving tray on top of the corn bread skillet. Using oven mitts, carefully pick up the skillet and the serving tray and slowly flip the corn bread out of the skillet and onto the tray.

PANTRY NOTE: This corn bread holds well in the fridge, covered, for three days. Reheat in the oven before serving. You can also cut the corn bread into small pieces and dry them out in the oven for corn bread croutons, brushing them with oil so they don't burn.

Ricotta–Squash Dumpling Soup

MAKES 6 SERVINGS

I love cooked soup in summer. Call me crazy, but I find something refreshing about eating hot food on a warm day. Here, a simple homemade chicken stock is used to poach a citrus-spiked ricotta dumpling. A chicken breast is added for healthy protein, and a big handful of squashes are tossed in for a hearty portion of veg. The secret to this soup is selecting the proper pot to cook it in. Look for a wide, shallow stockpot: you want to have enough room for the dumplings to cook without moving them around too much, lest they fall apart. The creamy-looking soup broth will become cloudy with the tasty cheese whey. You can swap out the lemon zest and add fresh herbs to the dumplings instead—chives and marjoram are two favorites.

1 cup ricotta cheese

1 egg

½ cup cornmeal

¼ cup all-purpose flour

1½ teaspoons salt

1 tablespoon lemon zest

1 tablespoon olive oil

1 tablespoon butter

1½ cups chopped yellow onion (about half a large onion)

1 teaspoon kosher salt

4 cups chicken or vegetable stock

1 boneless, skinless chicken breast (about 8 ounces)

1 carrot, peeled and cut into small, even dice

1 yellow squash, cut in half lengthwise, then into ½-inch half moons

1 small green zucchini, cut in half lengthwise, then into ½-inch half moons

In a large mixing bowl, combine the ricotta and egg. Add the cornmeal, flour, salt, and lemon zest, and fold until evenly combined. Move the bowl of dumpling dough to the refrigerator until ready to use.

Put the olive oil and butter in a 5-quart stockpot over medium heat. When the butter is melted, add the onion and salt. Cook until the onion is soft and just beginning to brown, about 7 to 10 minutes. Add the stock and chicken breast. Cover the stockpot with the lid slightly ajar, bring to a gentle simmer, and cook until the chicken breast is just cooked through, about 15 to 20 minutes. Remove the cooked chicken from the stockpot, let it sit until cool enough to handle, then shred it into strips. Set the chicken aside.

Add the carrot to the stockpot. Remove the dumpling dough from the fridge. Using a large soup spoon, scoop up a portion of dough and gently drop it into the stockpot. Do not crowd the stockpot by putting in too many dumplings. There should be a bit of space between each one.

Cover the stockpot and cook the dumplings over medium-low heat for 10 minutes. Remove the lid, gently turn the dumplings over with a soup spoon, and add the set-aside shredded chicken and the yellow squash and zucchini slices. Gently push aside the dumplings and submerge the chicken, squash, and zucchini. Cover the stockpot again and cook another 10 minutes, until the zucchini is just cooked through.

Serve immediately.

PANTRY NOTE: This soup holds very well in the refrigerator, covered, for up to four days. You may also freeze any leftovers. Be sure to defrost the soup before reheating, which will help keep the dumplings intact.

HOW TO IDENTIFY, HARVEST & COOK SQUASH BLOSSOMS

One of the most frequently asked questions I get every summer is when and how to harvest squash blossoms. These brilliant tangerine-colored flowers can be cooked in broths, sautéed, or more commonly stuffed and dipped in light batters and fried. Everyone loves fried squash blossoms!

Summer squash plants (all members of the Cucurbitaceae family, for that matter—cucumbers, pumpkins, melons, gourds, and so on) send out both male and female blossoms. Through pollination, male blossoms lend their pollen to the female blossoms, and those female blossoms turn into the fruit of the plant. A plant will create more male blossoms than are necessary for pollination, and some of these may be harvested and eaten. (But if you eat all of the male blossoms, you will not have any fruit to harvest!)

Identifying male versus female blossoms is a reasonably simple task. Male flowers have stamens—a long, slender "stalk" that runs up the center of the bloom, tipped with a thick carpet of pollen. Male blossoms grow on long, thin stems from the base of the squash plant—typically about six or seven inches in length. By contrast, female blossoms sit low to the plant and do not have a stamen. To harvest, cut the male blossoms at the base of their stems, as close to the plant as possible. You can use the stem in your cooking or trim it down to a few inches. (You may also harvest female blossoms, if you are trying to reduce the fruit of the plant or it's early in the season and you wish for the plant to fully establish itself before fruiting.)

Use harvested squash blossoms right away, as they wilt quickly. If you need to store them for a short time, line a storage container with a linen cloth or paper towel and mist it until just damp. Lay out the flowers in single layers, leaving space between the blossoms, and stack them between layers of moistened towel. Store in the fridge for up to two days.

To prepare squash blossoms for cooking, I like to remove the stamen, particularly if the anther is thick, as it can taste quite bitter. (The anther is the tip of the stamen and contains the pollen.) To do this, use a small paring knife and delicately open the blossom to remove the stamen at its base or as close to the base as possible. Cook squash blossoms by dipping them into a light egg batter and frying, briefly, in a shallow pool of oil. Make sure the heat is high, as they cook quickly and you need only let the batter brown slightly before serving. For more crunch, roll them in bread crumbs (after dipping them into the batter) before frying.

You can also chop squash blossoms and add them to soups, such as Ricotta–Squash Dumpling Soup or Carrot Peel Soup. I have also had squash blossoms in a simple, light quesadilla. Heat a tortilla in a dry pan; when both sides are golden, add cheese and several squash blossoms to one side and fold in half, pressing the sides together. The cheese will melt and the blossoms will steam. Delicious!

Creamy Parsley Risotto with Zucchini

MAKES 6 SERVINGS

Instead of using arborio rice for a traditional risotto, this creamy version parboils farro, then cooks it with chicken stock until toothsome and earthy. Zucchini slices and chopped parsley, added toward the end, offer up a verdant twist, while a few spoonfuls of mascarpone cheese bring a decadent richness. You can substitute nonfat sour cream or even plain yogurt for the mascarpone if you'd like a less rich dish.

Salt
1½ cups farro
2 tablespoons olive oil
2 tablespoons butter
½ large yellow onion, chopped (about 1½ cups)
1 teaspoon salt
4 cups chicken or vegetable stock
2 to 3 medium zucchinis, cut into thin half moons to make 2 cups
½ cup mascarpone
½ cup chopped fresh parsley
Salt and pepper

Fill a large saucepan with water and salt until it tastes like sea water. Set over high heat and bring to a boil. Drop in the farro and cook, uncovered, for 20 minutes. Remove from the heat and drain the farro. Set aside until ready to use.

In a deep-sided skillet, set the olive oil and butter over medium heat. Once the butter is melted, add the onion and the teaspoon of salt and cook, stirring occasionally, until the onions are soft and translucent, about 8 to 10 minutes. Add the cooked farro to the skillet, along with 1 cup of the stock, and cover. Cook for 10 minutes, then remove the lid.

Continue cooking until all of the stock has been absorbed, stirring often, about 10 to 15 minutes more. Add another cup of stock and cover the skillet, cooking for 10 minutes before removing the lid and stirring until all the stock is absorbed. Continue cooking in this fashion until all the stock is used and absorbed and the farro is tender but still al dente. (Farro is cooked when it no longer squeaks against your teeth but is still slightly chewy.) From start to finish, this process will take about 1 hour and 10 minutes.

Once the farro is cooked, add the zucchini to the skillet and cover, cooking until the zucchini is just cooked through, about 10 to 12 minutes. Remove the skillet from the heat and stir in the mascarpone and parsley. Season to taste with salt and pepper and serve immediately.

PANTRY NOTE: Leftover risotto holds very well in the fridge for up to three days. Before serving, reheat and refresh with a few slices of zucchini and a handful of chopped fresh parsley.

Zucchini–Coconut Cupcakes

MAKES 12 TO 15 CUPCAKES

I am in *love* with these cupcakes! Moist, flavorful, and light, they feature shredded coconut and zucchini, which add an addicting richness to the batter. Perfect for kids' parties, as they offer a less sugary cake than the kind made from a boxed mix, these treats are just right for adult soirees as well. You can use buttermilk in place of the plain yogurt in this recipe with stellar results.

CUPCAKES
1 tablespoon softened butter and
    1 tablespoon all-purpose flour (or
    15 cupcake liners), for preparing
    the baking pan
1½ cups all-purpose flour

½ cup unsweetened coconut flakes or
    shredded coconut
1 teaspoon baking powder
1 teaspoon baking soda
½ teaspoon kosher salt
½ cup (1 stick) butter, softened
1 cup sugar
1 cup plain nonfat yogurt
1 tablespoon vanilla extract
1½ cups grated zucchini (about
    1 medium)

ICING
½ cup cocoa powder
1 cup (2 sticks) butter, softened
¼ cup milk
1 teaspoon vanilla extract
5 cups confectioners' sugar

Preheat the oven to 350 degrees F. Prepare a cupcake baking pan by lightly greasing the inside of the pan with the softened butter and a sprinkle of all-purpose flour (alternatively, use cupcake liners).

In a large mixing bowl, combine the 1½ cups of flour with the coconut flakes, baking powder, baking soda, and salt. Set aside.

In the bowl of an electric stand mixer with the paddle attachment (or with a handheld mixer), mix together the softened butter and the sugar until pale, about 3 minutes. Add half of the dry ingredients to the butter-sugar mixture and mix until just combined. Add the yogurt and vanilla extract to the batter and mix until well incorporated. Add the remaining dry ingredients and mix until just incorporated. Finally, fold in the zucchini with a rubber spatula until it is just incorporated.

Spoon the batter into the prepared cupcake pan and bake for about 20 minutes, or until lightly brown and a wooden skewer inserted into the middle of a cupcake comes out dry. Remove from the oven and let cool on a wire rack for 10 minutes before taking the cupcakes out of the pan.

While the cupcakes are baking, make the chocolate icing. In a medium-sized bowl, combine the cocoa powder and butter, and stir a few times to incorporate the cocoa. (This prevents the cocoa powder from puffing up in a dust cloud when you turn the mixer on.) Mix on high until well blended and fluffy. Add the milk and vanilla extract and blend completely. Adding 1 cup at a time, mix the confectioners' sugar with the butter mixture and beat until well combined. Set aside, covered, at room temperature, until ready to use.

Once the cupcakes are cool, use a butter knife or an offset spatula to cover each cupcake with a thin layer of icing, and serve.

PANTRY NOTE: Leftover cupcakes store well, covered in a plastic container and left at room temperature, for about three days. Simply double the batch for more indulgence.

Sugar-Cured Cucumber & Onion Salad

MAKES 6 SERVINGS

This dish is one of the few vegetable dishes my vegetable-hating sister makes and loves. My family has been making it for years, and it's at every summer barbecue, though everyone has a slightly different version. My sister's is pretty perfect, as it leaves time for the flavors to meld and the onions to soften slightly. It is easily embellished with fresh herbs—dill, mint, or even fennel fronds go perfectly. You may also add nuts or cheese to bulk it up, though it's delicious as is.

> 4 cucumbers, peeled and sliced paper thin
> 1 small white onion, about the size of a baseball, sliced super thin into half moons
> ¼ cup distilled white vinegar
> 2 tablespoons olive oil
> ¼ teaspoon sugar
> Salt and pepper

Put the cucumbers and onions in a large sealable container (you can also use a resealable plastic bag). Pour in the vinegar, olive oil, and sugar, and cover. Shake vigorously until all cucumbers and onions are well coated and put it in the refrigerator overnight, or for at least 6 hours. Season with salt and pepper to taste. Serve the salad in a shallow bowl.

PANTRY NOTE: This salad holds for up to two days in the fridge, covered.

Pork Loin with Bing Cherries & Charred Onion

MAKES 4 SERVINGS

I worked with a Seattle chef for many years, and he made this cherry-onion relish for grilled salmon. I have used many variations of the same two ingredients over the years, rotating the protein and adding flavor with spices and fresh herbs. Here, charred onions are tossed with fresh cherries—their heat cooking the cherries slightly. Basil complements the flavors in both and is ripe and ready in summer. You may vary the spices on the pork rub to your liking—fennel and coriander work well. You may also add some vegetables to the pan with the onions—fennel bulbs are a great complement to the meal.

> 5 torpedo onions (or other small, oval-shaped onions), cut into ½-inch slices
>
> 4 tablespoons olive oil, divided
>
> 2 cups Bing cherries, pitted and halved
>
> 1 teaspoon honey
>
> 1 teaspoon apple cider vinegar
>
> 1 tablespoon chopped fresh basil
>
> 1 teaspoon salt, divided
>
> ¼ teaspoon pepper
>
> 1 teaspoon ground cumin
>
> ¼ teaspoon ground cinnamon
>
> 1½ pounds pork tenderloin
>
> 1 tablespoon butter

Preheat the oven to 450 degrees F.

Place the onions on a sheet pan and toss with 3 tablespoons of the olive oil. Roast them in the oven until the onions are charred and the edges are blackening, turning them halfway through, about 20 minutes total.

While the onions are cooking, combine the cherries, honey, vinegar, basil, and ½ teaspoon of the salt in a large bowl. Toss to combine and set aside. When the onions are done cooking, add them to the bowl and cover with a plate or piece of plastic wrap. Leave the oven on. Set the onion mixture aside to cool.

On a large plate, combine the remaining ½ teaspoon salt with the pepper, cumin, and cinnamon, and stir with a fork to combine well. Roll the pork loin in this spice mixture, coating all sides. In a large sauté pan, set the remaining tablespoon of olive oil and the butter over medium-high heat. When the butter has melted and the pan is hot, add the pork tenderloin and sear on each side until dark brown, about 2 minutes per side. Put the pan in the oven (or transfer pork to a roasting pan if you do not have oven-ready pans) and roast until the meat is cooked through, about 15 to 20 minutes. Remove from the oven and let rest for 10 minutes before slicing.

Slice the pork into thin medallions, and fan them out on a serving platter. (It is okay if the center of the pork is slightly pink.) Pour cherry-onion relish over the top of the pork and serve immediately.

PANTRY NOTE: Leftover relish and pork will hold in the fridge for up to two days.

AUGUST

TOMATOES

AS AN URBAN FARMER, I ask my clients for a "grow list" every year—basically a wish list of veggies they would like to have in the garden. I encourage them to think big and be bold, and ask for produce they would never imagine growing. Do you know what every single person requests? Tomatoes. There is a compelling reason for this: nothing beats the taste of homegrown tomatoes eaten fresh off the vine. I always gorge on them in late summer, and by mid-September I never want to see a tomato again—and I won't until the next summer. Tomatoes imported during the winter are a far cry from the sun-ripened fruits grown closer to home. Commercial tomato production breeds varieties more for durability, disease-resistance, and consistency in shape and color. For the most part, this process sacrifices taste.

Tomatoes are universally appealing and make regular appearances in many global cuisines. Italians rely on them for sauces; tomatoes are eaten raw and fresh throughout southeast Asia; in the United States, Southerners fry up green tomatoes; heck, despite their cool climate, even the British commonly enjoy roasted tomato halves with their breakfast eggs.

In most tomato-friendly climates, tomatoes start to ripen in midsummer. The ramp-up to tomato season often starts with early-ripening varieties, but I have always found it better to wait a few weeks before indulging. The longer the sun hits a fruit, the more sugars it will have when harvested. For tomatoes, this guarantees a rich and juicy bite. Early-ripening tomato plants will set fruit even when the nights are cold, but they pay the price in flavor, as the fruits are less sweet and the flavor not as interesting.

Tomatoes are grown in a rainbow of colors, and the flavor varies with each hue. Growers are continually creating new varieties by cross-pollinating tomatoes, so the fruits can be grown in shades of purple-green, purple, red, orange, yellow, and deep burgundy. Of course that means not all tomatoes are created equal, and I encourage you to choose your tomato based on the recipe you're making. Red- and orange-hued fruits are typically sweeter than their yellow and green counterparts. The earlier a tomato is harvested, the more acidity it will carry as well. Soft, mushy, overripe tomatoes are perfect in such dishes as Halibut & Lovage with Ginger-Tomato Broth. A firmer cherry tomato is necessary for Tomato-Melon Soup with Poached Shrimp & Summer Herbs, so the flesh doesn't bleed out into the broth.

There are three overarching categories for all tomatoes: slicer, cherry, and paste tomatoes. Big, fat slicers are meant for eating fresh in salads or sandwiches. Many of the "heirloom" varieties found at farmers markets are slicer tomatoes, as are beefsteak tomatoes. Shapes, colors, and flavors vary widely, but all slicing tomatoes are known for their juicy nature.

Cherry tomatoes are also meant for fresh eating. They make impeccable, bite-sized salads and range in shape from teeny round fruits to pear-shaped. Also known as grape tomatoes, these little fruits are the best choice for roasting recipes, as they have a smaller flesh-to-skin ratio, so the flavor is amplified when their water evaporates in a hot oven (as in Grilled Corn with Tomato Butter). Campari tomatoes are not technically a cherry tomato; they're a bit larger than a cherry tomato but smaller than a plum tomato, and are grown for fresh eating.

Paste tomatoes are best for cooking and preserving. These are typically oblong and have firm, starchy flesh and little water. They are a meatier fruit and the flavor is subtly different: they aren't very tasty eaten raw but are the only tomato to use for canning or making sauces (see Crushed Tomatoes and Tomato Jam). Once cooked, paste tomatoes hold their flavor far better than tomatoes meant to be eaten fresh. Romas are probably the most common paste tomato variety, but San Marzanos or anything labeled "paste" at the farmers market will work well. For canning, I almost exclusively use "seconds" (slightly bruised or overripe tomatoes), which are often a third the price of a more perfect tomato—you're going to pulverize them anyway.

As the summer season wanes and the days get shorter, many tomatoes will sit on the vine and stay green. You can harvest mature-sized green tomatoes and ripen them indoors. Tomatoes will continue ripening off the vine—a good "note to self" for any late harvests or underripe tomatoes you pick up at the farmers market. If you harvest a lot of them, pile them in a bucket and set them outside or in a cool, dark room to ripen. If you have only a small batch, set them on a sheet pan and leave them indoors. You can also use them in my Green Tomato Salsa recipe.

Whether eaten fresh, deeply roasted, turned to broth, or preserved, tomatoes are an incredibly flexible fruit that offers vibrant diversity to your meals. You'll find all of these techniques and a few more in this book, but don't stop here! Make a traditional Italian marinara sauce, spoon large amounts of tomatoes onto grilled bread for a summer bruschetta, and, of course, enjoy a fresh caprese salad. You say tomato, I say . . . let's eat!

AUGUST RECIPES

Tomatoes

Honey–Tomato Scones with Lemon–Lime Glaze
Beet & Tomato Salad with Pickled Watermelon
Grilled Corn with Tomato Butter
Seared Salmon with Minted Peach & Tomato Salad
Halibut & Lovage with Ginger–Tomato Broth
Tomato–Melon Soup with Poached Shrimp & Summer Herbs
Minestrone Verde with Tomato Leaf Broth
Crushed Tomatoes
Tomato Jam
Perfect Tomato Salsa
Green Tomato Salsa

Seasonal Extras

Spicy Cucumber, Melon & Cilantro Gazpacho
Peach–Cardamom Smoothie

Honey-Tomato Scones with Lemon-Lime Glaze

MAKES 8 TO 10 SCONES

Scones make for a festive weekend brunch and are easy to make and bake quickly. The last time I made these, for my friend's fortieth birthday weekend, everyone loved them—even the kids who thought it was crazy to eat tomatoes in a scone. Cherry tomatoes are cut into small pieces and doused in honey, then left to slow roast and candy in a low oven. Folded into scone batter crisped with cornmeal and covered in citrus icing, they offer a refreshing take on breakfast. Choose ripe cherry tomatoes for this recipe, which bake up into small candied pieces—like tomato "crack."

SCONES

1 pint cherry tomatoes
2 tablespoons honey
$\frac{1}{2}$ cup all-purpose flour
$\frac{1}{2}$ cup cornmeal
$\frac{1}{4}$ cup sugar
2 teaspoons baking powder
$\frac{1}{4}$ teaspoon baking soda
8 tablespoons cold butter, cut into
   small chunks
$\frac{3}{4}$ cup buttermilk
1 egg

ICING

1 cup confectioners' sugar
2 tablespoons orange juice
2 teaspoons lemon zest
2 teaspoons lime zest

Preheat the oven to 300 degrees F.

To prepare the tomatoes, quarter them and roughly chop so there are no pieces larger than about $\frac{1}{2}$ inch. Line a baking sheet with parchment paper and place the chopped tomatoes on it. Pour the honey over them and stir or toss to combine well, spreading the tomatoes so they are in a single layer. Roast this mixture in the oven, turning once halfway through, until caramelized and dried, about 45 to 60 minutes. They will be chewy and candy-like when finished. Remove from the oven and set aside to cool.

Increase the oven temperature to 350 degrees F.

In the bowl of a food processor, pulse the flour, cornmeal, sugar, baking powder, and baking soda until just combined. Add the butter, dispersing evenly over the top of the flour mixture. Pulse until combined and crumbly, but big pieces of butter still remain, about 20 times.

Beat the buttermilk and egg together in a bowl. With the food processor running, pour in the buttermilk mixture in a steady stream and process just until the dough comes together, forming a large ball in the processor—about 1 minute.

Remove the dough from the food processor and put it in a large bowl. Sprinkle the tomato "candy" over this and, using a wooden spoon, fold it in until just combined and even throughout the dough. Place the mixed dough in the middle of a parchment-lined baking sheet. Pat the dough out into a round disc, about $\frac{3}{4}$ to 1 inch thick. Using a sharp knife, precut the scones

TIPS FOR GROWING TOMATOES

Come summertime, when the air is hot and the sun is high, everyone comes down with a case of tomato fever. I'm not sure how this plant grew to such epochal proportions as to be the measure of success for a home gardener, but it has. That said, it is also a somewhat demanding plant and needs a bit of attention to produce good-tasting fruits over the course of several weeks. Here I share tomato tips and tricks to improve your chances of success—from pruning for maximum yield to building easy DIY trellises to watering your plants.

Pruning Those Suckers. Tomato suckers are the small sets of leaves that grow between the main stem and a leafy branch of a tomato plant. These suckers, if left to grow, become additional flowering and fruiting stems for the plant. That's good, right? Not exactly. If allowed to bloom and fruit, these additional tomatoes will ultimately compete for nutrients from the plant. Over time, this lessens the overall chances of all the fruit coming to delicious maturity. Cooler and shorter seasons (like those in the Pacific Northwest) cannot support such prolific tomato production, but regardless of your local temperature, all tomatoes do well with a little pruning.

Pruning, in this case, refers to snapping off those little suckers. When the stems are new and short (say, three to four inches), you can snap them off with your fingers by bending them back quickly. If you let them get much larger, it's best to use a set of shears so you don't tear the main plant stem in the process. Starting in early August (after the plants have some good strong growth and the weather is consistently warm), I snap off suckers—no hesitation, no regrets—from the top half of the plant. If you planted a smaller tomato variety or a cherry tomato plant, leave more suckers on the plant. Because cherry tomatoes are smaller, they ripen faster and the plant can support more production.

In addition to trimming suckers, August is a great time to prune about 30 percent of the green leaf stems from the tomato vine. This sends the plant's energy into fruit production rather than upward growth. It allows for air to pass through and for sun to shine on the fruit, which helps develop sweetness. More practically, pruning also allows a gardener to clearly see when tomatoes are ripe. Be aggressive and fear not: pruning will seldom cause damage to the plant or overall tomato production. As home cooks and gardeners, our "job" is to produce the most luscious tomato for our table. Keep that in mind, and you won't have a problem getting rid of suckers and excess leaves.

→

One last note: Some people (like me) find the leaves of tomato plants highly irritating to their skin, especially with prolonged contact. For this reason I *always* wear gloves and long sleeves when dealing with tomato plants.

Building a DIY Trellis. A structured tomato trellis offers support to climbing or tall plants and is perfect for maximizing and managing your space—it keeps tomato stems from breaking and allows for easier pruning. August is the time to get in the garden and build tomato supports, if you haven't already. Perhaps you're one of the many who purchase tomato "cages," but I find that plants often grow over the confines of the cage and drag it down.

Instead, I build a support system of bamboo for all of my tomato beds. DIY trellising is very efficient and less expensive than buying cages. It allows for easy pruning, good air circulation, and delicious fruit maturity (the sun sits on individual tomato fruits, ripening and sweetening them up). There are other options for trellising—reusing a fence, for instance. If you have supportive items like this around, get creative and repurpose them.

Constructing a Bamboo Trellis. You'll need five lengths of 6-foot bamboo. Crossing two pieces of bamboo, tie string about five inches down, creating a small X at one end. Once the pieces are tied, splay the bamboo apart, making a large X—this will act as the foundation for the trellis. Do this twice and position the bamboo legs about 5 feet apart in the bed. Position the remaining piece of six-foot bamboo across the frame and voilà! You now have a super-durable and strong trellis for trailing tomato vines.

Supporting & Watering Tomatoes. Use garden twine and loosely make a knot around the main stem of the tomato, winding the string up to the top of your bamboo trellis (or other support system) and tying off. Do this in one or two places along the main stem, gently twisting the tomato plant around the string for extra support.

For heat-loving tomato plants, it is best to water in the morning. This leaves time for plants to soak it up before the heat of day (and evaporation) take over. Watering in the evening results in a drop in soil temperature, which these heat-lovers do not appreciate. You wouldn't like to sit outside in wet socks at nighttime, would you?

into small triangular pieces, like you're cutting a pizza pie, but leave the dough in the same place.

Bake the scones for 20 minutes. Remove from the oven and cut the scones again, moving them apart slightly so the sides get crisped. Return the pan to the oven and continue cooking until the tops are golden brown, about another 5 to 7 minutes. Set aside to cool until just warm.

While the scones are cooling, make the icing. In a small bowl, combine the confectioners' sugar, orange juice, and lemon and lime zests. Whisk with a fork until well blended and smooth. When the scones are still slightly warm, drizzle a portion of icing over each and serve.

PANTRY NOTE: Leftover scones keep well for one day if covered loosely with a piece of parchment and left on the counter. Heat up in the oven before serving, if so inclined. Tomato "candy" can be used in place of raisins or dried fruit in most recipes—try some in morning granola or as an ingredient in oatmeal-ginger cookies.

Beet & Tomato Salad with Pickled Watermelon

MAKES 4 TO 6 SERVINGS

Make this dish immediately—it's the most delicious salad you'll ever eat! Several summers ago, I had a version of this at JCT Kitchen in Atlanta, and I made notes on the flavor profile to try to re-create it back at home. The surprise ingredient is the heavily spiced pickled watermelon rind. This salad is sheer perfection in balance—mellow, earthy beets combine with sweet, fresh watermelon and acidic cherry tomatoes, along with generous portions of avocado, almonds, and basil. It is a texture-lover's dream—soft, firm, fresh, crispy, fatty, crunchy, sweet, sour.

½ small seedless watermelon
1 cup apple cider vinegar
1 cup sugar
2 whole star anise pods
1 tablespoon whole cloves
2 thin slices peeled fresh ginger
3 small red beets, about 3 to 4 inches in diameter
½ pint of red cherry tomatoes
½ large avocado
¼ cup chopped fresh basil
¼ cup chopped almonds
¼ cup olive oil
⅛ teaspoon salt
⅛ teaspoon pepper
4 ounces feta, crumbled into big bits

Using a vegetable peeler, peel off the dark green outer skin of the watermelon, leaving the white rind intact. Cut the peeled watermelon in half, lengthwise, and remove the red inner flesh from each half. You can do this with a spoon or run a knife just under the red flesh and above the white rind. Leaving a bit of red flesh on the rind is okay. Chop the red watermelon flesh into 1-inch cubes and set aside. Cut the white watermelon rinds into thin, even strips, about ¼-inch wide, and then chop them into a small, even dice and set aside.

In a small saucepan, combine the vinegar and sugar. Tie the star anise, cloves, and ginger in a small cheesecloth spice bag and add it to the vinegar-sugar mixture. Bring to a boil over high heat, stirring to disolve sugar. Once the vinegar is boiling, remove the saucepan from the heat and add the small cubes of watermelon rind. Set aside to cool, allowing the rind to pickle in the brine.

Put the beets in a medium-sized saucepan and just cover with water. Bring to a boil over high heat, then reduce the heat to a low boil and cook until the beets are just tender, about 20 to 30 minutes. Drain the beets and set aside to cool. When they are cool enough to handle, rub off their skins using a paper towel or linen cloth. Chop the peeled beets into 1-inch cubes and set aside.

Once the watermelon rind pickles are cool enough to handle, drain the brine, reserving 3 tablespoons. Discard the spice bag.

Put the beets, watermelon flesh, rind pickles, cherry tomatoes, avocado, basil, and almonds in a large bowl. Add the olive oil, the reserved watermelon pickle brine, and the salt and pepper. Fold to combine. Place the salad on serving plates and sprinkle equal portions of feta crumbles over each. Serve immediately.

PANTRY NOTE: This salad holds well in the fridge up to two days, but the feta and almonds will turn pink from the beet juice. To serve leftovers, refresh with some new feta crumbles and a sprinkle of fresh basil.

Grilled Corn with Tomato Butter

MAKES 6 SERVINGS

Grilled corn is a favorite summertime side dish and, although I don't have a grill at my apartment, I make this dish whenever I visit friends with big backyard barbecues. The secret to grilled corn is letting the whole ear of corn sit over high heat for long stretches without moving or turning it. The corn comes out blackened, charred, and slightly chewy—an excellent partner to sweet, creamy tomato butter. Tomato butter is made easily by whisking roasted tomatoes (which are slightly dehydrated and crinkly) with a dollop of softened butter.

½ pint cherry tomatoes
1 tablespoon olive oil
2 sticks (1 cup) unsalted butter, at room temperature
6 ears of corn

Preheat the oven to 450 degrees F.

Place the cherry tomatoes in a single layer in a shallow baking dish and toss with the olive oil. Make sure the tomatoes are not overlapping and that there is a bit of room between each. Roast until the tomatoes are split and the juices are condensing, about 20 to 30 minutes. Remove from the oven and set aside to cool completely.

When the tomatoes are completely cool, put them (and all of the juices from the baking dish) in a large mixing bowl. Add 1 stick of the butter to the bowl and, using a hand-held electric mixer or a stand mixer, mix on high until the butter and the roasted tomatoes are well incorporated. Don't be worried if the butter looks chunky. Add the second stick of butter and continue mixing on high until the tomatoes emulsify into the butter and there is no separation between the fat and the liquid. Put the tomato butter in a small bowl in the fridge until ready to use.

Prepare the corn by peeling back the husks and removing as much of the corn silk as possible. Pull the husks back up over the corn and wrap the entire husk in aluminum foil. Do this for all 6 ears of corn, until each is individually wrapped in foil.

Preheat the grill to high and arrange the corn ears directly over the heat. Cover and cook for 8 to 10 minutes before rotating the corn a quarter turn. Continue in this fashion—you will turn the corn three times and cook it for about 30 to 40 minutes total.

Remove the ears of corn from the grill and set aside to cool. When they are cool enough to handle, remove the foil and the husks. Serve warm corn alongside the bowl of tomato butter (let people help themselves).

PANTRY NOTE: Tomato butter will keep in the fridge, covered, for several days. Use any leftover butter on sandwiches or in egg dishes, or smear it on a grilled cheese sandwich! Grilled corn holds well in the fridge for several days as well.

Seared Salmon with Minted Peach & Tomato Salad

MAKES 4 SERVINGS

In this dish, fresh herbs are muddled to a thick paste and tossed with a handful of in-season fruits—tomatoes, peaches, and cantaloupe. Served at room temperature, this savory-sweet salad is paired with seared salmon fillets. Many fish runs are prolific in summer months, an excellent time to purchase wild fresh salmon. This meal delivers maximum flavor: the acidity in the fruits makes a nice counterbalance to the fattiness of the fish. Easy to pull together, this tasteful dinner uses a mix of tomatoes for a harmonious texture—big, colorful heirlooms cut into wedges and small, sweet cherry tomatoes left whole. If desired, you can mix the proportions of fruit in this recipe. Double up on peaches and omit the cantaloupe, or stick with an all-tomato mix.

¼ cup fresh mint leaves
¼ cup fresh cilantro leaves
2 cups cubed cantaloupe
1 peach, cut into thin wedges
1 pound assorted tomatoes, larger tomatoes cut into wedges
¼ teaspoon salt, plus more for seasoning
⅛ teaspoon pepper, plus more for seasoning
3 tablespoons apple cider vinegar
5 tablespoons olive oil, plus more for sautéing
Four 4-ounce salmon fillets

DIY SUN-DRIED TOMATOES

Along with freezing and canning, drying tomatoes for pantry stocking is an excellent and easy form of food preservation. Tomatoes retain their flavor well, and dehydrated tomatoes are a real treat because that flavor is amplified by removing the fruit's moisture. Similar to the flavor of a roasted tomato, dried tomatoes have a sharp acidity and an intensely fruity flavor profile. Although they are excellent when rehydrated, dried tomatoes work beautifully in recipes when left dried and finely chopped. Add a handful of dried tomato bits to sauces for richness and brightness, or fold some into scone batter for a savory morning pastry.

I dry tomatoes in one of two ways, depending on both the time I have available for the task and on the weather. Yes, the weather. They don't call them sun-dried tomatoes for nothing! Using heat from the sun or from a low-temperature oven, it's easy to dry a large batch of tomatoes with little effort. To successfully store dried tomatoes, make sure they are completely dry before covering and sealing in any way. Any residual moisture left in the tomatoes before packing will lead to decay and mold, ruining the batch. Other than that, the rules are few. Make a huge batch using different varieties and dry both puréed tomatoes and sliced tomatoes so you have options for cooking later on.

The process for drying will fluctuate depending on the time of year and the juiciness of the fruits, so there are no specific instructions to follow. Here I offer a loose how-to guide. Rely on your own judgment to know when tomatoes are dry enough for storage. There is a bit of preparation before you embark on tomato drying, but once you have all of your materials assembled, this project is easy to manage.

Drying Tomatoes in the Sun. You'll need a large screen (window screens work well, as long as they are completely clean). You could also build a simple timber frame and stretch a screen across, using a staple gun to hold the screen in place. Paste tomatoes work best for drying, as they have less liquid than a tomato bred for fresh eating.

Once you have a screen ready, use a food processor to pulverize the tomatoes into a thick pulp. Strain the pulp for a few hours, or overnight, in a colander or fine-mesh strainer. This helps remove some moisture from the fruits. Cover any pulp you are straining to keep out insects (place a plate or a piece of cheesecloth over your colander).

Once the pulp is strained, use a rubber spatula to spread out the tomato pulp evenly on the screen. Cover the purée with a thin layer of cheesecloth or a kitchen linen to keep insects off, and set the drying racks out in the sun. Set the screen on top of bricks or a frame so that air can get under and around the screen. Dry until the tomato purée is paste-like and thick. Using a spatula or knife, scrape up the dried tomato paste and form into 1-inch balls. Sun-dried tomato balls can be frozen (lined up on a sheet pan and frozen until hard before storing in a resealable plastic bag) and kept for several months. You can also submerge them in olive oil in a glass jar and store the jar, covered, in the fridge. Use within two to three weeks.

Drying Tomatoes in the Oven. Preheat the oven to 175 degrees F. Cut paste tomatoes into even slices—no fatter than ½-inch thick. Set a metal cooling rack over a sheet pan and place the slices on the rack (make sure the pieces do not overlap). If you have time, lightly salt the tomato slices and set them aside for several hours or overnight before oven roasting—this will help draw out some moisture. Roast in the oven until the tomatoes are crispy and completely dry. Let them cool on the rack overnight. Make sure the oven-dried tomato slices are cool throughout before storing in the freezer or pantry.

With a mortar and pestle, muddle the mint and cilantro by smashing them until they are broken down and juicy. Transfer to a large bowl, then add the cantaloupe, peach, tomatoes, salt, pepper, vinegar, and olive oil. Fold gently to combine, making sure everything is covered with the herbs. Set aside for the flavors to develop.

Season the salmon fillets with salt and pepper. Cover the bottom of a large skillet with a thin layer of olive oil and heat over medium-high heat. When the olive oil is hot but not quite smoking, add the salmon fillets, skin side down. Cook for 4 minutes.

While the salmon is cooking, fold the salad once more and then portion out helpings onto 4 plates. Set aside.

Don't move the salmon fillets around the pan, but instead let them sit and sear. Flip and cook the second side of the fillets about 4 minutes more, until the salmon pieces are nearly cooked through but slightly underdone in the center. Remove from the heat and place one salmon fillet over each salad portion. Serve immediately.

PANTRY NOTE: Leftover salad can be held in the fridge, covered, for one day. Fresh herbs should be added to liven up the flavors before serving leftovers.

Halibut & Lovage with Ginger–Tomato Broth

MAKES 4 SERVINGS

Every year I have a harvest party with some of my farmer friends. Our goal is to celebrate what's in season and give thanks for a successful growing year. This quick-cooking broth, rich and bursting with flavor, can be made in advance, making it an excellent choice for such a summer dinner party. Fresh tomatoes are cooked down and infused with an excessive amount of aromatics—star anise, fennel, and ginger. Just-cooked celery and herbaceous lovage leaves are beautiful complements to the halibut. Any fish can be substituted for the halibut, so use what's local and in season.

4 tablespoons olive oil, divided
2 leeks, trimmed, washed, and chopped
4 cloves garlic, smashed
1/8 teaspoon salt
6 roma tomatoes, diced
2 whole star anise pods
8 cardamom pods, crushed
1 teaspoon fennel seeds
2 slices peeled fresh ginger
4 cups water
1/4 cup rice wine vinegar
2 tablespoons sugar
Four 4-ounce halibut fillets
Salt and pepper
1/2 cup diced celery
1/4 cup fresh lovage leaves (or celery leaves)

In a large saucepan, heat 2 tablespoons of the olive oil over medium-high heat. Add the leeks, garlic, and salt and cook until the leeks are soft and just starting to brown, about 7 to 10 minutes. Add the tomatoes, cooking until they just release their juices, about 4 to 5 minutes. Tie the star anise, cardamom pods, fennel seeds, and ginger in a small cheesecloth spice bag and place it in the saucepan. Add the water, vinegar, and sugar, and bring to a boil. Cover the saucepan and reduce the heat to low. Cook for another 30 minutes, allowing the flavors to infuse.

While the broth is cooking, prepare the halibut. Season all sides of the halibut with salt and pepper. In a large sauté pan, set the remaining 2 tablespoons of olive oil over medium-high heat. When the oil is hot, add the halibut pieces, skin side down. Cook until the undersides of the fish are brown and the sides are becoming opaque, about 4 minutes. Turn the halibut pieces over and brown the other sides, about 4 minutes more. Remove the fish from the heat and set aside on a plate until ready to serve.

After the broth has cooked, remove it from the heat and pour it through a fine-mesh strainer set over a large bowl. Discard the spice bag and vegetables. Put the strained broth back in the saucepan and return it to the stovetop. Add the celery, cooking until just cooked through but still crispy, about 8 minutes. Remove the saucepan from the heat and set aside.

Place the fish in 4 shallow bowls and pour equal amounts of broth and celery over each. Garnish with a sprinkling of lovage leaves and serve immediately.

PANTRY NOTE: This broth can be made well ahead of time, but don't add and cook the celery until you're ready to serve. Leftovers store well in the fridge for up to two days—reheat briefly before serving.

Tomato–Melon Soup with Poached Shrimp & Summer Herbs

MAKES 6 SERVINGS

This dish screams "summer!" Soup is an excellent make-ahead meal that will fool anyone into thinking you've slaved away in the kitchen for hours. The preparation here is beyond simple, the flavor outstanding, and the final soup bowl very elegant. The only "work" involves waiting—the tomatoes and melon must be pulverized and then strained overnight, resulting in a delicate broth. These fruit "waters" are then paired with a handful of fresh, tender herbs and a light helping of poached shrimp. Feel free to vary the fresh herbs in this soup—use what you have available, but steer clear of woody herbs like rosemary and sage.

3 pounds tomatoes, quartered
1 small honeydew melon (about 3 to 4 pounds)
4 cups water
½ lemon, cut into thin slices
1 tablespoon salt
Ice cubes, for water bath
12 large unpeeled raw shrimp
18 to 20 mixed cherry tomatoes, cut in half
3 tablespoons mixed tender fresh herbs

(such as cilantro, marjoram, dill, and tarragon)
Salt and pepper

Chop the quartered tomatoes in a food processor or blender until smooth. Set a fine-mesh strainer over a deep, large bowl and pour in the pulverized tomatoes. Let them strain overnight. You may have to empty the bowl once if it fills quickly and liquid comes in contact with the bottom of the strainer, preventing proper drainage.

Repeat this process with the honeydew melon, allowing it to strain into another bowl. (Alternatively, you can also line a large bowl with cheesecloth four layers thick and pour in the fruit purée. Gather the corners of the cheesecloth and tie them together, creating a large bag of fruit pulp, and hang over a large bowl to collect the "water.") Both the tomato and the honeydew will slowly release their juices—the longer you leave them hanging, the more you will collect. Do this at least overnight, or up to 24 hours.

The next day, discard the fruit solids. You may need to re-strain the tomato water if red pulp has collected on top of the clear water. Once you have two bowls of tinted but clear fruit water, measure out 3 cups of tomato water and 1½ cups of honeydew water and set aside. (Use any leftover water for drinking, or in another recipe.)

To prepare the shrimp, heat the 4 cups of water in a medium-sized saucepan over high heat. Add the lemon slices and salt, and bring to a boil. While the water is coming to a boil, prepare an ice water bath—add several ice cubes to a large bowl of cold water and set aside. Once the water in the saucepan is boiling, drop in the shrimp and cook until just cooked through, about 2 minutes. Do not overcook! Remove the shrimp after 2 minutes using a slotted spoon, and immediately put them in the ice water bath to halt cooking. Once they are cool enough to handle, peel and set aside.

While the shrimp are cooling, combine the tomato water with the honeydew water and stir until blended. To each of 6 shallow soup bowls add a handful of halved cherry tomatoes and three shrimp. Divide the fruit water evenly among the bowls. Sprinkle with equal portions of fresh herbs and season to taste with salt and pepper. Serve within an hour.

PANTRY NOTE: Fruit waters hold for several days in the fridge, covered, but maintain the best flavor when consumed within two days of straining.

Minestrone Verde with Tomato Leaf Broth

MAKES 4 TO 6 SERVINGS

Minestrone verde is a thin soup made of broth and lots of green vegetables and herbs. Here, the leaves of a tomato plant infuse the chicken stock, lending the broth a vibrant tomato note that is both distinct and heady. The secret to this recipe's success lies in not overcooking the vegetables. Adding them in the last fifteen minutes of cooking ensures they will keep their shape and not break down. If you like, garnish with a float

of olive oil and freshly grated Parmesan to add a rich sharpness. Or purée some green tomatoes and make juice out of them, spooning a small portion over the soup before serving—this works just like a squeeze from a lemon. You can add any vegetables you like or have in the pantry—corn, turnips or green beans work well. If you don't have tomato leaves, you can omit them.

Olive oil
½ onion, chopped, plus ½ cup finely diced onion
1 cup dried broad beans or other large bean, soaked overnight and drained
5 cups chicken or vegetable stock
1 tablespoon salt
10 tomato plant leaves
Salt and pepper
½ cup peeled and chopped carrot
½ cup chopped zucchini
½ cup roughly chopped flat-leaf Italian parsley (about ½ bunch)
½ cup roughly chopped fresh mint (leaves from about 7 sprigs)

Cover the bottom of a large stockpot with a layer of olive oil and set over medium heat. When the oil is hot, add the chopped onion, cooking and stirring until soft, about 5 to 7 minutes. Add the beans and stock and bring to a boil. Stir in the tablespoon of salt.

Reduce the heat to medium-low, and simmer until the beans are soft and can be mashed easily with the back of a spoon, about 2 to 4 hours. (Cooking time varies widely depending on the bean.) When the beans are soft, place the tomato leaves on top of the soup broth and let them steep for 20 minutes. Using a slotted spoon, remove the tomato leaves and season the broth with salt and pepper to taste.

Stir in the carrot and the finely diced onion. Cook for about 10 minutes, then add the zucchini and continue until just cooked, another 5 minutes or so. When the veggies are cooked through but still toothsome, add the parsley and mint. Serve immediately.

PANTRY NOTE: This soup holds well in the fridge, covered, up to two days. This soup freezes reasonably well, but tastes better reheated if you add a few handfuls of fresh herbs and vegetables.

Crushed Tomatoes

MAKES ABOUT 9 PINTS

This recipe makes a decent amount of sauce (meant for stocking your cupboards), but don't be intimidated by the quantity of tomatoes. The work is quick and the results rewarding. Tomatoes vary greatly in their acidity, so acid must be added to each jar to ensure a safe canned product. The final product is a batch of pure tomato flavor that's very flexible in its use. Use these tomatoes as a base for an Italian marinara sauce, as braising liquid for meats or legumes, or as an addition to soups and broths. A pinch of salt is optional. For a step-by-step guide to canning at home, check out Water-Bath Canning 101 in June: Berries.

9 to 10 tablespoons fresh lemon juice
15 pounds paste tomatoes, such as roma
Salt (optional)

Fill one large pot with water, leaving a 3-inch allowance on top, and bring to a boil for the tomatoes. Set up another large pot for your water bath canning. Put 2 large glass bowls and one small glass bowl on a counter within reach, along with a slotted spoon, a mesh strainer, and canning tongs. Line up 9 pint jars and add 1 tablespoon of lemon juice to each jar. Set aside.

Once the water is boiling, add as many tomatoes as can fit in the pot and cook, stirring occasionally, for 1 to 2 minutes—just long enough for the tomato skins to start splitting. Use a slotted spoon to remove the tomatoes, letting the water drain off completely. Place these blanched tomatoes in one of the large glass bowls and set aside to cool. Continue working in this fashion until all of the tomatoes have been blanched.

When the tomatoes are cool enough to handle, remove the skins while working over the bowl of blanched tomatoes. Working over the same bowl allows any residual juice and tomato flesh to collect without being wasted. Put the skins into the smaller bowl (juice will also pool in this bowl, and you'll add it back later) and then remove the seeds from the tomatoes. To remove the seeds, grasp the top (stem) end of a tomato and, using your other hand like a claw, dig into the flesh and scrape down, exposing the quadrants of the tomato and releasing the seeds. Once all of the seeds have been removed, put the "clean" tomato in the second large bowl and set aside. Continue working like this until all of the tomatoes are skinned and seeded.

Seeds, tomato water, and some tomato flesh will have collected in both of the processing bowls. Using a fine-mesh strainer to keep out the seeds and skins, pour any collected liquid into the bowl with the tomatoes. Using your hands, crush the tomatoes until the desired consistency is reached. (I typically crush tomatoes just until there are no overtly large pieces, which takes about 2 minutes to accomplish.)

Put the crushed tomatoes in a large pot and set the pot over medium-high heat. Stirring often, cook the tomatoes until just at a low boil. Once the tomatoes have started boiling, reduce the heat to medium and cook another 5 minutes. Add salt to taste, if using. Skim off and discard any thick foam that collects on the surface.

Fill the pint jars with the cooked tomatoes, leaving ¾ inch of headspace. Wipe the jar rims and seal the jars. Place the jarred tomatoes in a prepared water bath and process for 20 minutes. Remove the jars with tongs and let them cool on the counter overnight.

PANTRY NOTE: You can also follow this same process and leave the tomatoes uncrushed. You may also add herbs to the jars just before sealing, if you prefer to preserve a sauce to be used for marinara. Oregano, marjoram, and basil are the standards.

Tomato Jam

MAKES 1 CUP

My friend Lynda made this jam for me years ago and I thought about it for months afterward. As was typical, any time I got together with her for dinner I'd bring a notebook and ask her how she made things—after all these years, this tomato jam is still one of my favorite recipes. Tomatoes are dry-roasted in a pan to remove all of their liquid. From there, ginger, cinnamon, honey, and orange zest are added, making a savory yet sweet spread. This jam is amazing smeared on sandwiches or under the skin of a chicken before roasting it, but I prefer it on its own with some toasted crackers and a wedge of sharp cheddar cheese. You must use a large pan while cooking this jam so that the tomatoes dry out. To double the batch, use two pans and cook simultaneously.

> 2 pounds paste tomatoes (such as
>   roma), halved
> ¼ teaspoon salt
> 2 tablespoons honey
> 1 tablespoon sesame seeds, toasted
> 1 teaspoon orange zest
> 1 teaspoon grated fresh ginger

Set a large sauté pan over medium-low heat and add the tomatoes and salt. Stir occasionally, making sure the tomatoes do not stick (adjust the heat if they are cooking too quickly). The tomatoes will release water and break down slowly.

After 30 to 40 minutes, the tomatoes should be dry and condensed, their skins slightly sticking to the sauté pan. Remove from the heat and add the honey, sesame seeds, orange zest, and ginger, stirring until well combined. Serve immediately or store in a small jar in the fridge, covered, until ready to use.

PANTRY NOTE: This jam holds in the fridge for well over a week, but it's so delicious, I can't imagine you'll have any leftovers.

Perfect Tomato Salsa

MAKES 4 TO 5 CUPS

My friend Michelle makes the best salsa ever. She combines juicy, diced roma tomatoes with a handful of roasted peppers, a generous portion of fresh cilantro, and a bit of lime juice to create the perfect flavor balance. Everyone who eats this salsa raves. You would do well to double the batch and save some for midweek snacking. You can increase the heat of the salsa by adding more jalapeño peppers or including the seeds of the peppers (they store the heat).

2 Anaheim peppers
1 jalapeño pepper
1 poblano pepper
7 roma tomatoes
½ bunch fresh cilantro, finely chopped (about 1 cup)
Juice of 1 to 2 limes
Salt

Turn the broiler on high. Put the peppers on a sheet pan and set it on the rack directly below the broiler coils. Roast the peppers until completely black and charred, about 7 to 10 minutes, turning occasionally so all sides roast. After the peppers are roasted, remove them from the oven, put them in a deep bowl, and cover it with a large plate or piece of plastic wrap (this allows the peppers to steam and soften). Set aside until cool.

While the peppers are cooling, dice the tomatoes into small pieces and put the pulp, seeds, and juices in a large bowl. Add the cilantro, lime juice, and a pinch of salt, and stir to combine. Set aside.

Once the peppers are cool, remove the charred skin, along with the core and seeds. Dice the cleaned peppers into small pieces and add them to the tomatoes. Stir to combine well and taste for salt and lime juice, adding more if so inclined. Let the mixture macerate a bit longer, which develops flavors, or serve immediately.

PANTRY NOTE: This salsa is best after a few hours of maceration and holds well in the fridge, covered, for several days.

Green Tomato Salsa

MAKES ABOUT 2 PINTS

It is inevitable that anyone growing tomatoes at home will wind up with a bucketful of green tomatoes come fall. Outside of breading and

191

frying them (a traditional Southern technique), unripe green tomatoes can be used in salsas. This herb-laden salsa makes an amazing garnish for stewed black beans and can also be used as a dip for chips. Often I'll pour some in a small sauté pan and crack in an egg, effectively poaching the egg. It also makes a spicy and colorful stewing sauce for pork. Using the green tomato salsa as a braising liquid promises the meat will come out fork-tender, with a hint of heat from the poblano and jalapeño peppers. You can also use tomatillos in place of the green tomatoes.

> 2 poblano peppers
> 1 jalapeño pepper
> 1 medium red onion, outer skin peeled, sliced into rings
> 1 tablespoon olive oil
> 2½ pounds green tomatoes
> 2 cloves garlic, peeled
> ½ bunch fresh cilantro, chopped (about 1 cup)
> Juice of 1 to 2 limes
> 2 teaspoons salt

Preheat the oven to 450 degrees F.

Coat the poblano and jalapeño peppers and the onion rings with the olive oil and place on a sheet pan. Roast in the oven until charred and cooked through, about 20 minutes, turning occasionally. Transfer the roasted peppers and onions to a bowl, and cover to let steam and cool, about 20 minutes. Once they are cool enough to handle, remove the stems and seeds from the peppers. Peel off the skins. Roughly chop the peppers and onions, and set aside in a small bowl.

Meanwhile, cut the green tomatoes in half. Heat a heavy skillet over medium-high heat. When the skillet is hot, put a batch of the green tomatoes in the hot, dry skillet in a single layer, cut side down. Don't move them around in the skillet—let them sit and char, about 8 to 12 minutes. When they are fully charred, move the green tomatoes to a small bowl and cover them to let steam until soft. Put the garlic in the skillet and char in the same fashion. Continue charring the green tomatoes in batches as need be until all are cooked and softened through.

Put the peppers, onion, green tomatoes, garlic, cilantro, lime juice, and salt in the bowl of a blender. Blend on low speed until all the ingredients are just combined, or purée to a super-smooth salsa if you prefer. Serve immediately or store in the fridge until ready to serve.

PANTRY NOTE: This salsa will keep well in the fridge for about a week. The more lime juice you add, the longer it will keep, as the acid acts as a preservative.

Spicy Cucumber, Melon & Cilantro Gazpacho

MAKES 8 SERVINGS

Satisfying and refreshing, this soup is a superb and easy summer meal. Jalapeño adds a little heat, and the cilantro helps to cool your palate. Add more of both, if so inclined. This makes a huge batch—enough for a family dinner with leftovers—but works well if you prefer to halve it. You can substitute buttermilk for the yogurt and another spicy pepper for the jalapeño—try Anaheim.

> 1 ripe honeydew melon, seeded and removed from rind
> 3 to 4 cucumbers, peeled and seeded
> 1/2 cup plain yogurt (either whole or non-fat)
> 1/2 jalapeño, seeded and minced
> 1/2 cup fresh cilantro leaves
> 1/4 cup fresh lime juice
> Salt

Purée the honeydew flesh in a food processor until smooth. Line a large, deep bowl with cheesecloth, and pour in the purée. Gather up the ends and suspend the purée over the bowl, tying the cloth around a wooden spoon so that the juices can collect in the bowl below, at least 4 hours or overnight.

Measure out 4 cups of melon liquid and set aside.

Purée the cucumbers in the food processor until smooth. Add the yogurt, jalapeño, cilantro, lime juice, and honeydew juice, and purée until they're well combined and the cilantro is broken down into small bits. Add salt to taste and chill for at least 1 hour before serving.

PANTRY NOTE: This soup holds well in the fridge, covered, for three days.

Peach–Cardamom Smoothie

MAKES 1 SMOOTHIE

I make this smoothie nearly daily for breakfast. It offers a lean but nutritious start to the day and allows me to get out the door when I'm in a hurry. Using peach pie as inspiration, I purée one whole peach with fresh ginger and cardamom for a flavorful morning drink. Almond milk and almond butter add a nutty flavor and healthy fat—a great start to the day. I freeze peaches by the bushel and throw them in for an icy beverage, but feel free to use a fresh peach and a handful of ice for the perfect smoothie texture.

> 1 peach, halved and pitted
> 1 tablespoon fresh diced or grated ginger
> 1/2 teaspoon cardamom seeds
> 1 tablespoon almond butter
> 1 cup almond milk

In the bowl of a blender, whiz all ingredients on the lowest setting for 1 minute. After the peaches (and ice, if using) are fairly broken up, turn the blender on a higher speed (purée or liquefy) for 1 to 2 minutes more. Drink immediately.

PANTRY NOTE: If you have any leftover smoothie, it will hold in the fridge for one day. Add more ingredients the next morning and mix as above. I often leave the blender in the fridge and simply add more fruit and milk the next morning.

FALL

AUTUMN IS A GENTLE SEASON, one that comes on slowly in the shape of cooler temperatures and glowing light. There's an undeniable chill in the morning air, but it burns off by noon, so it is easy to forget, if only briefly, the seasons are changing. Autumn officially begins on September 21st, and since the first few weeks straddle summer, it's a chore to consider the new produce that the cooler temperatures bring when there are still tomatoes fighting to ripen on the vine. And while it's time to start shifting gears and buckling down for another long, cool season that turns to winter on December 21st, it is also a time to be mindful of the last bounty you can snatch from your local farms. Autumn is the perfect time to take advantage of produce that won't hold over through winter. Tender lettuces, sweet baby carrots, earthy eggplants, and water-crisp radishes are all pulled from the ground by October at the latest, so it's your last opportunity to gorge. These late-harvested vegetables might appear beat up from the cooler weather or nicked and bruised, but this shouldn't affect the flavor much, so don't be put off.

Once those summer goods are no longer available, it's time to embrace all that autumn has to offer, and, thankfully, fall vegetables and fruits have the ability to hang on until you're ready. Brussels sprouts are usually available from September through November, while long-lasting kale is ready to harvest from September through December (or even during winter in some climates). Broccoli and celery are also exceptional fall finds that really introduce the season. Autumn is also a time when there is much to harvest from the wild. Mushrooms abound, for anyone with nose enough to forage safely, and in urban confines rosehips sweeten up after the first frost. The season also ushers in bushels of fruits—apple varieties, crisp pears, and quinces are relied upon to supply our universal sweet tooth with a healthy sugar. While we tend to think of these fruits as dessert-ready eats, there are plenty of savory dishes to be made of the lot as well. Apples offer a refreshing palate cleanser to winter stews—try a few slivers as garnish. Pears are lovely in savory salads, particularly when partnered with toasted nuts. Braised alongside a lamb shank, quince offers a sweet-tart bite that is perfectly complementary.

Interestingly, most vegetables available in fall and winter are planted in summer, so it is also a quieter time on farms and in gardens, the pause after the late summer bustle of September when much of the work is done. By now, farmers have likely transitioned their fields from fast-growing, warm-temperature crops to cover crops or slow-growing, overwintering varieties. In autumn, it's a race to get every last inch of earth planted before frost sets in, but work done now is for produce to eat next spring. Such is the cyclical way of growing food. The pantry, much like the fields, is ever changing.

PEPPERS

PEPPER SEASON HITS, AND IT is always an exciting time in the kitchen. There's nothing more appealing than basket after basket of multihued peppers at the farmers market. I can't get enough and keep going back for more but, I admit, it's a love-hate relationship. Sometimes I love them (pickled peppers on steak—yum!), and sometimes I can't stand them (raw bell peppers on a crudité platter—yuck). But their draw is undeniable, and they go well with so many other foods, I'd be a fool to disregard them.

Peppers come in all shapes and sizes. Bell peppers—large, sweet globes found the world over and the most popular pepper used in almost all cuisines—can be grown in a rainbow of colors: red, yellow, orange, green, purple, brown, and white. These sweet and mild peppers lack the chemical capsaicin, which produces the heat found in hot peppers (like jalapeños, habañeros, and cayennes). Their flavor varies in pungency along with their color—green and other dark bell peppers are particularly acidic and savory, whereas the red and lighter-hued bell peppers are sweeter. Bell peppers can be eaten raw or cooked, as they have thick flesh and add a substantial consistency to many dishes, but not all sweet peppers are large and round. The Jimmy Nardello sweet Italian pepper—ubiquitous at farmers markets—is a long, thin-skinned sweet pepper that can be used in sautés. The thin skin gives this pepper a nice, chewy texture. Substitute a long, sweet pepper for any cooked bell pepper recipe in this book for a slightly novel result.

Hot peppers are an entirely different fruit—and so varied in shape, size, color, and heat value that it's impossible to cover them all here. Most hot chiles have a traditional sweet pepper flavor when first tasted but then immediately turn hot. I recommend seeking the expertise of farmers or produce specialists; use their guidance for the level of heat you desire. Jalapeño, poblano, Anaheim, and serrano peppers are widely available in most grocery stores across the country, making them accessible to all. Farmers markets will offer a more diverse range of chile peppers in an evolving lineup—new varieties are created almost annually. All hot peppers will range in their heat level on any given day—some jalapeños will barely burn your lips, whereas others will quickly overpower your palate. It is rumored that one of every twenty of the recently popular Hatch peppers virtually explode with nearly over-whelming spiciness. There is no surefire way to guarantee a specific level of heat, so start with small amounts in recipes whenever they are called for and add as you prefer.

Poblanos are mildly spiced with only gentle heat. Their flesh is dark, and they lend an almost smoky flavor to dishes, especially when roasted. I use poblanos anytime I want a strong, roasted pepper. Anaheim peppers tend to be in the mild-medium heat range and are hued lime green. Their flesh is sweeter than that of poblanos, and they work well when a raw hot pepper is needed. Jalapeños and serranos will definitely add some kick to a recipe, with serranos being the hotter of the two. Serranos are sold in both green and red flesh. The green serranos are underripe and will have slightly less heat than their red counterparts. Habañeros and cayenne peppers are also found commercially and are on the super-hot end of the spectrum.

Peppers can be used interchangeably for most any dish, but I make notes in recipes when I've found a pepper that works particularly well. In any recipe, use whichever variety you prefer or are currently growing, as long as you stick to sweets when sweets are called for and hots when hots are preferred. Any pepper variety in that flavor profile will work beautifully, so whether you're shopping at the grocery store or at farmers markets, you have options galore.

Peppers can be eaten raw, but I am partial to cooked peppers because this preparation mellows their astringent bite and turns them velvety, as in rich and smooth Baked Peppers, Tomatoes & Eggs. Pickling peppers also reduces their bitter bite, and I always add a touch of sugar to the brine to sweeten them up. Try a sweet-hot pepper with grilled meat or a sweet bell pepper with seafood (as in Chilled Squid with Pickled Peppers & Summer Herbs). Although I prefer not to eat peppers raw, sampling them in their original state is a great way to gauge flavor, sweetness, and level of heat, and to determine your personal tastes.

SEPTEMBER RECIPES

Peppers

Baked Peppers, Tomatoes & Eggs
Turkish Stuffed Peppers
Chilled Squid with Pickled Peppers & Summer Herbs
Sesame–Pepper Relish
Cauliflower Steaks with Peppers & Anchovy
Seafood Bake with Fennel Bulb & Peppers
Chickpeas with Peppers & Fennel Seed
Mango–Habañero Hot Sauce
Whole Pickled Peppers

Seasonal Extras

Concord Grape & Lavender Shrub
Burnt Cauliflower with Whipped Feta
Roasted Eggplant with Miso Butter

Baked Peppers, Tomatoes & Eggs

MAKES 4 SERVINGS

My perfect breakfast pairs a mass of vegetables with baked or fried eggs. Here, tomatoes and bell peppers stew with a generous mix of spices, drawing on the traditional North African dish *shakshuka*. A raw egg is cracked into the stewlike mixture and poached until just done. The goal is for the yolk to break and bleed into the peppers. You can bake this dish in individual ramekins or crack four eggs into a large sauté pan, as described in this recipe, and cook them all together to serve a crowd.

> 1 tablespoon olive oil
> ½ medium onion, cut into thin slices
>   (about 1 cup)
> Pinch of salt
> 1 red bell pepper, cut into thin slices
>   (about 1¼ cups)
> 1 tablespoon chopped fresh rosemary
>   or sage
> 1 cup tomato sauce
> 1 teaspoon red chile flakes
> 4 eggs
> Yogurt, for garnish

In a large sauté pan, set the olive oil over medium-high heat. When the oil is heated, add the onions and pinch of salt. Cook and stir the onions until just soft, about 5 minutes. Add the bell peppers and fresh herbs, and cook and stir until the peppers are just soft, about 10 minutes more. Reduce the heat to low and add the tomato sauce and red chile flakes. Cook until the vegetables are soft and the mixture is thick and sauce-like, about 15 minutes.

Make four small spaces in the vegetable mixture and carefully crack a whole egg into each. Cover and cook until the whites are just set and the yolks are still runny. Portion into 4 small bowls, garnish with yogurt, if desired, and serve immediately.

PANTRY NOTE: Leftover stewed bell peppers can be used as a poaching mixture for more eggs, a thin chicken breast, or small turkey meatballs—get creative. If the mixture is too thick, add a bit of water, broth, or tomato juice to thin it out before using again. This bell pepper-tomato mixture will keep in the fridge, covered, for up to three days.

Turkish Stuffed Peppers

MAKES 6 SERVINGS

Several years ago, my Turkish bombshell friend, Aliye, taught me how to make this dish. To me, Turkish cuisine is modest—ingredients are roughly chopped and baked or sautéed with spices to make a satisfying meal. Although the recipes may be uncomplicated, the final dishes are nothing short of complex: toasted spices and big flavors brighten the plate. Here, bell peppers are stuffed with savory rice and herbs before baking into a velvety dish that can be served straight out of the oven or made in advance—a solid vegetarian dish for a crowd.

1 cup cooked wild rice

1/4 cup pine nuts, toasted

1/4 cup finely chopped dried fruit (apricots, raisins, or currants)

1/2 cup chopped fresh mint

2 green onions, chopped (about 1/4 cup)

1/4 teaspoon ground cinnamon

1/4 teaspoon freshly ground nutmeg

1/2 teaspoon smoked paprika

1/4 teaspoon salt

1/2 teaspoon sugar

3 green or purple bell peppers, cut in half, ribs and seeds removed

2 tablespoons butter, cut into 6 equal chunks

1 cup water

1/4 cup olive oil

Juice of 1/2 lemon

2 teaspoons honey or agave syrup

3 cloves garlic, peeled and smashed

Preheat the oven to 375 degrees F.

In a large bowl, mix together the wild rice, pine nuts, dried fruit, mint, green onions, all of the spices, the salt, and the sugar. Place the bell pepper halves cut side up in a medium-sized baking dish. Fill each pepper half with a few spoonfuls of the wild rice-spice mixture, pressing down to fill completely. Top each pepper with a chunk of butter. Pour the water, olive oil, lemon juice, and honey or agave syrup into the baking dish around the peppers, and add the garlic to the broth. Put the baking dish in the oven and cook until the bell pepper halves are soft and beginning to char along the edges, about 35 to 45 minutes.

Remove the baking dish from the oven and let the stuffed peppers cool slightly before serving. Discard the steaming broth or spoon a bit over each bell pepper half before serving, to moisten the rice mixture.

PANTRY NOTE: Extra wild rice stuffing can be used as a side dish on its own or used to stuff any other veg you have around—zucchinis, tomatoes, or mushroom caps work great. Leftover stuffed peppers can be stored in the fridge and eaten within three days.

Chilled Squid with Pickled Peppers & Summer Herbs

MAKES 4 SERVINGS

This dish reminds me of a meal I ate in Croatia, along the coast where my cousins live. It draws on the fresh flavors of olives and parsley, and pairs both with a few slivers of pickled peppers. Little squids (aka calamari) can be intimidating for home cooks, but they are fast-cooking and actually quite easy to work with. Most fishmongers sell squid already cleaned, so you need worry only about the timing. Cooked too long, squids go rubbery and are hard to chew. Cooked briefly, they are supple and lend a fabulous texture and flavor to this simple summer salad. This salad is also a great packed meal—make it ahead of time and bring it camping or on a picnic. Use any olives you prefer, or a mix of greens and blacks, but don't scrimp on the olive oil. You want a nice grassy-tasting olive oil for this recipe, as with most salads.

4 medium Yukon Gold potatoes, peeled
   and cut into quarters
1 green bell pepper, cut into thin strips
   (about 1¼ cups)
1 red serrano pepper, cut into thin strips
1-inch piece fresh ginger, cut into thin
   slices
1 cup rice wine vinegar
½ cup sugar
1 pound cleaned squid, patted dry
¼ cup olive oil for frying, plus 3 tablespoons for salad
½ teaspoon salt
¼ teaspoon pepper
3 cloves garlic, smashed and minced
1 teaspoon red chile flakes
2 cups chopped fresh parsley (mint,
   cilantro, or basil also work well)
1 cup whole olives (green, black, or
   mixed)

Set water to boil in a medium-sized saucepan. Add the potatoes and boil them until cooked through, about 30 to 35 minutes. Drain the potatoes and set aside to cool in a large bowl.

Put the bell pepper, serrano pepper, and ginger in a medium-sized bowl and set aside. In a small saucepan, heat the vinegar and sugar until boiling; stir until all the sugar has dissolved. Pour this over the peppers and set them aside to pickle while they cool.

To prepare the squid, cut the body portion into 1-inch rings. To cook the squid, heat ¼ cup of the olive oil over high heat in a large sauté pan. You want the oil to be rippling and very hot. Drop in the squid and sprinkle it with salt, pepper, garlic, and red chile flakes. Stirring constantly, cook the squid until just cooked through, about 1 minute. The squid may splatter and pop when it hits the heat, so be careful and wear an apron! Do not overcook the squid—it is ready quickly, when just opaque. You may have to cook the squid in batches if the saucepan is too full.

Remove the squid from the sauté pan, using a slotted spoon, and add it to the cooled potatoes. Add the parsley and olives to the squid and potatoes. Drain the pickled peppers from the brine, reserving 3 tablespoons of the brine and discarding the ginger. Add the peppers and reserved brine to the squid-potato-parsley-olive salad. Add the remaining olive oil and fold gently to combine all ingredients well—be careful not to break down the potatoes. Serve immediately.

PANTRY NOTE: This salad holds well in the fridge, covered, for one day. Any longer and the squid loses its fresh flavor.

Sesame–Pepper Relish

MAKES 4 TO 6 SERVINGS

This is a rustic spin on *ajvar*—a red pepper relish commonly used in Croatia. Eggplant, red onions, and bell peppers are cut into even pieces and roasted in the oven until just charred, after which they are tossed with apple cider vinegar and sugar, resulting in a flavorful late-summer relish. Here, in the final minutes of roasting, a hearty dose of sesame seeds is added, lending a nutty flavor and a pleasing crunch to the mix. Use this relish as a garnish for sandwiches, as a bruschetta topping, or as a tasty addition to cheese and crackers. For a sweeter version, add ½ cup of soaked raisins. For a more savory adaptation, add toasted chopped nuts—pine nuts and almonds work well.

1 large eggplant (about 1 pound), cut into small cubes (about 3 cups)

1 large red onion, cut into small cubes (about 2 cups)

3 red, yellow, or orange bell peppers, cut into small cubes (about 3½ cups)

6 tablespoons olive oil

1 teaspoon salt

½ teaspoon pepper

¼ cup sesame seeds

1 tablespoon sugar

2 tablespoons apple cider vinegar

Preheat the oven to 450 degrees F.

Put the eggplant, red onion, and bell peppers on a large sheet pan and toss them with the olive oil, salt, and pepper until well coated. Distribute evenly across the sheet pan so everything is in a single layer—you may need to use 2 sheet pans.

Put the sheet pan in the oven and roast until all the vegetables are just beginning to char, about 40 minutes. Sprinkle on the sesame seeds and continue roasting until the seeds are golden, another 10 minutes more.

Remove the sheet pan from the oven and put the vegetable mixture in a large bowl. Sprinkle the sugar over the top and add the apple cider vinegar, stirring to combine well and until the sugar has dissolved. Transfer to a small bowl and serve when ready.

PANTRY NOTE: Because this relish has some vinegar in it, it will hold in the fridge, covered, for several days.

Cauliflower Steaks with Peppers & Anchovy

MAKES 4 SERVINGS

I am a one-trick pony where roasting vegetables is concerned. Pretty much any veg roasted on high heat with some oil, salt, and pepper results in an awesome and healthy side dish. For this cauliflower "steak," instead of breaking the head into small florets, the entire cauliflower head is sliced vertically—stem and all. This results in a thick and large piece of cauliflower that can be charred in a hot pan on the stovetop. This crispy "steak" is then paired with a salad of roasted bell peppers, salty anchovy, toasted hazelnuts, and fresh parsley for a light but satisfying meal. You can play with the flavor profile in this dish by using a mix of bell peppers—green, red, yellow, or orange—in the salad.

2½ cups thinly sliced bell peppers

3 tablespoons olive oil, divided (plus more if needed)

8 toasted hazelnuts, crushed

1 anchovy fillet, mashed

¼ cup chopped fresh parsley

1 teaspoon apple cider vinegar

1 teaspoon honey or agave syrup

1 tablespoon butter (plus more if needed)

1 large head cauliflower, cut vertically into 1½-inch-thick "steaks"

3 cloves garlic, smashed

¼ teaspoon salt

Preheat the broiler on high. Place the bell peppers on a sheet pan and toss with 1 tablespoon of the olive oil. Put the sheet pan directly under the broiler until the bell peppers are charring and roasted, turning them occasionally, about 8 minutes total. Remove from the oven and scrape the peppers and oil into a medium-sized bowl.

Preheat the oven to 450 degrees F.

While the peppers are still hot, add the hazelnuts, anchovy, parsley, vinegar, and honey or agave syrup. Stir well until all of the ingredients are evenly coated and the anchovy is mixed in. Set aside.

In large cast-iron or heavy-bottomed pan, set the remaining 2 tablespoons of olive oil and the butter over medium-high heat. When the butter is foaming, add two cauliflower steaks and the smashed garlic and cook, without moving, until the bottoms are deep golden brown, about 2 minutes. Using a large spatula, carefully flip the steaks so as not to break off any florets and continue cooking until the second side is deep brown, about another 2 minutes. Stir the garlic constantly so it does not burn. Place the browned cauliflower steaks and garlic on a sheet pan and set aside.

Continue cooking the remaining cauliflower steaks in the same fashion, adding more olive oil or butter to the pan as needed. When all the steaks are browned, sprinkle them with salt and put the sheet pan in the oven until

A WORD OF CAUTION

Use care when working with hot peppers. The capsaicin will stay under your fingernails and on your skin for hours, and a casual wipe of your eye can do harm. As a general rule, always wear gloves when working with hot peppers. If your hands come into prolonged contact with the seeds and become irritated, soaking them in a bowl of cold milk or buttermilk may help ease the pain. It's best to work in well-ventilated areas, whether you're cooking garden-fresh hot peppers or grinding dried chiles—turn the stove fan on and open a window for some fresh air. This helps flush airborne irritants.

the cauliflower steaks are just cooked through, about another 4 minutes.

Remove the sheet pan from the oven and place the individual steaks on plates. Distribute equal amounts of pepper-anchovy-parsley salad and garlic over all. Serve immediately while still hot.

PANTRY NOTE: Leftover cauliflower steaks can be held in the fridge, along with the pepper-anchovy-parsley salad, for up to three days. The dish tastes great at room temperature.

Seafood Bake with Fennel Bulb & Peppers

MAKES 4 SERVINGS

I love this recipe for both its effortlessness and promised piquancy. An abundant portion of seafood is paired with a savory, thick pepper and tomato sauce spiked with preserved lemon, an ingredient found often in north African dishes. Caramelized onions and fennel bulb add yet another layer of flavor. Cut the fish into approximately the same size as the scallops and shrimp so they cook simultaneously.

This elegant but quick-cooking meal is sure to impress. Healthy, light, and simple on its own, it can also be served with a bowl of pasta, the sauce spooned over the top. Feel free to cook with the freshest picks from the market—any type of fish and shellfish works well. For a super-savory sauce, toss a ham hock, a few slices of prosciutto, or even bacon ends into the onions while they cook. If you don't have preserved lemon, add a spoonful of freshly grated lemon zest instead.

2 tablespoons olive oil
1 tablespoon butter
½ large onion, cut into thin half-moon slices (about 1 cup)
½ teaspoon salt
1 medium fennel bulb, fronds removed and cut into thin, half-moon slices (about 1 cup)
1¼ cups red bell pepper slices
2 tablespoons finely chopped pre-served lemon
2 cups tomato sauce
Salt and pepper
4 ounces firm fish fillet (salmon, halibut, or snapper), cut into 1-inch cubes
4 sea scallops
4 large shrimp, whole (shells on)

In a large sauté pan, heat the olive oil and butter over medium-high heat. When the butter has melted, add the onions and salt, cooking and stirring until just softened, about 5 minutes. Add the fennel and continue cooking until very soft and starting to brown lightly, another 10 minutes more. Add the bell pepper and the preserved lemon, cooking and stirring until the peppers are just beginning to soften and the fennel and onions are starting to stick to the bottom of the sauté pan. Pour in the tomato sauce and cover. Reduce the heat to a simmer and cook another 20 minutes. Check for seasoning and add salt and pepper to taste.

HOMEMADE RED CHILE FLAKES

On occasion I come across a new hot pepper variety at the farmers market with excellent flavor and the perfect amount of heat. I like to purchase a few extra and dry them at home by hanging them or using a drying rack. You've likely seen this process before, if you've left small peppers indoors and on the countertop too long—green peppers change to red and eventually dehydrate and wrinkle. It is that moisture-free fruit that is crumbled into pieces to produce what we think of as a spice—red chile flakes. The flakes are always red (even green peppers eventually turn red with age).

To dehydrate, choose smaller red peppers. Selecting a variety of peppers with varying heat will give you flakes with the most depth of flavor. Trim off the stems and cut the peppers down the middle. Do not discard the seeds—this is where most of the heat comes from. Lay the peppers on a parchment-lined baking sheet and bake overnight on the lowest temperature setting your oven has. It helps to turn the peppers once or twice during drying. Conversely, you can sun-dry peppers on drying racks—just make sure to cover them with a thin linen cloth or cheesecloth so no bugs get in them.

To turn the dried chiles into flakes, you can either hand crush them or pulverize them in a food processor or blender. If using your hands, be sure to wear gloves so the oils do not irritate your skin. If using a machine to pulverize, be sure to do so in a well-ventilated area, so the dust does not assault your eyes or olfactory system. Store the chile flakes in an airtight container (canning jars work great), in a cool, dark spice cupboard.

Preheat the oven to 400 degrees F.

Remove the sauté pan from the stovetop. Pour half of the vegetable and tomato sauce mixture into a large, shallow baking dish. Distribute the fish, scallops, and shrimp evenly throughout the baking dish, tucking them in between the onions, bell peppers, and fennel. Top with the remaining sauce and bake in the oven until the seafood is just cooked through, about 8 minutes—fish, scallops, and shrimp should be just about opaque. They will continue cooking after you pull them from the oven, so do not overcook.

Remove the baking dish from the oven and serve immediately, dishing out equal portions among the plates.

TOP Seared Salmon with Minted Peach &
Tomato Salad, p. 183
BOTTOM Tomato Jam, p. 190

OPPOSITE
TOP Turkish Stuffed Peppers, p. 202
BOTTOM Chilled Squid with Pickled Peppers
& Summer Herbs, p. 203

Mango–Habañero Hot Sauce

TOP Chickpeas with Peppers & Fennel Seed, p. 209
BOTTOM Whole Pickled Peppers, p. 210
(Photo by Kenneth Dundas)

TOP Biscuts & Kale Gravy,
p. 220
BOTTOM Kale Bubble &
Squeak, p. 221

TOP LEFT Raw Kale Salad with Apples & Cheddar, p. 223
TOP RIGHT Lemon–Kale Gratin, p. 225
BOTTOM Asian Noodles with Kale & Avocado–Miso Dressing, p. 226

Steps for making
Kale-Stuffed Turkey
Breast with Prosciutto,
p. 228

TOP Cumin Flatbread
with Beet Purée, p. 236
BOTTOM Beet-Pickled
Eggs, p. 237

Beet & Sage Ravioli, p. 241

PANTRY NOTE: Cooked seafood holds for about one day in the fridge, covered.

Chickpeas with Peppers & Fennel Seed

MAKES 4 SERVINGS

Homemade stock and perfectly cooked beans are always a winning combination. I prefer to rehydrate and cook dried chickpeas for this soup—they hold together better and have a creamier texture than canned beans. Here, chickpeas are slowly cooked in broth, while pepper slices are added in the last few minutes so they are just cooked through and retain some bite. A dollop of plain yogurt adds some fat to this lean soup, and whole fennel seeds provide some crunch. All together, it's a delicious bite! You can vary the peppers in this recipe—red, yellow, and gold bells are the sweetest and best tasting.

2 tablespoons olive oil

½ large onion, diced (about 1 cup)

1 teaspoon salt

1 cup dried chickpeas, soaked overnight and drained

4 cups chicken or vegetable stock

1 yellow or red bell pepper or poblano, cut into thin slices (about 1¼ cups)

Salt and pepper

½ cup chopped fresh mint

1 tablespoon fennel seeds

4 tablespoons plain nonfat yogurt

In a large stockpot, heat the olive oil on medium-high. Once the oil is warmed, add the onions and salt, and cook and stir until the onions are soft and just cooked through, about 10 minutes. Add the chickpeas and the stock and bring to a boil. Reduce the heat to simmer and cover. Heat until the chickpeas are completely cooked through and creamy, about 1 hour. Next, add the bell peppers or poblanos to the stockpot and cover, cooking another 15 minutes. Season with salt and pepper to taste.

Remove the soup from the heat and ladle into 4 individual bowls. Sprinkle each serving with a generous portion of mint, a pinch of fennel seeds, and 1 tablespoon of nonfat yogurt. Serve immediately.

PANTRY NOTE: Leftover soup holds in the fridge, covered, for up to three days. Refresh any leftovers with a spoonful of yogurt and a sprinkle of fennel seeds.

Mango–Habañero Hot Sauce

MAKES ABOUT 4 HALF PINTS

A few years back, a friend kept requesting hot sauce at meals in my apartment, but I never had the Tabasco commonly found in many kitchens. I experimented all summer and finally came up with this combination of sweet mango and deathly hot habañeros—a golden hot sauce that packs intense heat and flavor into even the smallest dash. Be careful when working with habañeros, and be sure your kitchen is well ventilated. These will burn your eyes, wreak havoc on your olfactory system, and sting your fingers for days. I *always* open doors and a window, and you must *wear rubber gloves* when handling raw habañeros—they are lethal. For a step-by-step guide to canning at home, check out Water-Bath Canning 101 in June: Berries.

> 1 large carrot, peeled and cut into 1-inch
> pieces
> 1 small onion, quartered
> 7 small orange habañeros, seeds and
> membranes removed
> 2 ripe mangoes, peeled and pit
> removed (about 2 cups)
> 2 teaspoons salt
> 1 teaspoon light brown sugar
> 1 cup distilled white vinegar
> ½ cup water

Put the carrot pieces in the bowl of a food processor and grind them until finely shredded. Add the onions and process until finely chopped. Add the habañeros to the food processor and finely chop. Next, add the mangoes, salt, and brown sugar, and blend until completely pureéd, about 2 minutes.

Transfer the pureé to a medium-sized saucepan and stir in the white vinegar and water. Set the mixture over medium-high heat and bring to a low boil. Reduce to a simmer and cook, about 25 minutes, stirring often. Remove the hot sauce from the stovetop and pour into clean canning jars, leaving ½ inch of headspace. (If you would like a perfectly smooth consistency,

strain the hot sauce first.) Process in a water bath for 10 minutes.

PANTRY NOTE: Store this hot sauce in a cool, dark cupboard for up to one year. You may also put it in small bottles with lids and store in the fridge for up to two months. These make exceptional hostess gifts for the holidays, so double the batch if you know you'll give some away. For most households, one half pint of this hot sauce is plenty for the year.

Whole Pickled Peppers

MAKES 4 PINTS

Peter Piper picked a peck of pickled peppers, and now so can you! Whole pickled peppers add vibrancy and bite to winter roasts, stews, and salads. I use them up quickly, as they work well with so many dishes. These pickled peppers are among the sweet-hot variety. You can amp up the heat or tone down the sweetness to your liking without affecting the safety of the preserve. For a step-by-step guide to canning at home, check out Water-Bath Canning 101 in June: Berries.

> 8 whole allspice berries
> 8 whole cloves
> 4 cloves garlic, peeled
> 4 pounds small mixed peppers, with 2
> small slashes made in each
> 2½ cups rice wine vinegar or white
> wine vinegar
> ¾ cup sugar

Place 2 allspice berries, 2 whole cloves, and 1 clove of garlic in each of 4 clean pint jars. Trim the stem tips off the peppers, leaving a bit of stem intact, and pack the peppers in the jars as densely as possible (the peppers will deflate when the hot brine is poured over them). Set aside.

In a medium-sized saucepan, bring to a boil the vinegar and sugar, stirring until all the sugar has dissolved. Pour this hot brine over the peppers in each pint jar, filling them halfway. Tap the jars on the countertop to compress the peppers and refill if needed, making sure to leave ½ inch of headspace. Cover the pint jars and process in a water bath for 10 minutes.

PANTRY NOTE: Store these pickled peppers in a cool, dark cupboard for up to one year. Once the jars are opened, store them in the fridge, where they will keep for about three weeks. Use pickled peppers in panzanella, as a garnish for roasted meats, or as a topping on scrambled eggs.

Concord Grape & Lavender Shrub

MAKES 1 QUART

Concord grapes are perfect for juicing—no surprise, given their popularity as a flavor in kids' snacks and juices. Sadly, this bold, grape-y flavor falls to the wayside as we age, and it is more difficult to come by in grown-up drinks. This drinking vinegar, or shrub, is an excellent throwback to grape juice, but largely appeals to adults. Grape juice is paired with sweetened vinegar and laced with a subtle floral aromatic. Concord grapes are only available for a short time in early fall, so get them when you see them, lest you miss the season.

> 3½ pounds Concord grapes, rinsed
> 4 to 6 cups hot water
> ½ to 1 cup sugar
> ¾ cup apple cider vinegar
> ¼ cup lavender blossoms

Place the grapes (stems and all) into a large stock pot and cover with the hot water. Set the pot over medium heat and bring to a low simmer. Reduce heat to low and cook, stirring occasionally, until the grape skins are split and soft, about 20 to 30 minutes. Set a mesh strainer over a large, deep bowl and drain the liquid from the grapes. Press down on the grape solids to release any residual juice, then discard the solids.

Measure the juice, which should be about 1 quart. Stir in ½ cup of the sugar until it's dissolved, then taste. Add the remaining ½ cup if you'd like a sweeter juice. Add the apple cider vinegar and stir to combine. Add the lavender blossoms to the warm juice and steep until the desired potency is reached, anywhere from 15 to 45 minutes. Strain out the leaves before storing the juice. Pour the juice into a large glass jar.

Cover with the lid and put the juice jar in the refrigerator to cool completely before serving. To serve, fill a tumbler with ice and add 2 or 3 large spoonfuls of grape shrub. Fill with sparkling water and serve.

PANTRY NOTE: Grape shrub will hold in the fridge, covered, for several months. Use as a beverage, or add a spoonful to a bowl of crushed berries or sliced peaches for an easy and interesting fruit topping for ice cream, cheesecake, or yogurt.

Burnt Cauliflower with Whipped Feta

MAKES 4 SERVINGS

Deeply roasted cauliflower is surprisingly delicious and very easy to make. Small florets cook up in a thick swath of oil at very high heat, burning the edges irresistibly. Paired with a smear of creamy whipped feta, this cauliflower dish makes a quick-cooking and delicious side for summer meals.

1½ cups crumbled feta cheese

½ cup plain yogurt

2 tablespoons olive oil

Zest from 1 lemon

¼ cup fresh basil leaves

1 medium head cauliflower (1½ to 2 pounds)

3 tablespoons olive oil

½ teaspoon salt

¼ teaspoon pepper

Lemon wedges, for drizzling

Put the feta and yogurt in the bowl of a food processor and pulse to combine, about 15 to 20 pulses. Add the olive oil and lemon zest and blend to combine, about 1 minute. Add the basil and pulse until just mixed in and coarse, about 10 times. Remove the whipped feta from the food processor and set aside.

Preheat the oven to 450 degrees F.

To prep the cauliflower, cut the head into quarters. Lay each quarter on its side and cut out the stem and core. Chop the stem and core into 3-inch pieces and place them on a large baking sheet. Break up the cauliflower head into florets, using your knife or hands, and add them to the baking sheet. Drizzle the cauliflower with olive oil and sprinkle with the salt and pepper. Using your hands, toss to combine, making sure all the cauliflower is glossy and coated. Spread the cauliflower evenly across the pan, making sure no pieces overlap.

Put the baking sheet in the oven and cook until the edges are charred and crispy, turning and redistributing once or twice, for about 15 to 17 minutes total. Remove the pan from the oven and let it cool slightly.

To serve, dollop the whipped feta onto a serving platter and, using the back of a spoon, spread it out into a thin layer. Pile the cauliflower over this evenly, and squeeze some lemon juice over it before serving.

PANTRY NOTE: Leftover roasted cauliflower holds in the fridge, covered, for up to three days. Extra whipped feta can be used as a dip for crudité or toasted pita.

GROWING PEPPERS INDOORS, ALL WINTER LONG

Most crop gardeners tend to think of pepper plants as annuals (those that must be planted annually in order to produce a fruit or green to harvest), but they are actually perennial. A few years ago, I cooked a private wintertime dinner for my friend Hillary. To my amazement, she proudly displayed her potted winter jalapeño plant—in full fruit production and showing vigor. Until then, I had no idea that peppers were perennial plants. Hillary had received the container plant as a gift and just left it alone through autumn, as the leaves were quite green. As the temperatures dropped, she took the plant inside, set it in a sunny windowsill, and kept it watered. Come January, she had several jalapeño peppers—quite the surprise!

To extend your own pepper season—and make the most of your budget—try taking your pepper plants inside this year when temps begin to dip regularly into the mid to low sixties. Here's how:

Dig Up the Plant from the Garden. Make sure to use a wide girth—about 8 to 10 inches out from the stem of the plant—and shake the soil from the roots. In a large pot (remember, the larger the pot, the more room you give the plant to grow and produce), replant the pepper plant in potting soil. I do this by holding the plant's stem in one hand, its roots centered in the pot and dangling, and then filling it with soil using a large scoop or hand trowel. This assures the roots are facing down and you're not packing the soil too densely.

Prune the Pepper Plant. To encourage growth, prune the plant by trimming any minor branches and most of the leaves. Leave intact those branches that are showing buds—particularly those that grow directly off the main stem. Keep the pepper plant indoors, where it is warm, and place it in a sunny window.

Pollinate Any Blooms. Because the pepper plants are indoors, you'll need to hand-pollinate any blooms. Do this by tapping the stems with your hands to shake out pollen, or turn it into a science experiment for kids and have them pollinate flowers precisely by using a cotton swab.

Actively Harvest. The pepper plant should produce fruit throughout winter. Remember to actively harvest, which encourages new growth, and prune any weak branches as the plant grows. Next summer, when daytime temperatures are consistently warm (in the seventies), you can transplant the pepper plant outdoors for another season of garden growing and harvesting.

Roasted Eggplant with Miso Butter

MAKES 4 TO 6 SERVINGS

Eggplant is one of my all-time favorite vegetables—as kids we demanded that my mom fry them up in super-thin slices. "That's too fat," my sister and I whined (mostly her, of course). For a healthier version, I now prefer roasted eggplant. Tossed in olive oil and roasted in a hot oven, eggplant turns supple with a concentrated flavor. A small amount of miso butter melts into the eggplant, hot out of the oven—a concept I borrowed from Momofuku in New York City.

> 2 large globe eggplants or 5 small Thai
>   eggplants, sliced thin
> 1 teaspoon salt
> 3 tablespoons olive oil
> 1 tablespoon butter, softened
> 2 tablespoons white miso

Preheat the oven to 450 degrees F.

In a large bowl, toss the eggplant slices in the salt, coating the eggplant well. Set aside and let sit for at least 30 minutes.

Remove the eggplant from the bowl, squeeze out any excess moisture, and pat it dry. Place the eggplant in a single layer on a sheet pan and cover it with olive oil, using your hands to turn and coat the pieces well.

Put the sheet pan in the oven and roast, turning once, until the flesh is soft and translucent and the skin is blackened and charred, about 35 to 45 minutes.

While the eggplant is roasting, make the miso butter. In a small bowl, combine the butter and miso and, using the back of a spoon, mash them together until well combined. Set aside until ready to use.

Remove the eggplant from the oven and dot the slices with miso butter. Toss and stir them gently, until the butter has melted and all the pieces are well coated and glossy. Serve immediately.

PANTRY NOTE: Leftover eggplant can be held in the fridge, covered, for up to three days. It can be chopped and used as a relish on sandwiches or as a garnish for steamed or roasted fish.

OCTOBER

KALE

AS A CHILD, I LOVED hearty greens. I actually enjoyed eating my vegetables—anything green was good by me. But my mom only made her delicious braised greens when her parents were visiting. My grandfather, an immigrant from Yugoslavia, had a penchant for vegetable dishes. Mom would braise them down, along with bacon or a ham hock, into a soft heap. My grandmother still eats her greens this way.

Kale is one of the garden's more nutritiously decadent greens, and I'm always thrilled to eat something so nutrient-dense. Kale's deep green color means it is full of chlorophyll, which translates to fiber and power nutrients such as iron and calcium. Each leaf is packed with vitamins A and C, among other beneficial compounds. Nutritionally speaking, kale can't be beat!

Understanding the seasonality of kale requires a bit of gardening education. As a cold-tolerant crop, kale has two main growing seasons—spring and autumn. Spring kale at the farmers market is the product of the previous year's summer sowing. Kale is planted in late summer and puts on minimal growth before winter sets in. Winter is a dormant time for all plants, but in the late days of the season, as days start getting longer, kale (and other overwintering crops) begins to put on leafy growth. This late-winter surge in garden activity provides something green during a season that is otherwise quite barren. The sweet bite of late-winter kale (frost actually sweetens up the leaves) provides a welcome relief from the dulling flavor of root vegetables.

In contrast, the kale available in fall is often the product of sowing in spring or early summer. These strong leaves are the last of the summer crop, their vigor pronounced in every robust bite of thick, sun-fortified goodness—perfect for a fall meal, as they have a distinct textural difference from summer's light, airy lettuce or watery chard leaves. Kale announces the seasonal change in temperature and weather, providing a hearty density to autumn's favorite dishes. Baked gratins, like my cook-off-winning Lemon–Kale Gratin, and rich soups, like Kale & Turnip Soup with Pork Shoulder, are fall friendly—a bit too rich for the warmer days of summer. Cooler weather demands heartier meals, and kale is the perfect ingredient.

There are several kale varieties to choose from. Frilly or curly kales provide a robust texture and demand a serious jaw workout if eaten raw. The very popular Lacinato kale—also known as dino, dinosaur, or Tuscan kale—is a long, narrow, flat-leafed variety available at farmers markets and in grocery stores across the country. This variety has thinner leaves, so it is more tender. Also popular is a variety of Russian kale—this flat, oakleaf variety is often found in purple or red, which can add beautiful color to a raw dish, although it cooks down to green.

Whichever kale you choose, you can use these varieties interchangeably in the recipes in this book. Here, I offer kale in as many ways as there are to prepare it: roasted, braised, blanched, and eaten raw. Kale's versatility shows in this diversity of recipes—it suits everything from Asian to Southern cuisine and can be used in place of collard or mustard greens. Work your way through these recipes and keep going! For breakfast, braise a batch of greens and stems, then toss in an egg to poach. Add a single leaf of kale to your next fruit smoothie to boost up the nutrition factor. For dinner, finely chop a few leaves and fold them into your mince—hiding a little kale in your hamburger is a great way to increase its healthful benefits for the whole family.

OCTOBER RECIPES

Kale
⁓

Biscuits & Kale Gravy
Kale Bubble & Squeak
Kale & Turnip Soup with Pork Shoulder
Raw Kale Salad with Apples & Cheddar
Lemon–Kale Gratin
Asian Noodles with Kale & Avocado–Miso Dressing
Kale-Stuffed Turkey Breast with Prosciutto

Seasonal Extras
⁓

Apple Parfait with Anise Biscotti Crumbs
Caramel–Vanilla Seckel Pears

Biscuits & Kale Gravy

MAKES 8 TO 12 BISCUITS

For most of us, the allure of biscuits and gravy for brunch is undeniable. The dish on its own seems overly indulgent, but a healthy dose of kale lightens the meal a bit. Here, traditional biscuits are coupled with a kale-based breakfast gravy that has all the lusciousness of a thick sausage gravy but fewer calories. No longer a gut bomb in the morning, these biscuits and gravy are still plenty hearty and flavorful. For non-meat eaters, omit the sausage from this dish or add a vegetarian substitute. Choose whole-fat or low-fat milk but do not use nonfat milk—the gravy will not thicken up.

BISCUITS
1¾ cups all-purpose flour, plus more for rolling out the dough
2½ teaspoons baking powder
1 teaspoon salt
7 tablespoons cold butter, cut into small pieces
¾ cup buttermilk or milk

KALE GRAVY
1 tablespoon olive oil
1 cup ground turkey sausage
5 tablespoons butter
4 tablespoons all-purpose flour
4 cups milk, warmed
5 kale leaves, stems removed and discarded, finely chopped
Salt and pepper

Preheat the oven to 350 degrees F.

To make the biscuits, put the flour, baking powder, and salt in the bowl of a food processor and pulse a few times to blend well. Add the cold butter pieces, then pulse again until the dough resembles coarse crumbs, about 30 times if you're counting. Add the buttermilk or milk and pulse another 20 to 30 times, until the dough is just starting to come together. The dough will blend itself into two or three large portions.

Flour a clean work surface liberally, dusting your hands to prevent sticking, and turn out the dough. Using your palms, push together the dough, forming one big mass. Form a rectangular block of dough by pushing in the opposite sides of the dough. Do not knead.

Flour a rolling pin and roll out the dough to about a ¾-inch thickness, working from the center. Using a 4-inch biscuit cutter (or a straight-edged juice glass), cut out as many biscuits as possible and put them on a parchment-lined baking sheet. Place the biscuits close to each other, with their sides just touching; this helps them to bake tall. Leftover dough can be pushed into another rectangle, rolled out again, and cut into more biscuits. Put the baking sheet in the oven and bake until the biscuits are just starting to brown, about 15 to 20 minutes. Remove from the oven and set aside.

While the biscuits are baking, prepare the kale gravy. Set a large sauté pan over medium-high heat, add the olive oil, and crumble in the turkey sausage. Cook the sausage, breaking up any clumps, until golden brown, about 8 to 10 minutes. Using a slotted spoon, remove the sausage from the sauté pan and set aside. Wipe the pan clean with a paper towel.

Return the sauté pan to the stovetop and reduce the heat to medium. Add the butter and cook until just melted. Sprinkle in the flour and, using the back of a fork, stir until the flour is smooth and paste-like. Continue cooking, stirring continuously, until the butter-flour mixture is just beginning to brown, about 5 to 7 minutes.

Add the milk to the pan, just a few tablespoons at first, stirring or whisking continuously, until all of the milk has been added. Pour slowly and keep stirring so the gravy remains smooth and the milk is incorporated, about 2 minutes. Add the kale to the pan and stir in the cooked sausage. Cook another 10 minutes, until the gravy is thick and the kale is just cooked through. Remove the gravy from the heat and season to taste with salt and pepper. To serve, put a biscuit or two on each plate and pour on a few ladlefuls of kale gravy.

PANTRY NOTE: Leftover gravy holds well in the fridge for two days or can be frozen for up to one month.

Kale Bubble & Squeak

MAKES 4 SERVINGS

This traditional British breakfast is made from leftover roast dinner fixings—mashed potatoes and vegetables—mashed together and fried into savory cakes. My mom made a version of this when I was a kid, using whatever veg she had handy. Here, I've updated the recipe to make a quick meal. Potatoes are boiled with onion and kale, drained, and blended, then hand-shaped into patties. These fried cakes, packed with kale, make for a robust weekend breakfast. This flexible recipe can include any combination of vegetable; try cabbage or Brussels sprout leftovers. For a more decadent kale cake, fold some cooked bacon into the patties and fry the cakes in the leftover bacon fat.

1 pound boiling potatoes, peeled
½ large onion, finely chopped (about
    1½ cups)
2½ cups chopped kale
1 teaspoon salt
½ teaspoon pepper
2 to 3 tablespoons olive oil, for frying

Put the potatoes in a large pot and cover them with water. Set over high heat and bring to a boil. Once the water is boiling, reduce the heat to medium and add the onions. Cook the onions for 5 minutes, then add the kale. Continue cooking another 15 minutes or so, until the potatoes are soft.

Drain the potato-onion-kale mixture, and put it in the bowl of a food processor. Add the salt and pepper, and pulse until well combined, about 30 seconds. Set aside to cool.

While the mixture is cooling, set a large sauté pan over medium heat and add 2 tablespoons of the olive oil (enough to cover the bottom of the pan; add more if needed). When the oil is warm, use your hands to shape the potato-onion-kale mixture into small cakes, about 4 inches wide, and carefully place them in the olive oil. Cook the cakes until golden brown, about 4 minutes on each side. Remove the cakes from the sauté pan and serve immediately.

PANTRY NOTE: Leftover kale cakes hold in the fridge for about two days, or they can be frozen for up to one month.

Kale & Turnip Soup with Pork Shoulder

MAKES 6 SERVINGS

Although this simple soup is easy to make and the final dish is humble, it does not disappoint on flavor. My friend Rusty made it for me over summer, using the last of the spring kale, and I've been thinking about it ever since. Here, pork shoulder is braised in a bath of water with only salt and pepper to add flavor. Once it's cooked through, the pork is removed and shredded, added back in only at the final stage before serving. The strained broth is returned to the pot and used to braise turnips, carrots, and kale—a quintessential autumnal trio. You can change the ingredients of this dish depending on what you have on hand—potatoes, celery, collards, and rutabaga are all in season in fall and will taste great. The only real trick is timing their cooking so you don't overcook and mush out the veg.

2 to 3 pounds pork shoulder
1 tablespoon salt
1 teaspoon pepper
3 tablespoons olive oil
6 small turnips, cut into quarters or eighths
4 carrots, peeled and sliced in half lengthwise, then cut into 3-inch-long batons
4 kale leaves, stems removed and discarded, chopped into 3-inch pieces

Season the pork shoulder with the salt and pepper, covering all sides, and set it aside on the counter to cure for at least 30 minutes. In a large Dutch oven, set the olive oil over medium-high heat. When the oil is hot, place the pork shoulder in the Dutch oven and brown all sides until golden and crispy, about 3 minutes per side. Add water to the Dutch oven, just covering the pork shoulder, and cover. Allow to boil and then reduce the heat to medium-low, cooking until the pork is tender and comes apart easily, about 3 hours.

Remove the pork from the broth and set aside on a plate to cool slightly before handling. Strain the pork broth and wipe out the Dutch oven to remove any left-behind bits. Return the broth to the Dutch oven and set over medium heat. Add the turnips and carrots and cover, cooking for 5 minutes. Add the kale and cover, cooking until all the vegetables are al dente, another 10 minutes. Do not overcook the veggies! You want them with a little bite so they bring texture to the soup.

While the vegetables are cooking, trim any fatty bits from the pork shoulder and then, using two forks, shred the pork into bite-sized pieces. After the vegetables are just cooked, put the pork pieces back in the soup broth and serve immediately.

PANTRY NOTE: Leftover soup can be stored in the fridge, covered, for up to four days, or it can be frozen and used within a month.

Raw Kale Salad with Apples & Cheddar

MAKES 4 SERVINGS

I have had the great fortune of growing up in the restaurant industry; many of my friends are chefs, cooks, pastry chefs, and bartenders. Melissa Nyffeler, owner of one of my very favorite Seattle restaurants, Dinette, made this salad for a friend's dinner one night, and I was compelled to pick her brain for a quick recipe. I enjoyed it so much that I lived off of it for an entire winter. Raw kale is massaged with salt, which helps tenderize the leaves, and then tossed with intense apple vinaigrette made from cooked-down apple cider and caraway. Like me, you'll flip over this salad—it is a perfect fall dish. You can vary the cheese to alter the flavor— blue cheese works nicely. Try this salad with sliced pears or dried fruits.

1 bunch kale, stems removed and dis-
    carded, cut into 1-inch ribbons

1 teaspoon salt
1 cup apple cider
2 tablespoons apple cider vinegar
3 tablespoons olive oil
2 teaspoons caraway seeds, crushed
¼ cup green pumpkin seeds
1 apple, peeled and cored, cut into
    small, thin matchsticks
4 ounces sharp cheddar cheese, diced

Put the kale and salt in a large bowl. Using your hands, massage the salt into the kale, tossing it as you go and pulling the salt up from the bottom of the bowl to mash it into the leaves. When all of the kale has been coated and the leaves start to break down and release water, about 2 minutes, set the bowl aside.

In a medium-sized saucepan, set the apple cider over high heat. Bring to a boil and reduce the heat, keeping at a low simmer until the apple cider is reduced to ¼ cup, about 15 to 20 minutes.

Remove the apple cider from the heat and pour it over the wilted kale. Add the vinegar, olive oil, caraway seeds, and green pumpkin seeds, and toss to combine thoroughly. Add the apples and cheddar to the bowl and toss to combine. Serve immediately.

PANTRY NOTE: This salad holds well overnight in the fridge.

HOW TO GROW KALE

Kale is a prolific plant to add to any vegetable garden. As soon as the plant puts out some leaves, harvest commences and will last several months if you time it right. Kale is a member of the Brassicaceae family of plants, along with broccoli, cabbages, Brussels sprouts, and rutabagas. This family of veg thrives in cooler weather and can overwinter in mild climates, making it a great plant for a fall or early spring sowing.

Autumnal plantings produce a few green leaves as we head into winter but really kick up production in the new year, depending on where you live. Kale is meant to be eaten in the late winter and early spring (northern states that have deep freezes may not be able to overwinter kale), when there is little else to choose from in terms of green vegetables. Kale leaves soften up and sweeten after a frost, so any fall-planted spring kale offers a sweeter leaf than spring-planted kale, which produces strong, thick leaves that soak up sun as the plant grows. Because of this, kale eaten in late spring and early summer is often more chewy and dense. The leaves are more tender when used imme-diately after harvest, which is all the more reason for growing kale at home.

Kale plants grow tall and have thick, sturdy stalks. I've seen some crest over two feet! Because of this height, they demand space in the garden, and it's best to plan ahead to make sure there is room in your plots. Leave at least eighteen inches between plants. In prepared beds and raised gardens, plant kale in a criss-cross pattern, diagonally from one another. This saves space in small beds and allows you to sow more plants.

Kale comes in a handful of varieties and falls into two visual camps—either flat-leaf or curly. The curly kales have crimped and frilled leaves, and they offer an incompa-rable texture to meals. Their ruffled form makes them an excellent addition to soups and braises. Common varieties are all clumped under the name of simply curly kale, or they are sold as Starbor. In the flat-leaf varieties, Red or White Russian kale is a popular seed and start, putting out an oakleaf-shaped leaf with purple hues. These kales are harvested off one short main stalk and grow out into a bushy shape. Lacinato kale (aka dino, dinosaur, Tuscan, or Italian kale) grows off a tall stalk. This leaf, looking similar to a palm tree leaf, is wildly popular in grocery stores and farmers markets. It's excellent for salads or wraps, as the flat leaves are easy to cut and work with.

As for feeding kale plants, note that they are greedy crops. Fall sowings need a few weeks in the ground before fertilizing, which will help toughen them up for a cold winter. Mix in a light, nitrogen-dense fertilizer when you first plant your starts or seed and then do so again, lightly, in early fall. Plan to side dress (that is, to place nutrients on the soil surrounding the plants) each plant heavily in spring—right about late February or early March. This should increase late winter production, and the plant will grow many leaves and get taller throughout spring.

To harvest kale plants, simply cut individual leaves as needed. Try working from the bottom up, though the small leaves are most succulent and mild. The plants will inevitably flower in late spring or early summer, and these flowering stalks can be cut and harvested and eaten as you would broccoli rabe or purple sprouting broccoli.

Kale plants are best left for field sowing and don't do well in pots. They require a wide bed, in addition to deep soil, to grow tall and stretch their roots wide and long. This thick and webbed root system allows kale to produce prolifically. Growing kale in a pot inhibits this process, though it's not impossible. If you're dead set on growing kale at home and have only a patio, choose the biggest pot you can find and don't overcrowd it with other plants! Be sure to feed the start when you first plant it, and mulch the soil or wrap the entire pot over winter to help protect the plant from temperature changes.

Lemon–Kale Gratin

MAKES 4 TO 6 SERVINGS

My friend Jody, owner of a cupcake shop in Seattle, hosts a day-after-Thanksgiving football match every year. At one of her parties she had a casserole cook-off, where we all made and then voted on the best casserole; the winner got a gift certificate for her cupcakes. Instead of going traditional Americana for my entry, I came up with this creamy kale dish—and won! Spiked with a lavish amount of lemon zest to lift the flavor, this gratin makes for a fresh-tasting side dish to balance out fall's heavier dishes. You may use whole milk or reduced-fat milk, but do not use nonfat milk as the sauce will not thicken well.

5 tablespoons butter
¼ cup all-purpose flour
4 cups milk, warmed
2 teaspoons freshly grated nutmeg
2 tablespoons lemon zest
2 teaspoons salt
¼ teaspoon pepper
1 bunch kale, stems removed and discarded, chopped into 1-inch-wide ribbons
½ cup bread crumbs
½ cup freshly grated Parmesan
2 tablespoons olive oil

Preheat the oven to 375 degrees F.

In a medium saucepan, melt the butter over medium heat. Add the flour and, using a whisk, stir until smooth. Cook, stirring constantly, until the flour-butter mixture turns a light golden color, about 6 to 7 minutes, and is paste-like and thick.

Slowly add the milk to the saucepan, 1 cup at a time, whisking continuously until very smooth. Bring the sauce to a low boil and cook, stirring constantly, about 10 minutes. Remove the sauce from the heat and add the nutmeg, lemon zest, salt, and pepper. Taste the sauce and adjust the flavor as you wish—the lemony note should be strong. Put the kale in a large bowl and pour the sauce over it. Stir to combine well. Pour the mixture into a shallow gratin pan and set aside.

In a small bowl, combine the bread crumbs and the Parmesan. Sprinkle evenly over the top of the gratin. Drizzle the olive oil over the top of the gratin and put the pan in the oven. Cook until the bread crumbs are golden brown and the kale is tender, about 30 to 40 minutes. Remove the gratin from the oven and let it cool a bit before serving.

PANTRY NOTE: Leftover gratin holds well in the fridge, covered, for two or three days.

Asian Noodles with Kale & Avocado–Miso Dressing

MAKES 4 SERVINGS

A cold noodle salad makes for a perfect weekday lunch. Throw it together in the evening and pack it for work the next day. It also holds well in the fridge, so this is a perfect recipe to double for plan-ahead meals. For this salad, a handful of buckwheat noodles are tossed with a spoonful of toasted sesame seeds and blanched kale. An avocado-miso vinaigrette coats these healthful ingredients, and a scoop of green pumpkin seeds adds crunch. You can find miso in the refrigerated sections of most grocery stores. For a spicier bowl, substitute half the amount of miso paste with chile sauce. You could also replace the miso with nut butter.

> One 12-ounce package of buckwheat
>   soba noodles
> 4 kale leaves, stems removed and dis-
>   carded, chopped into thin ribbons
> 1 avocado
> 2 tablespoons lime juice
> ¼ cup white miso paste
> 2 tablespoons olive oil
> 2 teaspoons sesame oil
> 2 teaspoons honey
> ¾ to 1 cup water
> ½ cup green pumpkin seeds
> 2 tablespoons toasted sesame seeds

Bring a large pot of water to a boil. Once the water is boiling, drop in the soba noodles and

COOKING WITH KALE STEMS

Many recipes in this book call for kale with the stems removed and discarded. I have found that most people prefer the softer version of kale in their recipes and are put off by salads and sautés peppered with chewy stems. In truth, though, I love eating kale stems, and they are easy to prepare—and better in your stomach than in the compost, as far as I'm concerned!

For sautés, kale stems can simply be added to the mix. Remove the stems as suggested, then cut and discard the last hard inch or so. Chop thick stems into small dice and add them to your sauté pan before you add the leaves. Stems are rife with fibrous threads and need more cooking time to break down properly. Adding them first ensures they will cook through. You're aiming for a stem piece that easily melts in your mouth and provides a velvety texture to dishes. Soup dishes are treated the same way. Add chopped kale stems first and allow them to cook for 5 minutes before continuing with the recipe instructions.

There are a few instances where kale stems are best left out, however. They will not break down properly in raw salads, so unless you want to really chew and work at it, keep them out of your salad bowl.

You may save kale stems, rolled in a single layer of linen (or paper towel) in your refrigerator's crisper, where they will keep for three to five days. After you have a big bunch, chop them into small pieces and use in sautés like Biscuits & Kale Gravy or in soups like Kale & Turnip Soup with Pork Shoulder.

cook according to package instructions. When the noodles are cooked completely, drain and run cold water over them, which helps prevent sticking. Set aside.

Bring another large pot of water to a boil. Once the water is boiling, drop in the kale, stirring occasionally. Cook until the kale is bright green and soft, about 2 to 3 minutes. Strain the kale and set aside to cool. When the kale is cool enough to handle, squeeze any excess water from the leaves and set aside.

While the kale is cooling, make the vinaigrette. Put the avocado, lime juice, miso paste, olive oil, sesame oil, and honey in the bowl of a blender. Add half of the water and blend on medium speed until the vinaigrette is creamy, about 3 minutes. You may have to push the ingredients down if they come up and cling to the sides of the blender. Taste for flavor and consistency. If you'd like a thinner vinaigrette, add more of the water and blend to combine.

In a large bowl, toss together the soba noodles, kale, and several spoonfuls of the vinaigrette. Add more vinaigrette if desired. To serve, sprinkle a handful of green pumpkin seeds and some toasted sesame seeds over the noodles.

PANTRY NOTE: This salad holds well in the fridge, covered, for two to three days.

Kale-Stuffed Turkey Breast with Prosciutto

MAKES 4 TO 6 SERVINGS

I love roasted poultry, and Thanksgiving is my favorite holiday, so I came up with this rolled turkey breast to satisfy my midyear cravings. Turkey breast is an affordable, lean protein that is too often overlooked as a main ingredient. Here, a simple stuffing made of blanched kale and Parmesan is rolled up with prosciutto inside of the turkey. The roll is baked, wrapped in cheesecloth, and soaked in butter, which keeps the meat moist and allows for a deep brown roast—a flavorful and gorgeous dish to present. You can vary the cheese in the stuffing—chèvre or ricotta lend creaminess to an otherwise lean dish. This recipe works with butterflied meat of all kinds—pork, lamb, or chicken. Try them all!

8 kale leaves, stems removed and discarded, chopped

½ cup freshly grated Parmesan
2 cloves garlic, minced
2 tablespoons olive oil
1 split turkey breast, skin removed and reserved, breast butterflied
3 or 4 slices prosciutto or ham
4 tablespoons butter, room temperature

Bring a large pot of water to a boil. Once the water is boiling, drop in the kale, stirring occasionally, until the kale is just cooked through, about 4 to 5 minutes. Taste a small leaf and make sure the kale is easy to chew. Cook longer if need be. (Kale leaves differ in their toughness, so cooking times will vary.) Strain the kale and set aside to cool. When the kale is cool enough to handle, squeeze any excess water from the kale, then set aside. You should have about 2 cups of kale.

Preheat the oven to 450 degrees F.

Place the cooled kale in a medium-sized bowl, along with the Parmesan, garlic, and olive oil. Stir to combine well and set aside. Lay the butterflied turkey breast between two sheets of parchment paper and pound out (using a kitchen mallet or rolling pin) to a uniform thickness, about ½-inch thick. Remove the top layer of parchment and line the inside of the turkey breast with the prosciutto (or ham). Don't worry if you don't cover every inch of turkey—just a few slices are perfect. Pour the kale mixture over the prosciutto and spread evenly across the turkey breast, leaving about a 1-inch allowance at the edges.

To form the roll, start on one end and, lifting the parchment to help you, roll the turkey breast lengthwise. Don't worry if some stuffing falls out the sides—you can stuff it back in once the roll is formed. End with the seam side facing down and push any stuffing that fell out back into the middle of the roll. Place the reserved turkey skin over the top of the roll.

Set a 4-layer-thick portion of cheesecloth (about 10 inches wide and 12 inches long) next to the turkey roll. Moving in the same direction as before, roll the turkey onto the cheesecloth. Tuck the edges under the turkey. Secure the cheesecloth with kitchen twine, tying it as you would a ribbon around a package. Rub the softened butter all over the cheesecloth, coating all sides. Place the turkey roll in a small but deep baking dish and put it in the oven.

Roast for 20 minutes, then, without opening the oven door, reduce the heat to 350 degrees F. Continue cooking until the internal temperature of the roll is 155 degrees F, about 1 hour and 15 minutes. Begin checking the temperature after 1 hour, and periodically baste the turkey.

Remove the baking dish from the oven and let the turkey roll cool slightly, about 10 minutes. Cut the twine and remove the cheesecloth. To serve, place the stuffed turkey breast on a serving platter and slice into 1-inch-thick portions.

PANTRY NOTE: Leftover turkey can be stored in the fridge, covered, for up to three days. Slice thin pieces for sandwich filling, or reheat, covered and in a shallow pool of chicken stock to keep the turkey from drying out.

Apple Parfait with Anise Biscotti Crumbs

MAKES 6 SERVINGS

This is the perfect throw-together dessert, because it's easy to make all of the components ahead of time and have them lying in wait. I made this dessert at a local-food charity dinner years ago, pulling from whatever garden scraps I could find at the time—only one apple tree and some sad-looking anise plants. But it worked. This parfait is layered with soft whipped cream, crushed biscotti cookies, and poached caramel apples—the epitome of an autumn dessert. You can substitute almond oil for the anise oil, but cut the measurement to ½ teaspoon.

BISCOTTI
2 eggs
Zest from ½ lemon, plus 1 tablespoon
    lemon juice
½ tablespoon vanilla extract
1 tablespoon anise oil
1½ cups barley, emmer, or whole wheat
    flour
½ cup brown sugar
½ teaspoon baking soda
1 small pinch salt
1 tablespoon whole anise seed

POACHED APPLES
2 cups water
1 cup sugar
½ vanilla bean pod, split
3 apples, peeled, cored, and diced
1 cup heavy cream

Preheat the oven to 350 degrees F.

Using an electric mixer, combine the eggs, lemon zest and juice, vanilla extract, and anise oil. On medium speed, add the flour, brown sugar, baking soda, salt, and anise seed until everything is well incorporated. Let the dough stand for 5 or 10 minutes.

Line a baking sheet with parchment paper or grease it with a bit of olive oil. Using a dough scraper or a large rubber spatula, scoop out half of the batter and drop it onto the baking sheet. Shape the dough into a rectangular mound, about 3 to 4 inches wide. Do the same with the remaining dough, using a second baking sheet if needed.

Bake on the center rack for 30 minutes. Remove the baking sheet from the oven and reduce the oven temperature to 300 degrees F. Slice the dough into pieces of biscotti about ¼-inch to ¾-inch thick, depending on your preference. Place the biscotti pieces cut side down on the baking sheet and bake for another 10 to 15 minutes, until golden brown. Remove from the oven and allow to cool. In the bowl of a food processor or blender, or using a meat mallet and some elbow grease, crush all of the biscotti cookies into small crumbs.

While the biscotti are baking, poach the apples. Put the water, sugar, and vanilla bean pod in a small saucepan and set over medium-high heat. Bring to a low simmer and stir to dissolve the sugar. Once the sugar has dissolved, add the diced apple and turn the heat to medium-low.

Poach until the apples are easily pierced and translucent in color, 20 to 30 minutes. Remove from the heat and set them in a bowl in the fridge to cool completely.

Once the apples are cool, drain them from the syrup. (You can reserve the leftover syrup for later use.) Put the heavy cream in a large bowl and whip to soft peaks. To assemble the parfait, gather 6 short, wide glasses or parfait cups. In the bottom of 1 glass, put 1 large spoonful of whipped cream, about ½- to 1-inch deep. Over the whipped cream, add 1 heaping spoonful of poached apple, followed by another big spoonful of biscotti crumbs. Make another layer of whipped cream, apples, and biscotti crumbs. Garnish the tops with 3 or 4 pieces of apple and continue assembling the rest of the parfaits in the same manner. Serve immediately.

PANTRY NOTE: You may store extra diced apples in their syrup, in a jar or container in the fridge for up to three weeks. Leftover biscotti crumbs can be placed in an airtight plastic bag and held in the freezer for up to four weeks. Leftover apple syrup can be reduced down and used as pancake syrup, or drizzled over other desserts or tarts.

Caramel–Vanilla Seckel Pears

MAKES 6 TO 8 PINTS

Seckel pears are diminutive pears with olive green to muddy-colored skin and a firm texture. Their tiny proportion makes them impossible to resist, as well as the perfect size for a light dessert after a rich fall meal. They come into season toward the end of September, so be on the lookout, as the season is short. If you can't find Seckel pears, it's okay to use any firm pear for this recipe—try small-sized D'Anjous split in half, instead. Use wide-mouth pint jars for this recipe—this size fits pear halves the best. When you finally crack open the jars, the pears' exteriors will have taken on a gorgeous caramel hue, whereas the centers stay cream-colored. I like to serve the pears whole with a dollop of cream or mascarpone and a drizzle of caramel-vanilla syrup. For a step-by-step guide to canning at home, check out Water-Bath Canning 101 in June: Berries.

2¼ cups sugar

5½ cups warm water

1 vanilla bean pod, cut in half lengthwise,
    beans scraped out and reserved

5 pounds Seckel pears

Place the sugar in a large, completely dry saucepan, and shake the pan gently to level it out. Set the saucepan over medium to medium-high heat. Without touching it, leave the sugar to melt and brown; do not stir it. The sugar will begin to brown at the edges. Once the sugar is starting to brown, gently swirl the pan slightly, making sure to keep the sugar level so it does not coat the sides of the saucepan. The sugar will caramelize and become dark brown and amber at the edges. Stir the melted sugar slowly, incorporating the dry sugar, until all of the sugar is melted and amber colored. Wearing an oven mitt and long sleeves (molten sugar will spit and pop), carefully pour in the warm water while simultaneously stirring. Any sugar crystals that form will melt in the water. Add the vanilla bean pod pieces and the reserved seeds, and set the pot aside.

Peel the pears, leaving a small piece of each stem intact. Immediately drop the pears into the syrup. When all of the pears have been added, return the pot to medium-high heat. Bring the syrup to a low boil and then reduce the heat to medium. Cook the pears for 10 to 15 minutes, until they are just beginning to soften but are not cooked all the way through. The exterior flesh will be easily pierced, but the core of the pear will be firm.

Remove the pears from the heat and, using a soup spoon, immediately put them into clean jars, lowering each pear gently to prevent bruising. You will have about 6 pint jars full. Pack the jars as densely as you're able, leaving 1 inch of space. Once the jars are packed, pour the caramel-vanilla syrup over the pears so they are submerged, leaving ½ inch of headspace in the jars. Cut the vanilla pod into even pieces and add a small piece of it to each jar. Gently tap the jars on the counter to release any air bubbles. Wipe the rims and seal the jars. Place them in a prepared water bath and process for 20 minutes. Remove the jars with tongs and let them cool on the counter overnight.

PANTRY NOTE: Jars should be stored in a cool, dark location for up to a year. After opening, hold pears in the fridge and use within a few weeks.

NOVEMBER

BEETS

IT TOOK ME A LONG time to warm up to beets. We never had them as kids, and I don't even remember my dad planting them in our big vegetable garden out back. I started eating them a little over ten years ago when I worked in a restaurant, and my manager used to make me have them for staff family meal. "They're so good for you!" he insisted. I would stand in the back of the restaurant, eating my dinner and choking them down. As an urban farmer, I grew beets in the first garden I ever planted, so naturally I had to eat them. Then it became a matter of not letting something go to waste. Over time, I acclimated and eventually started to enjoy eating beets, though it obviously took a while!

Beets are the quintessential root vegetable, growing just underground in damn near every season. They stand up to summer heat and withstand near-freezing temperatures in winter, making them a year-round staple. We tend to think of beets as winter produce, but I think that has more to do with their strong earthy flavor than anything else. Beets are quick growing and can be harvested as tiny baby beets or left to grow into globe-like spheres. As with most vegetables, the younger beets are more tender and sweeter, while older, fatter beets can be woody and taste more of dirt or even turn bitter.

As an added bonus to this nutrient-packed root—you can eat the beet tops. Beets are in the same plant family as chard, and so the leaves can be treated the same way. Trim them off and use them in sautés. On small beets, you can roast the entire plant and serve it whole, which makes for a lovely display on the plate.

While most everyone is familiar with dark red beets, this sugary root vegetable does grow in several shades ranging from deep purple to magenta. Golden beets are also available, though mostly in the warmer months. These beet variations can mostly be used interchangeably in recipes, although golden beets should be chosen for broths or soups, as their color won't leach out. Beets also come in a striped version, with red and white spherical rings stemming from the center out.

These beets are sold as "striped" beets—Chioggia (a variety), Candy Cane, and likely more—but they're all the same vegetable, so don't bother too much over the name.

It is good to know, before you get cooking, that red beets will bleed. Once cut open or peeled, red beets dye anything they touch—cutting boards, hands, shirts, countertops—so be careful when working with them. This ability to strongly color something has benefits too, like the gorgeous Beet-Pickled Eggs.

Beets can be eaten raw or cooked. They also make for an excellent pickling ingredient, as their texture remains firm even after cooking. Beets also work well in relishes and chutneys, like Caraway-Beet Chutney, due to their inherent fortitude and structure—they add a crisp bite to a meal. Eaten raw, beets are best cut into small dice or matchsticks, or shaved thin on a mandoline. (Cutting paper-thin slices of beet with a knife will prove difficult.) Beets are also an excellent item for juicing, providing both a high level of vitamins and a sweet note to fresh-pressed juices.

Beets are equally delicious when cooked, which brings out their sweetness even more. Boiling, steaming, or roasting are the easiest ways to cook whole beets, and I prefer to leave them al dente. Roasted beets take time but result in a velvety texture that is easy to mash, while also keeping all nutrients intact. Beets may be boiled, the water saved and used for dye on any crafty DIY projects, and boiling is the preferred method for very large beets. Try to choose beets of about the same size, so the cooking time is consistent for all.

Beets should be well scrubbed before cooking or storing—a vegetable brush comes in handy for this. If using the whole beet, the tops can be submerged in water to loosen any soil that clings there. Once they're clean, store the beets in the fridge, wrapped between layers of linen or paper towel, which will protect them from dehydrating. Beets will last for several weeks in the crisper if stored properly. They may also be held, long-term, in a cool cellar or garage. It is best to pack them loosely in a box of sand, but pending that, in between layers of paper. For any budget-conscious cooks: buy a box of beets in bulk at the onset of winter, which will reduce the price greatly and keep you stocked up for months.

Once you've got your hands on some beets, the options are plentiful. I love beets in salads all year long. In winter, I like roasted beets as a side to meats and poultry—they offer a different taste outside of traditional roasted carrots, onions, and potatoes. While they are excellent winter storers, they really are an all-season vegetable, so don't neglect them come spring.

NOVEMBER RECIPES

Beets

Cumin Flatbread with Beet Purée
Beet-Pickled Eggs
Shaved Chioggia Beet Salad with Lemon–Horseradish Yogurt
Roasted Beets with Pistachio Powder
Fennel–Beet Borscht
Beet & Sage Ravioli
Caraway–Beet Chutney

Seasonal Extras

Korean Ribs with Pumpkin Purée
Toasted Pecan & Cranberry Relish

Cumin Flatbread with Beet Purée

MAKES 10 TO 12 FLATBREADS

It's nice to have snacks ready and available around the house, and this beet "hummus" is the perfect nibble. Roasted beets are puréed with a small amount of steamed lentils and a liberal amount of spices, making for a thick, flavorful, and satiating dip that is paired with homemade flatbread. Homemade wheat flatbread is easy to make and cooks quickly, so don't shy away from making and baking your own dough!

FLATBREADS

1½ cups whole wheat flour
½ cup all-purpose flour
1 tablespoon olive oil, plus more for brushing (or use melted butter)
Scant ¾ cup warm water
½ teaspoon salt
1 tablespoon cumin seeds

HUMMUS

12 ounces beets (about 3 medium), roasted and chopped
¼ cup red lentils, washed
¾ cup water
1 tablespoon pomegranate molasses
1 tablespoon olive oil
¼ teaspoon salt
¼ teaspoon pepper
1 teaspoon ground coriander
1 teaspoon paprika
1 teaspoon red chile flakes
1 teaspoon orange zest

To make the flatbreads, combine the flours, olive oil, and water in the bowl of an electric mixer fitted with a dough hook, and knead on medium-slow speed for 5 to 7 minutes, until all the flour is incorporated and the dough is elastic, not wet. Remove from the bowl, cover with a cloth, and set aside to rest for 1 hour.

While the dough is resting, make the beet hummus. Put the chopped beets in the bowl of a food processor or blender. Put the lentils in a small saucepan and cover them with the water. Bring to a boil over high heat and reduce to a simmer, cooking covered until the lentils are soft and easily mashed with the back of a fork, about 15 minutes. Drain any residual water and add the hot lentils to the food processor. Add the pomegranate molasses, olive oil, salt, pepper, coriander, paprika, red chile flakes, and orange zest, and process until all the ingredients come together in a thick purée and are well incorporated, about 1 minute. Scrape down the sides of the bowl, if necessary. Transfer all of the beet hummus to a small serving bowl.

Preheat the oven to 400 degrees F. Set a sheet pan in the oven to heat.

Cut off pieces of flatbread dough and shape them into small balls—each about the size of a Ping-Pong ball. On a lightly floured surface, roll each ball into a thin, flat disc about 5 inches across. When you have five or six discs of dough, remove the sheet pan from the oven and place the discs on the hot pan. Bake until the edges are just golden brown, 8 to 10 minutes. Continue baking the rest of the dough in this fashion.

While the flatbreads are still warm, brush one side with olive oil, sprinkle with salt, and finish with a sprinkling of cumin seeds. Serve warm alongside the beet hummus, or hold at room temperature until ready to use.

PANTRY NOTE: You can change the legume in the hummus; just make sure it is a soft bean that can be easily mashed. Cooked chickpeas and cannellini beans work well. Leftover hummus can be held in the fridge, covered, for up to three days. Leftover flatbread should be used within one day or can be frozen and later warmed under the broiler or in a toaster.

Beet-Pickled Eggs

MAKES 6 EGGS

This is a fun recipe to try when you're looking for something festive and obscure to serve. Here, hard-boiled eggs are dropped into a spiced and spicy pickling brine made up of beet-infused water and vinegar. Left to cure for several days (or longer) the pickled eggs turn bright pink and firm. Serve pickled eggs as you would a deviled egg, or slice them and use in salads. Bring eggs up to room temperature before serving.

1 small red beet, peeled and sliced in half
2 cups water
½ cup sugar
2 whole star anise pods
1 tablespoon whole black peppercorns
1 cup apple cider vinegar
2-inch piece jalapeño, serrano, or dried chile
1 small shallot, sliced (about ¼ cup)
1-inch-long piece fresh ginger, cut into thin slices
6 eggs, hard-boiled and peeled

In a medium saucepan, combine the beet halves, water, sugar, star anise, and peppercorns, and cover. Bring to a boil over high heat. Once it's boiling, reduce heat to low and cook until the beets are just cooked through, about 15 minutes.

Strain the beets from the water, reserving both. In a large glass jar or container, mix the hot beet water, vinegar, chile pepper, shallot, and ginger. Drop in the eggs. Finely chop the boiled beet and add the pieces to the jar.

Set aside on the counter until cool, about 2 hours. Once the mixture is cool, cover the jar and move it to the fridge, allowing the eggs to pickle for at least 2 days (and up to 2 weeks) before serving.

PANTRY NOTE: Beet-pickled eggs will keep for up to four months in the fridge. You can change the pickling aromatics to suit any flavor you prefer. Dill seed, caraway, fennel, and cloves are great choices. You may also make the brine more or less sweet, per your tastes.

HOW TO GROW BEETS

Beets are a standard root crop grown in many gardens, supplying the gardener with both a proper crop rotation (which equals healthy soil) and a massive amount of harvestable nutrients. Easy to grow year-round, this vegetable can be sowed from early spring through autumn in a variety of soils and climates. Beets may be overwintered in mild climates, but will need to be harvested before winter if your region is prone to freezing.

Beets grow right at the surface of the soil, their thick tops often protruding, so the soil does not need to be deeply worked before sowing. Beetroots do not demand large amounts of nutrients either, and I will often plant them without adding any amendments. All plants, however, do best in a light and loamy soil, so dig in a bag or two of well-composted manure if you have heavy clay soils.

In rows, plant one or two beet seeds every inch along the row, about half an inch deep, and cover with a light broadcast of soil or compost. As beet seeds germinate and grow, you will need to thin the plants, allowing the beetroots to develop. With beets, the final spacing depends on the size of beet you ultimately desire. For large beets, best for winter storage, leave about six inches between plants. Leave at least four inches for medium-sized beets with round roots. For small beets, thin to one plant every inch—this allows you to harvest baby beets early, well before the maturity date on the seed packet.

To harvest, simply pull beets from the soil when you see fit. Leave behind any small beets or weak-looking starts. They will often take hold and mature, offering a second round to harvest later. Wash beets thoroughly before cooking—a good vegetable brush works well. The greens can be trimmed and used as you would chard.

To store just-harvested beets, trim the tops and wrap the beets in a thin linen cloth, holding them in the crisper of the fridge, where they will keep for many weeks. For late-season beets, you may also store them in a sand box or outdoor pit, where the sand and soil act as insulation and the winter temperatures act as refrigeration.

The larger the beet, the more fibrous the flesh and the less sweet the flavor. This is not to say that old, large beets aren't tasty—use them in winter borscht, or for purées or roasting. Baby beets benefit from thin skins and delicate greens, which allows you to eat the entire plant. Without trimming the greens, submerge baby beets in a bowl of water to remove all of the soil, changing the water several times until it runs clear. When they are clean, cook the whole beets, greens and all, in sautés, braises, or simply roasted in the oven.

Shaved Chioggia Beet Salad with Lemon–Horseradish Yogurt

MAKES 4 SERVINGS

Raw beets are pretty delicious when shaved very thin and tossed in vinaigrette. To get beets super thin, a mandoline is key. Chioggia beets make a great salad because of their variegated stripes and varying color tones. If you can't find Chioggia, you can use golden or red beets, which are slightly sweeter. Fresh horseradish, found in most grocery store produce sections, is grated into yogurt to make a creamy and pungent dressing.

3 tablespoons olive oil

$1\frac{1}{2}$ tablespoons lemon juice

$\frac{1}{2}$ teaspoon lemon zest

1 tablespoon grated fresh horseradish

$1\frac{1}{2}$ teaspoons honey

2 tablespoons yogurt

$\frac{1}{4}$ teaspoon salt

1 pound Chioggia beets

To make the dressing, in a small jar with a lid, combine the olive oil, lemon juice, lemon zest, horseradish, honey, yogurt, and salt. Shake vigorously until well blended, about 1 minute, and set aside.

To prepare the beets, remove any knobby bits from the beet tops and peel off any dirt-clogged skin or rough patches with a vegetable peeler. Using the thinnest setting on a mandoline (and using the hand guard!), shave the beets into fine, round slices until all beets have been cut.

Put the beets in a shallow salad bowl and pour the dressing on top. Use your hands to toss the salad and coat all of the slices, fanning the beets out flat across a platter or shallow bowl before serving.

PANTRY NOTE: Shaved and dressed Chioggia beets hold in the fridge for up to one day before going soggy and limp. Refresh with some fresh beets before serving.

Roasted Beets with Pistachio Powder

MAKES 4 SERVINGS

Beet salad with blue cheese is pretty pedestrian these days—it's on nearly every restaurant menu come winter. Here, the same flavors are dissected and presented in a new, refreshing way. Beets are roasted and split in half before being pressed lightly into homemade pistachio powder. The powder is easy to make—simply grind the nuts to a fine dust, making sure not to over-process, lest you wind up with pistachio *butter*.

$1\frac{1}{2}$ to 2 pounds small beets, about
    4 inches in diameter (about 8 to 12)

$\frac{1}{2}$ cup pistachio nuts, toasted

1 tablespoon olive oil

1 tablespoon apple cider vinegar

$\frac{1}{8}$ teaspoon salt

$\frac{1}{8}$ teaspoon pepper

2 ounces veined blue cheese (optional)

Preheat the oven to 400 degrees F.

Put the beets on a small, shallow baking pan and fill the bottom with enough water to reach about ½ inch up the sides. Cover the baking pan with aluminum foil and place it in the oven. Roast until the beets are just tender, when you can pierce the outer edge of a beet easily, but the center has some resistance to it—al dente—about 45 to 60 minutes. Remove the beets from the oven and let them cool until warm.

While the beets are roasting, make the pistachio powder. Put the pistachios in a blender or food processor and pulse to chop roughly. Once the pistachios are large crumbs, turn the blender to high and mix until the pistachios are a fine powder, less than 1 minute. Watch closely so you don't over-process them. Pour the pistachio powder onto a small, round plate.

When the beets are cool enough to handle, rub off the skins with paper towels, and dispose of the skins. Cut each beet in half. In a medium bowl, put the beet halves, oil, vinegar, salt, and pepper, and toss to combine. Working with one beet at a time, shake off any excess vinaigrette and press the cut side of the beet lightly into the pistachio powder. Plate immediately, pistachio side up. Keep working until all the beets are coated; you can either plate servings individually or serve all the beets on a platter, adding small pieces of blue cheese, if desired.

PANTRY NOTE: Leftover pistachio powder can be used for garnishing salads, dusting pies and tarts, or topping ice cream.

Fennel–Beet Borscht

MAKES 4 TO 6 SERVINGS

Borscht is a traditional eastern European soup, served hot or cold, and varies greatly in its preparation. Some preparations are long-cooked stews flecked with tender beef that take all day to prepare, while others rely simply on shaved beets and broth. For this hot, autumnal version I paired anise-scented fennel bulb with red beets and a small pinch of cayenne. A dollop of yogurt or sour cream is traditional and delicious—and will turn the soup from red-gem toned to fuchsia in seconds. You can add diced carrots or celery to the soup as well. Be sure to cut your veg the same size, so they all cook at the same rate.

> 1 pound red beets, peeled and cut into small, even dice (about 4 cups)
> ½ pound fennel bulb, cut into small, even dice (about 2 cups)
> ½ cup diced onion
> 2½ cups homemade stock (chicken, beef, or vegetable)
> ½ teaspoon salt
> ⅛ teaspoon cayenne
> Plain yogurt or sour cream (optional)

In a medium saucepan, combine the beets, fennel bulb, onions, stock, and salt. Set the pot over medium-high heat and bring to a boil. Reduce heat to low, cover, and simmer until all ingredients are just cooked through and still toothsome.

Remove from heat and taste for salt, adding if need be. Add cayenne to the broth and stir to combine well. Serve immediately, with a dollop of yogurt or sour cream, if desired.

PANTRY NOTE: Borscht holds in the fridge, covered, for up to five days. Reheat or serve cold.

Beet & Sage Ravioli

MAKES ABOUT 24 RAVIOLI (4 TO 6 SERVINGS)

Making pasta at home can seem overwhelming, but it is pretty easy to do, and you only need a rolling pin and some strong hands. Here, pasta is rolled into thin-as-possible sheets before being filled with a beet-ricotta mixture. These see-through ravioli, served with a sage-brown butter sauce, show off their brilliant red (or golden) filling and make for a simple and delicious pasta course.

PASTA
2 cups all-purpose flour
1 cup semolina flour
5 eggs

BEET FILLING
½ pound beets, roasted and peeled
½ cup ricotta
¼ cup grated Parmesan (optional)
¼ teaspoon salt
¼ teaspoon pepper

BUTTER SAUCE
4 tablespoons butter
8 fresh sage leaves
1 teaspoon lemon juice
Grated Parmesan (optional)

To make the pasta, mix the all-purpose flour, semolina flour, and eggs in an electric stand mixer fitted with a dough hook on low speed for about 5 minutes, or until the dough comes together and is fairly smooth. Turn it out onto a lightly floured countertop and knead by hand about 3 to 4 minutes, until the dough is elastic and shiny. Wrap it tightly in plastic wrap and refrigerate for at least 30 minutes and up to 1 hour.

While the pasta is resting, make the filling. Put the roasted beets, ricotta, Parmesan (if using), salt, and pepper in the bowl of a food processor or blender. Blend until the beets break down into a smooth purée, about 1 to 2 minutes. Chill in the fridge until ready to use.

Remove the dough from the fridge and divide it into three equal pieces. Work with one piece at a time, keeping the others well wrapped in plastic wrap. Lightly flour your work surface and roll out the dough, keeping its rectangular shape as much as possible (but don't worry too much if the dough takes on a different shape). Roll it out until quite thin—about 20 to 22 inches long and 8 to 10 inches wide (be sure to turn the dough over occasionally and roll the other side). Dust your work surface as needed so the dough does not stick. It should be thin, like a stick of gum, and should take about 8 minutes to roll out. Using a pastry brush, remove any excess flour.

COOKING WITH BEET GREENS

All beets are topped with sturdy stalks of greens that provide nutrients to the beetroot and take in sunlight, helping the beets to grow. Beets are closely related to chard and spinach, and lined up side by side their greens are similar in color and texture. In cooking, beet greens can be treated similarly as well.

As the beetroot grows, the plant produces "tops" of beet greens, which take in sunlight and produce nutrients for the plant, all of which are stored in the root. (This is why root vegetables are so nutritious.) The greens can be harvested from the plant as it grows with little damage or demise to the roots.

To trim greens from a plant, wait until a good root system is established after sowing, and the greens are hardy and plentiful—about four weeks. To cut, use scissors and trim off the beet greens as low to the beetroot as possible. Work your way around the plant, not taking too many off from one area. It is safe to harvest about 30 to 40 percent of greens from each plant without affecting the growth cycle too drastically.

To use beet greens, treat them as you would any sautéing green. Add to a pan with olive oil and garlic for a simple sautéed green side. A pinch of red chile flakes adds some kick. You may also use beet greens as a vehicle for stuffing—think cabbage rolls and update them. As they are tender, beet greens need not be blanched before filling, and require only a quick soak in hot water to soften the ribs. Add a spoonful of cooked and flavored grains or spiced ground meat (raw or cooked) to the center of the leaves before rolling and steaming. The filling for Butternut Squash and Shrimp Wontons will work beautifully here—the stuffed beet greens make a healthy and flavorful winter meal (and can be similarly poached in the broth, sparing the use of wonton wrappers for anyone with an aversion to wheat).

Beet greens, if tender, may also be sliced thin and added as a colorful (and healthy) garnish for soups. Using raw leaves, trim off the stems and stack and roll the leaves, slicing thinly into delicate strands. This green and fuchsia garnish can be used in summer for Ricotta–Squash Dumpling Soup or in winter as color for Turkey Meatball & Cabbage Soup. The leaves will cook quickly in the warm broth.

To make the ravioli, cut the sheet of pasta in half lengthwise, resulting in two sheets about 4 to 5 inches wide and about 20 inches long. Working about ½ to 1 inch above the long edge, drop a small spoonful (about 1 teaspoon) of beet filling every 4 to 5 inches. You will have 4 to 5 dollops of filling. Using your finger dipped in water, moisten the pasta all around each filling and fold the top edge of the dough lengthwise over the filling, pressing out any air pockets to form sealed ravioli.

Cut the dough into individual ravioli and crimp the edges, if desired. Set the ravioli aside on a semolina-dusted sheet pan and cover with a slightly damp kitchen towel. Discard any trimmed pasta dough. Keep forming ravioli until all of the dough is used. If not cooking immediately, store the sheet pan in the freezer until ready to use.

Just before serving, bring a large pot of heavily salted water to boil. Gently add about half of the ravioli and cook 8 to 10 minutes, until al dente but not too toothsome.

While the ravioli is cooking, quickly make the butter sauce. In a large sauté pan, melt the butter over medium-high heat. The butter will brown and caramelize. Add the sage leaves and remove the pan from the heat immediately. Add the lemon juice, stir, and set aside.

When the ravioli is cooked, use a slotted spoon to scoop it out and add it to the brown butter sauce. Cook the second batch of ravioli, then add those to the pan. Return the pan to the heat, and add a few spoonfuls of pasta water (about ¼ cup). Cook until the sauce thickens slightly, and then remove from the heat. Grate Parmesan into the sauce, if using, and serve immediately.

PANTRY NOTE: Ravioli can be filled and shaped, then laid out on a semolina-dusted sheet pan and frozen. Once they are completely frozen, store them in a resealable plastic bag in the freezer until ready to use, up to three months.

Caraway-Beet Chutney

MAKES ABOUT 2 PINT JARS

Chutneys are piquant condiments that can be used to enliven winter stews or colorfully garnish roasted meats and veg. This chutney is cooked quickly, so the beets remain crisp and toothsome. The citrusy, peppered bite of caraway offsets the warming spices used here. Combined, they bring out the sweetness in the beets. Feel free to amp up or tone down the sweetness to your liking—adjusting the sugar proportion if so desired.

> 1 medium red onion, finely chopped
>   (about 2 cups)
> 1½ cups water
> ¾ cup apple cider vinegar
> 1 teaspoon salt
> ½ cup sugar
> 1 teaspoon caraway seeds
> 1 teaspoon ground cinnamon
> ½ teaspoon ground cardamom
> ¼ teaspoon ground allspice

1 teaspoon red pepper flakes

2 medium firm apples, cored and
chopped

1 pound beets, trimmed, peeled, and cut
into medium dice

In a large pot, combine the onion, water, vinegar, salt, sugar, and all of the spices. Bring to a boil over medium-high heat, then reduce the heat to low, cooking for 5 minutes or until the onion is just cooked through and translucent. Add the apples and beets and cook for 20 to 30 minutes, until the apples are cooked through but firm and the beets are just soft.

Transfer the relish to clean jars.

PANTRY NOTE: This relish can be held in the fridge, covered, for up to a month.

Korean Ribs with Pumpkin Purée

MAKES 4 SERVINGS

Korean ribs are short ribs cut lengthwise across the bones into thin, long pieces of meat. Cutting the beef in this way assures a faster cooking time and more tender meat. Here, traditional Korean spices make an overnight marinade before the ribs are broiled and caramelized from the honey. Paired with a smooth pumpkin purée to tame the heat, this is fall eating at its best. This recipe can be made with any winter squash, though you may need to adjust the amount of liquid needed for a smooth purée.

1 cup soy sauce

½ cup mirin or white wine

1 lime, zested and juiced

½ cup honey

¼ cup sesame oil

½ head garlic, peeled and smashed

1 teaspoon grated fresh ginger

1 teaspoon chile sauce or red chile flakes

3 pounds Korean-style short ribs

1 small pie pumpkin, about 4 pounds

3 tablespoons olive oil

3 tablespoons chopped fresh thyme

½ teaspoon salt

¼ teaspoon pepper

1 cup water

2 to 4 tablespoons plain yogurt or milk

In large resealable plastic bag (or a large bowl), combine the soy sauce, mirin, lime juice and zest, honey, sesame oil, garlic, ginger, and chile sauce or pepper flakes. Shake to combine well, and then add all of the ribs to the bag. Set in the refrigerator to marinate overnight.

To prepare the dish, preheat the oven to 375 degrees F. Remove the ribs from the fridge and set aside until ready to use.

Using a sharp knife, cut the pumpkin in half from the stem end to the bottom. Pull off the pumpkin stem and discard it. Using a metal spoon, scoop out and discard the seeds and membranes.

Cut each pumpkin half into quarters and place in a shallow baking dish. Add the olive oil, thyme, salt, and pepper to the baking dish, and toss the pumpkin pieces, coating them evenly. Add the cup of water and bake, uncovered, until the pumpkin flesh is soft and tender, about 1 to 1½ hours.

Remove the pumpkin from the oven and let it cool until easy to handle. Using a metal spoon, scrape the pumpkin flesh into a large mixing bowl. Scrape up and add any brown bits from the bottom of the baking dish. Add 2 tablespoons of yogurt or milk and beat until smooth and creamy, adding more yogurt or milk if needed. Taste for seasonings and cover. Set aside until ready to use.

To cook the ribs, preheat the broiler. Line a baking sheet with aluminum foil and place a cooling rack or broiler pan on top. Shaking off any excess marinade, lay the ribs in a single layer on the rack. Place the baking sheet under the broiler, about 2 to 3 inches from the coils, and cook until browned and sizzling, about 3 minutes. Turn the ribs over and cook the other side until browned and caramelized. Place 3 or 4 ribs over a spoonful of pumpkin purée; serve immediately.

PANTRY NOTE: Leftover ribs and purée can be kept in the fridge, covered, for up to three days or frozen for up to two months.

Toasted Pecan & Cranberry Relish

MAKES 2 PINTS

This recipe is a traditional Thanksgiving cranberry sauce embellished with toasted nuts. Cranberries are quite tart (although I like them that way!), so feel free to add more sugar to taste. This relish is wonderful used as jam and even better when served as an appetizer alongside a delicate soft cheese like Brie or Camembert. Pecans are great, but pistachios would be equally delicious and walnuts also work well. For a step-by-step guide to canning at home, check out Water-Bath Canning 101 in June: Berries.

4 cups cranberries (about 1½ pounds)
1 cup water
2 cups sugar
½ cup currants or raisins
1 orange
½ cup toasted pecans, chopped

In a large saucepan, set the cranberries, water, sugar, and currants or raisins over medium heat. Zest the orange into the saucepan. Using a chef's knife, trim all the pith from the remaining orange and chop the flesh roughly. Add the orange flesh and the juice from the cutting board to the pot. Cook the mixture for about 20 minutes, until the cranberries begin to pop and the relish thickens. Taste for sweetness and add more sugar, if you like. Add the toasted pecans and cook another 5 to 10 minutes, or until the desired consistency is reached.

Fill your canning jars, leaving ¼ inch of headspace, and process in a water bath for 10 minutes.

PANTRY NOTE: Sealed jars will keep in a cool, dark cupboard for up to one year. Once it's opened, this relish will keep in the fridge for several weeks.

INDEX

ABOUT THE AUTHOR

AMY PENNINGTON is a cook, author, and urban farmer. She is the author of *Urban Pantry: Tips & Recipes for a Thrifty, Sustainable & Seasonal Kitchen*; *Apartment Gardening: Plants, Projects, and Recipes for Growing Food in Your Urban Home*; and *Apples: From Harvest to Table*. Pennington has been named one of *Seattle Magazine*'s 2013 Top 50 most powerful players in Seattle's food scene and as a 2012 *Bon Appétit* Tastemaker. She has been featured in *Bon Appétit*, *Wall Street Journal*, *Huffington Post*, GOOP.com, and ApartmentTherapy.com. She runs GoGo Green Garden, an urban farming service specializing in organic, edible gardens for homes and businesses. Pennington lives in Seattle. To learn more about Amy, visit www.Amy-Pennington.com.

ABOUT THE PHOTOGRAPHERS

DELLA CHEN is a photographer based in the Pacific Northwest. You can see her photos in *Urban Pantry* and at www.therighteyeopen.com.

KENNETH DUNDAS is a theater and portrait photographer based in Glasgow. His work has been shown in the prestigious Scottish National Portrait Gallery and regularly appears in print for the *Guardian*, Scottish Opera, and other publications. His work can be viewed at http://kkdundas.com.

ABOUT SKIPSTONE

Skipstone is an imprint of Seattle-based nonprofit publisher Mountaineers Books. It features thematically related titles that promote a deeper connection to our natural world through sustainable practice and backyard activism. Our readers live smart, play well, and typically engage with the community around them. Skipstone guides explore healthy lifestyles and how an outdoor life relates to the well-being of our planet, as well as of our own neighborhoods. Sustainable foods and gardens; healthful living; realistic and doable conservation at home; modern aspirations for community—Skipstone tries to address such topics in ways that emphasize active living, local and grassroots practices, and a small footprint.

Our hope is that Skipstone books will inspire you to effect change without losing your sense of humor, to celebrate the freedom and generosity of a life outdoors, and to move forward with gentle leaps or breathtaking bounds.

Our publications, as part of our 501(c)(3) nonprofit program, are made possible through the generosity of donors and through sales of more than 600 titles on outdoor recreation, sustainable lifestyle, and conservation. To donate, purchase books, or learn more, visit us online:

SKIPSTONE
LIVE LIFE
MAKE RIPPLES

www.skipstonebooks.org
www.mountaineersbooks.org

Other Skipstone titles you might enjoy!